THE
BODHISATTVA
PATH

THE
BODHISATTVA PATH

THICH NHAT HANH

Commentaries on the
Vimalakirtinirdesa and
Ugrapariprccha Sutras

PALM LEAVES
PRESS

Published by Palm Leaves Press
an imprint of Parallax Press

Parallax Press
2236B Sixth Street
Berkeley, California 94710
parallax.org

Originally published in Vietnamese as
Bồ Tát Tại Gia, Bồ Tát Xuất Gia
by Lá Bối, San Jose, CA, 2002.

Cover design by Katie Eberle
Text design and composition by Maureen Forys
Printed on Enviro Book Natural

ISBN: 978-1-952692-33-8
E-book ISBN: 978-1-952692-34-5

Non-English words are in Sanskrit unless
otherwise indicated or made clear by the context.

Library of Congress Control Number: 2022943251

1 2 3 4 5 / 26 25 24 23 22

CONTENTS

TRANSLATOR'S INTRODUCTION vii

I BUDDHISM AFTER THE PARINIRVĀṆA
OF THE BUDDHA

THE ŚRĀVAKA SANGHA AND THE
MONKHOOD 3

THE EMERGENCE OF MAHĀYĀNA SUTRAS . . 5

THE DEVELOPMENT OF OPPOSITION TO
THE ŚRĀVAKA PRACTICE 10

II THE UGRAPARIPṚCCHA SUTRA

SUMMARY OF THE SUTRA 19

EXPLANATION OF THE SUTRA 21

THE WAY OF PRACTICE FOR THE LAY
BODHISATTVA 23

THE LIFE OF THE MONASTIC BODHISATTVA . . 36

OBSERVING THE PRECEPTS 55

LIVING IN THE FAMILY AND PRACTICING
THE MONASTIC PRECEPTS 64

CONCLUSION 67

III THE VIMALAKĪRTINIRDEŚA SUTRA

THE MAIN FEATURES OF THE SUTRA 71

THE CHARACTERS PRESENTED IN
     THE SUTRA 74

INSIGHTS INTO THE SUTRA 79

    Chapter 1 The Buddha Land 79
    Chapter 2 Skillful Means 93
    Chapter 3 Hearer Disciples. 108
    Chapter 4 Bodhisattvas. 138
    Chapter 5 Manjuśri Asks after the Sickness . . 157
    Chapter 6 The Inconceivable Liberation 193
    Chapter 7 Meditation on Living Beings 209
    Chapter 8 The Destiny of a Buddha. 223
    Chapter 9 Entering the Door of Nonduality . . 235
    Chapter 10 Buddha Sugandhakūṭa 240
    Chapter 11 The Comportment of
       the Bodhisattva. 251
    Chapter 12 Buddha Akṣobhya 259
    Chapter 13 On Offering the Dharma 264
    Chapter 14 Entrusting. 267

IV CONCLUSION: THE ESSENCE OF THE
   VIMALAKĪRTINIRDEŚA

THE IDEAS 273

HANDING ON THE TEACHINGS 277

THE AIM OF THE SUTRA 281

READING AND UNDERSTANDING THE
    VIMALAKĪRTINIRDEŚA 283

This book is compiled from Dharma talks given in Vietnamese by the Venerable Thích Nhất Hạnh on the Mahāyāna sutras between November 10, 1991 and December 8, 1991, during the Winter Retreat in Plum Village, France.

If we analyze the word *bodhisattva* we see that *bodhi* means "awakening," "enlightenment," or "deep understanding," and *sattva* means a "living being." A bodhisattva is a being who enlightens others and enlightens themself. Enlightening oneself and enlightening others go together. This is something many of us have a deep aspiration to do. Understanding also means love. Once there is understanding there has to be love, and without understanding there cannot be true love.

This book contains the commentaries of the Venerable Thich Nhat Hanh on two early Mahāyāna sutras about what it means to be a bodhisattva. You can be a monastic bodhisattva or a lay bodhisattva, but these sutras stress the importance of being a lay bodhisattva. At the time they were written, the lay practice was often looked on as inferior to the monastic practice. These sutras are a manifesto for the effectiveness and significance of lay Buddhist practice.

The first sutra, the Ugraparipṛccha, "Questions of the Householder Ugra," is a comparatively gentle opening up of the way of esteeming a lay bodhisattva. It keeps respect for the value of the monastic path. The lay bodhisattva is even seen to model themself on the monastic bodhisattva. This sutra is a very solid, down-to-earth teaching. It encourages tolerance in the bodhisattva, whose role is not to judge those who do not practice but to help by example.

The second sutra, the Vimalakīrtinirdeśa is more iconoclastic. It does not spare even the most revered monastics of the time of the Buddha Śākyamuni. Nevertheless it has a very important message: that a bodhisattva must be engaged in helping the world and is not seeking personal enlightenment.

The Ugraparipṛccha is easy enough to follow because it remains firmly in the historical dimension. The Vimalakīrtinirdeśa tends to hop between the ultimate and the historical dimensions. On the one hand it praises nondiscrimination and on the other it discriminates between the Greater Vehicle (the Mahayana) and the Śrāvaka and Pratyekabuddha Vehicles.

One of the important aspects of the commentary by the Venerable Thich Nhat Hanh is that it helps us to see when the sutra is concerned with the historical dimension and when it is concerned with the ultimate dimension.

Although the Venerable Thich Nhat Hanh often suggests that we read the sutra itself rather than the commentaries on it, I have been very grateful to have been able to read this particular commentary, albeit with its lengthy citations from the sutras, before attempting to read the sutras themselves. The Mahāyāna sutras often can be a great ocean which we need a pilot to help us navigate.

In this book the citations of the sutras have been carefully chosen by the author to help us understand the essence of the sutras. Therefore the book becomes a guide on the path of training to become an authentic bodhisattva.

We do not want to become a store of knowledge about the sutras that we are not able to put into practice. The Venerable Thich Nhat Hanh is an engaged bodhisattva and has much valuable experience in the way of engaging the practice in the world. His experience helps us put these teachings into practice.

In my personal practice these sutras have been a great source of inspiration, especially in the teachings to treat adverse circumstances as opportunities rather than obstacles. Particularly interesting is the discussion of ill-health: how to practice with it and how to look deeply into it. Being a bodhisattva is not to run away from ill-health.

As the Venerable Thich Nhat Hanh remarks, reading the Vimalakīrtinirdeśa is like reading a play. Colorful and dramatic scenes reflect the culture of India of that time.* Those who wish to read the sutras in full can download from the internet the English translation of Kumārajīva's Chinese Vimalakīrtinirdeśa by Burton Watson. The Ugraparipṛccha has been translated into English by J. Nattier in her book *A Few Good Men*.†

As I finished translating this book I wrote the following lines:

> *A living being,*
> *a breathing being,*
> *earth, water,*
> *fire, air,*
> *space and consciousness.*
> *Evolving, dissolving,*
> *for the good of the world,*
> *for the good of all.*

We face a crisis now that Vimalakīrti and Ugra did not face. We do not know whether the human species or life on Earth can survive it. Still, in every moment that we have left to us, we can carry on the career of an awakening being and offer up the merit for the alleviation of suffering.

---

* It seems to have developed over the centuries and the earliest mention is at the end of the second century of the Common Era.

† Jan Nattier PhD, *A Few Good Men: The Bodhisattva Path according to the Inquiry of Ugra (Ugraparipṛcchā)* (Studies in the Buddhist Traditions), Hawaii University Press, 2005.

I
BUDDHISM AFTER
THE PARINIRVĀNA
OF THE BUDDHA

THE ŚRĀVAKA SANGHA
AND THE MONKHOOD

Śrāvaka is a Sanskrit word that means the disciple who listens. It is sometimes translated into English as "the Hearer." After the Buddha passed into *nirvāṇa* the word was used disparagingly by Mahayanists to describe a certain kind of monk who did not seem to them to embody the bodhisattva ideal.

About 150 years after the Buddha's *parinirvāṇa* Buddhism began to develop into many schools. This development continued for several hundred years, a period now called Schools' Buddhism. During that time there were some monks who started to live in a way which cut them off from the rest of the population. These were the monks referred to by Mahayanists as śrāvaka. Their primary concern was personal liberation. They were conservative, tending to make Buddhism into a series of doctrines and thus establishing a spiritual path which served their own group of monks. They believed that all laypeople needed to do was to make offerings and support the monks. Laypeople were not expected to benefit from and put into practice the teachings the Buddha had given. In this way Buddhism grew distant from the large majority of ordinary people.

Since quite a large number of monks had these narrow views and distorted ideas about the teachings, it deprived Buddhism of much of the esteem it had acquired while the Buddha was alive. The practice of a large number of monks was going in a negative direction and the nirvāṇa of the śrāvakas had become something very narrow in scope, reserved only for the minority of monks.

Consequently, also during this period, there arose amongst Buddhist practitioners, lay as well as monastic, the idea of popularizing Buddhism. From this sprang the Mahāyāna path. It was a movement aimed at promoting the deepest wellsprings of Buddhist thought, making *bodhicitta* energy (the mind of love) central again and bringing Buddhism back in touch with life in the world.

THE EMERGENCE OF
MAHĀYĀNA SUTRAS

As the ideas of the Mahayanists were taking shape, those who supported the Mahāyāna saw that if these deep teachings did not take root in the daily life of the monastic sangha they would not be effective in or acceptable to society. This meant that the teachings of the Mahāyāna should not just manifest as a way of thought but should be the basis of a sangha that included monks, nuns, and laypeople. Buddhism could not be presented as a spiritual path reserved for monks and nuns alone. About 50 BCE, Mahāyāna sutras began to appear, creating the right environment and a means for transmitting the Mahāyāna way of thought.

In the history of Mahāyāna literature the Prajñāpāramitā sutras were the first to appear. They were followed by the Ratnakūṭa collection and the Avataṃsaka. After that there came the Vimalakīrtinirdeśa and other sutras.

In the second century CE an eminent and wise scholar of Buddhism was born in Vidarbha (Berar), India, by the name of Nagarjuna. He was the author of many Buddhist works, the most outstanding of which is the Prajñāpāramitāśastra. This is the lengthy work that serves as a commentary on the Prajñāpāramitā sutras. In this work Nāgārjuna quotes from many Mahāyāna sutras which had appeared before he was born.

From a historical perspective we could choose as our starting point the parinirvāṇa of the Buddha, 480 years before the birth of Christ. About two centuries after the birth of Christ, Master Nāgārjuna was born. In the fourth century CE two renowned Buddhist teachers appeared, the two brothers Asanga and Vasubandhu. They systematized and developed the Buddhist teachings on the nature of consciousness.

Historically we can divide Mahāyāna sutras into three periods: First, there were sutras that appeared before the time of Nāgārjuna. They were quoted by him in the Prajñāpāramitāśāstra. Second, there are the sutras that appeared in the period that extended from the lifetime of Nāgārjuna until the time of Asanga and Vasubandhu. Finally, there are the sutras that appeared after the time of Asanga and Vasubandhu, which are the Mahāyāna sutras of the third period.

According to the Mahāyāna sutras, to be worthy of being a disciple of the Buddha one should be a bodhisattva. It is not enough to be a śrāvaka or a pratyekabuddha, (someone who realizes enlightenment without needing the help of others and without founding a sangha). The śrāvaka and pratyekabuddha practices are known as the two vehicles (*yānadvaya*). The Bodhisattva vehicle (bodhisattvayāna) is the third vehicle which is able to convey more people than the other two vehicles.

As far as Original Buddhism is concerned, the term bodhisattva refers to one person alone: namely Śākyamuni Buddha before he became the Buddha at his enlightenment under the Bodhi tree. With the development of Buddhist thought people began to ask why there should be just one bodhisattva. Buddha had said that there were many Buddhas in the past and in the present, and they had all been bodhisattvas. Therefore the idea of many bodhisattvas was quite reasonable both for Hinayanists and Mahayanists.

The Mahayanists held that an authentic disciple of the Buddha had the bodhisattva aspiration. Therefore whether monastic or layperson, any true descendant of the Buddha should be a bodhisattva. Mahāyāna Buddhism looked on everyone as equal. There was no discrimination between women and men. In chapter seven (Meditation on Living Beings) of the Vimalakīrti Sutra a goddess is portrayed as an outstanding practitioner of Mahāyāna Buddhism. In chapter four (Bodhisattvas) a very young bodhisattva by the name of Prabhāvyūha is portrayed as one of the very few who are able to converse on equal terms with the layman Vimalakīrti.

At the time when the Mahāyāna sutras had just began to appear, the senior disciples of the Buddha like Śāriputra, Mahāmaudgalyāyana, Subhūti, and others were looked on as Hinayanists. Only when the Saddharmapundarika (Lotus) Sutra appeared did people see that Śāriputra had no doubt or regret about practicing the Mahāyāna aspiration.

In the way the Vimalakīrti Sutra attacks the śrāvaka way of thought, it goes rather too far. It criticizes and maligns the way of practice and realization of the Buddha's senior disciples. In truth, Śāriputra was the trusted elder brother of the original sangha of the Buddha. As the elder brother he had the greatest responsibility of all the monks, teaching and caring for his younger brothers.

The Vimalakīrtinirdeśa is not a sutra that was taught directly by the Buddha. The sutra can be seen as a work written by a number of Buddhists who were active in transmitting Buddhism to a wide audience so that all could benefit from and take refuge in the teachings of the Buddha. The Mahayanists who compiled the Vimalakīrtinirdeśa wanted to compare the training and practice of the Hīnayāna with that of the Mahāyāna. They did this by portraying Śāriputra in sitting meditation and Mahākāśyapa on the alms' round in a way that was supposed to represent the Hīnayāna way of practicing. After that, to make the contrast, they presented the Mahāyāna teachings by way of answers and teachings given by the lay bodhisattva Vimalakīrti.

The aim of the sutra was to point out to the śrāvakas that the path of practice they were following was still narrow. The path of the Mahāyāna was the Great Path that could bring practitioners to the highest, right, and equal enlightenment.

It was not only laypeople who wanted to renew Buddhism; monastics too were involved in this movement, and they had a positive part to play. Nevertheless, it should be said that the majority of those who contributed to the movement were laypeople who wanted to bring śrāvaka Buddhism out of its ivory tower of monasticism. The śrāvakas for them were represented by Śāriputra, Mahākātyāyana, Upāli and so on. They wanted people to follow the wider and more open path of the bodhisattvas like Mañjuśrī, the bodhisattva of Great Understanding.

THE DEVELOPMENT
OF OPPOSITION TO THE
ŚRĀVAKA PRACTICE

In the beginning, the movement to oppose a privileged monastic order was promoted by monastics as well as by laypeople because they saw that the wonderful teachings of the Buddha were in decline. The appearance of the Vimalakīrtinirdeśa left a very important mark on this movement at a time when laypeople wanted to take the lead in bringing Buddhism back to the people by transmitting the teachings of the Mahāyāna.

If we look into the process of how the Mahāyāna sutras came into being, we shall see that the opposition to the śrāvaka vehicle can be divided into three stages:

The first stage was that of germination, when the Mahāyāna sutras were born. Their aim is to clear a path so that voicing opposition to a privileged monasticism could be possible. With this in mind, they describe on the one hand what the ideal life of a monk should be like and on the other hand give importance to a holy life (brahmacarya) that can be practiced by the lay bodhisattva. The first sutras to appear, which paved the way for the Vimalakīrtinirdeśa, were practical and tolerant in spirit and were therefore easily acceptable to everyone. Precisely because of this spirit of tolerance the Mahāyāna could take its first steps and then continue until our own time.

One of the sutras belonging to this first stage is the Ugraparipṛcchā, *Ugra's Inquiry*. It is no longer extant in Sanskrit but there are three versions in the Chinese canon. One version is the Dharma Mirror Sutra (法鏡經 Fajing Jing), meaning the mirror that reflects the Right Dharma. It can be found in the Taishō Tripiṭaka, number 322. Translated into Chinese in the year 181, the Sanskrit version from which it was translated must have been a very early Mahāyāna sutra. The Parthian monk 安玄 (An Xuan) translated the sutra, and the preface was written by a Vietnamese monk 康僧會 (Khương Tăng Hội; Kang Senghui). Senghui was born in Việt Nam and while a monk started translating Sanskrit texts into Chinese in Việt Nam. Later On in the middle of the third century CE, he went to Eastern Wu in the time of the Three Kingdoms and founded the First Temple. While residing there he wrote the short preface to this sutra which was also preserved in the Chinese Canon.

The second version is Ugra's Inquiry into the Bodhisattva Practice (郁伽越問菩薩行). In this sutra Ugra asks about the aspiration of a bodhisattva and how it is practiced. It can be found in the Taishō (Revised Chinese Canon) number 323, and was translated by Master Zhu Fahui (竺法會) in about 266. There is yet another equivalent sutra in the Chinese Canon called Ugra the Householder (郁伽長者) translated by Master Kang Senghui (康僧啟) into Chinese in 252. This is the nineteenth part of the Ratnakūṭa Sutra, which is entitled the Dharma Festival of Ugra the Householder (郁伽長者會).

Ugra was an intelligent person. He studied precepts and had a firm faith in the practice. He is described as the head of a family, which also means a successful man who held a certain position in society. Anāthapiṇḍika was also described like this. The Sanskrit word for householder (gṛhapati) means someone who is just, straightforward, truthful, honest, advanced in age, and wealthy; in Chinese it is 長者.

The next stage is the period of defamation (of the Hinayāna) and promotion (of the Mahāyāna). This was the time when Mahāyāna sutras like the Vimalakīrtinirdeśa appeared. These sutras applauded the Bodhisattva ideal and defamed the direction and the practice of the śrāvakas. All the Mahāyāna sutras that came out in the beginning of this phase, like the Prajñāpāramitā, the Ratnakūṭa, the Avataṃsaka and the Vimalakīrtinirdeśa attacked the śrāvaka way of training and practice and at the same time promulgated the teachings of Mahāyāna Buddhism. Among these sutras the Vimalakīrtinirdeśa delivers the strongest and most direct attack. It has no hesitation in condemning the teachings and practice of the ten most senior disciples of the Buddha.

In the Vimalakīrtinirdeśa, all the meetings, exchanges, and dialogues between the lay bodhisattva Vimalakīrti and the śrāvaka disciples like Śāriputra, Maudgalyāyana, and even the bodhisattvas like Maitreya are skillful means used by the authors to attack monasticism and applaud the teachings of the Mahāyāna. Nevertheless, as one reads the Vimalakīrtinirdeśa, one cannot fail to see that the reasoning of Vimalakīrti is deep and subtle in spite of the sharp criticism he uses to push home his point, effectively mocking the monastic disciples of the Buddha. I would suggest therefore that before you study the Vimalakīrtinirdeśa, you study the three sutras which come from the Sanskrit *Ugraparipṛccha* because these sutras put an emphasis on the practice of the precepts and the practice of the bodhisattva. If we have read these sutras, when we come to read the Vimalakīrtinirdeśa we shall know how to maintain our practice and not lose ourselves in lofty abstractions.

Finally, there is the stage of continued development when many more sutras made their appearance. These sutras bear a close resemblance to the Vimalakīrtinirdeśa and continue in the same vein. Their appearance was due to the enormous success of the Vimalakīrtinirdeśa in transmitting the Mahāyāna path. They include the Mahavaipulyanirdeśa (in Chinese, number 477 of the Taishō Tripiṭaka) that was translated into Chinese by Master Dharmarakṣa. It is a very interesting sutra appearing at the beginning of the third century C.E. Continuing on from the Vimalakīrti, its protagonist is Vimalakīrti's son who gives teachings on the Dharma. After that comes the Candrottarādārikāvyākaraṇa Sutra (in Chinese, number 480 of the Taishō). Here it is Vimalakīrti's daughter who gives the teachings, and she receives praise from the Buddha for the correctness of her teachings. The appearance of sutras featuring the son and daughter of Vimalakīrti prove the great success of the Vimalakīrtinirdeśa.

As far as the movement to promote lay practice and its relationship to the Vimalakīrtinirdeśa is concerned, the Śūraṅgama-samādhi should be mentioned. This sutra was strongly influenced by the Vimalakīrtinirdeśa, it's aim being the same. In it the Buddha predicts the Buddhahoood of Vimalakīrti in a future lifetime.

This sutra is not the Śūraṅgama Sutra that all Buddhists in Vietnam learn and recite. So far there is no evidence that the Śūraṅgama Sutra that is used in Vietnam today even appeared in Sanskrit. Most scholars agree that this sutra was compiled in China in the eighth century and the name of the sutra is the Great Heroic March, led by the Buddha for realizing the deep meaning of the ten thousand actions of the bodhisattvas. The beginning of the sutra tells the story of Ānanda going into the village and being caught by Matanga. At this point the Buddha uttered a mantra and ordered another bodhisattva to go and save Ānanda. The sutra continues with the Buddha teaching the Seven Abodes of the Mind. It is a very interesting sutra and we would do well to study it.*

Although modern scholars agree that the Śūraṅgama Sutra did not appear in Sanskrit and was composed in China, it can still be called a sutra as long as it teaches the way of thought of the Buddha. We should not discriminate against sutras because they did not first appear in Sanskrit. Next comes the Śrīmālādevi Sutra. Here a woman is again portrayed as the one who is teaching the Dharma. Her name is Śrīmālā. In the Vimalakīrtinirdeśa it is a layman, Vimalakīrti, who teaches. Then comes a sutra where his son teaches. After that, a sutra in which his daughter is teaching, and then yet another sutra where a woman is the protagonist. This time she is a queen, the daughter of King Prasenajit. She was married to the King of a region in southwest India as a child but that did not prevent her from being an excellent practitioner of the Buddha's teachings.

In the sutras that appeared later on, there is the Great Adornment Dharma Door Sutra (number 818 in the Taishō) translated in 583 CE. In this sutra it is again a woman who gives the teachings. Her name is Virtue of the

---

* *The Surangama Sutra: Sutra of the Indestructible*, translated by Ven. Master Hsuan Hua, Buddhist Text Translation Society, Ukiah, CA, 2009. *The Surangamasamadhi Sutra (T.642)*, *The Concentration of Heroic Progress*, translated into French by Étienne Lamotte, 1965, and into English by Sarah Boin-Webb, 1998, Motilal Banarsidass Publishers, Delhi, 2005.

Victorious Clarity Golden in Form. What is notable about this woman is that she had been a prostitute before she had a deep understanding of the Buddha's teachings. This demonstrates that anyone whether male or female, queen or courtesan, once imbued with the Buddhist teachings could transform and teach the Dharma as a bodhisattva.

The movement to make Buddhism a spiritual path for ordinary people had thus gone a long way. People discovered that a bodhisattva could be found not only in royal circles and among laypeople including women, but also among those who manufactured alcohol or who were courtesans. Buddhist teachings had begun to show just how engaged in the world they could be. We only need to look at a few sutras of that time to see this. They also show us in a historical way how the Mahāyāna path and the idea of a lay bodhisattva developed. They are linked together and continue each other in a clear way.

Besides the sutras that have been mentioned above there are many more that talk of the lay bodhisattva and his or her capacity to liberate beings from their suffering.

Before we go and visit the layman Vimalakīrti, the most talented of laypeople, let us go together to Anathapindika's monastery in the Jeta Grove to hear the words the Buddha taught to Ugra and a large assembly. He spoke about how to live a holy life of celibacy, either as a lay practitioner or as a monastic.

II

THE UGRAPARIPṚCCHA SUTRA

SUMMARY OF THE SUTRA

This sutra is said to have been taught by the Buddha in the Jeta Grove. In it, the Buddha talks about three ways a practitioner can lead the holy life (brahmacarya). The teaching was given in response to three questions asked by Ugra, a layman who had served and protected Buddhas over many lifetimes and was at that time present in the congregation.

The first part of the sutra instructs laypeople on how to make a living in a way worthy of a lay bodhisattva. The second part explains the training and practice of cultivation of a monastic bodhisattva. In the third part, Buddha talks about the five ways that make it possible for a fortunate layperson to train and cultivate their practice just like a monk or nun. This part of the sutra gives detailed instructions on how the lay bodhisattva should practice if they want to practice in the same way as a monastic bodhisattva, and what they should do if they want to take up the holy life of celibacy while still living in their family. However, without a sangha to practice with, the instructions given in the Ugra Sutra would not be easy to follow.

EXPLANATION OF THE SUTRA

The Vietnamese version of the sutra entitled "Ugra, the Householder," which we are using for the commentary given here, is from Chapter Nineteen of the Mahāratnakūṭa Sutra. The setting for the sutra is the Jeta Grove. On that occasion, although there were only 1250 śrāvaka monks present, there were also five thousand bodhisattvas in attendance.

Among the leaders of the bodhisattva assembly were the bodhisattvas Maitreya, Mañjuśrī, and Avalokiteśvara. All bodhisattvas whether of major or minor importance were present to support this Dharma festival. Apart from the śrāvakas and bodhisattvas there were hundreds of thousands of people in the audience who had gathered around the Buddha to hear the Dharma that day.

Amongst them was the householder Ugra who had come accompanied by five hundred of his relatives and friends from the nearby town of Śrāvasta, to pay his respects and to ask the Buddha about the Dharma. Ugra was the wisest of them all and acted as their spokesman. In the presence of the Buddha that day were other famous householders like Anāthapiṇḍika, who had previously donated the Jeta Grove monastery to the Buddha and the sangha.

After waiting until the whole community had assembled, Ugra then joined his palms, turned to the Buddha and asked: 'Lord Buddha, if there is someone who wishes to give rise to the mind of the Great Vehicle to practice liberating themselves and living beings, what path of practice should they follow? In other words: What precepts and practice should the lay bodhisattva follow?

This is a pragmatic sutra that draws a picture of the ideal lay bodhisattva as well as the ideal monastic bodhisattva. It is very interesting but for many years nobody has given it much attention.

THE WAY OF PRACTICE FOR
THE LAY BODHISATTVA

The Buddha gives very detailed instructions on how to practice as a lay bodhisattva. The teachings include taking refuge, recollection, protecting the Right Dharma, keeping the precepts, teaching the Dharma, and practicing in the family.

TAKING REFUGE

"To begin with, the lay bodhisattva should receive the Three Refuges and practice taking refuge in the Buddha, Dharma, and Sangha."

The Buddha then teaches in detail and in depth about the Three Refuges.

"When you take refuge in the Buddha, you must truly want to become Buddha. You should feel: 'I want to take refuge in you, but I also want to become like you. I want to be a Buddha

*adorned with the thirty-two beautiful signs.' Only then is it
appropriate to take refuge. If you just say: 'I take refuge in the
Buddha and for countless lifetimes to come, all I can do and all
I want to do is to hold the hem of the Buddha's robe,' you will
never be able to become a Buddha. If you think: 'All I can do
is be a śrāvaka and the most I can ever realize is the fruit of
arhatship,' then according to the teachings of the Mahāyāna, if
you have such an attitude and practice in accord with it, you
are not really taking refuge in the Buddha.*

"To take refuge in the Dharma means firstly to respect the
Dharma and the one who teaches the Dharma. One should
abide in the Dharma, train in the Dharma, and support the
Dharma. However that is not enough. One should use the
Dharma as a source of energy, a force, a tool to work with, an
instrument to liberate oneself and others. One should make
the vow that once one has realized the highest path, one will
bring the Right Dharma to share with all species. Only then is
it truly taking refuge in the Dharma. If you just bow your head
and say: 'I take refuge in the Dharma,' and you do not have the
strong aspiration to practice, then it is not really taking refuge
in the Dharma.

"To take refuge in the Sangha is to take refuge in one's own community of practice. One should respect monks and nuns even if
they are practicing the śrāvaka path."

Please notice this. This sutra belongs to the Mahāyāna,
but still it says that when one meets a śrāvaka monk one
cannot despise him; one treats him with all respect. At
the same time one's own aspiration goes further than
just becoming a śrāvaka. The sutra says that though you

respect the śrāvaka, your intention is not to stay always on the śrāvaka path. You always wish to go farther. This is what is meant by taking refuge in the Sangha.

Here the sutra mentions the need for a strong motivation and intention to go further than the śrāvaka path. Nevertheless there is a real respect for the śrāvaka as a part of the sangha jewel. This respect for the śrāvaka is never found in the Vimalakīrtinirdeśa.

"To take refuge in the Sangha is to recognize that the śrāvaka has realized merit and you need to be close to that merit, but deep in your heart you are seeking something greater. Those of you who have not yet realized the śrāvaka fruit should practice to realize that fruit first. When you do meet a monastic bodhisattva, you should be determined to take refuge in them."

Then the sutra adds that *"by being close to śrāvaka monks you could influence them, helping them give rise to bodhicitta and become a monastic bodhisattva."* This means there is every possibility that you would be able to encourage śrāvaka monks to follow the path of the Mahāyāna.

THE PRACTICE OF RECOLLECTION

The Buddha went on to teach:

"The lay bodhisattva should practice recollection (anusmṛti). First there is recollection of Buddha (Buddhānusmṛti), then Dharma (Dharmānusmṛti), and Sangha (Sanghānusmṛti)."

Having explained the principles of taking refuge and practicing recollection of the Three Jewels, the Buddha taught the path for the Eminent One. The Eminent One here means the Bodhisattva. This particular term "Eminent" is used in *the Inquiry of Ugra about the Bodhisattva Practice.* In the Dharma Festival of Ugra the Householder, the word "eminent" is not used. Instead there is the term "good and valiant one." Valiant One (丈夫),* like Eminent, signifies someone who has great motivation and a great aspiration.

"Such a person is within their right to own a house, possessions, and land but they should always use their possessions in a way that is in accordance with the law. They do not engage in unethical business and do not compete to become the richest or abuse their power by bullying anyone. The lay bodhisattva should always make their living in an ethical way. They should remind themselves constantly of impermanence, knowing that any business can at any moment go bankrupt. A lay bodhisattva should not intentionally store up riches for themselves. Rather they should find joy in sharing their wealth. They should respect and serve their parents and be a support for their family. They should offer their resources or at the very least a part of their resources as a donation for the benefit of living beings."

These teachings are very concrete and not just empty theory.

---

* 丈夫 is difficult to translate into modern English. Sometimes it is translated as 'hero' or 'gentleman,' meaning it is a man as opposed to a woman. 丈 can mean 'valiant' so I have translated 'Valiant One' here to avoid gender discrimination.

PROTECTING THE RIGHT DHARMA

The sutra continues with the Buddha saying:

"Although lay bodhisattvas need time to take care of their business affairs, they must also engage in the responsibility for the advancement of the Dharma. If someone uses all their time to build their personal career, they are not even Buddhist, let alone a lay bodhisattva. Your responsibility is to take care of the Dharma, bring all beings to the shore of liberation, bring the teachings of transformation to all beings without ever wearying of the task. The lay bodhisattva is not disturbed by profit and loss, praise and blame, suffering and happiness.

"You can be very rich but you should never be arrogant or negligent because of that. You should always practice the mindfulness trainings concerning speech, thought, and deed. Should you see someone who has received the mindfulness trainings but who is breaking them, it should not make you angry. You should feel compassion for such people and come to them to help them learn more about the mindfulness trainings, to revive their precepts' body and begin anew in the solid practice of the mindfulness trainings.

"The lay bodhisattva should always complete the task they have undertaken. They should feel gratitude and know how to repay gratitude. They should not be arrogant and do their best to help those who are sad or anxious to transform. They should respect and look up to those whose understanding and wisdom is vast so that they can learn from them. When they have studied the Dharma they should not keep it to themselves but share it with others. They should look on all worldly objects of sensual pleasure as impermanent. They should meditate to see that their *lifespan is like a drop of dew in the sunshine and their riches like a cloud. They should be careful that their partner, children, and associates do not become their prison.*

The sutra takes great care in teaching the lay bodhisattva not to spend their days preaching the theory without getting down to the correct practice.

KEEPING THE PRECEPTS

In this sutra the Buddha teaches that the lay bodhisattva should observe the mindfulness trainings.

"The first mindfulness training concerns non-harming— protecting life. A bodhisattva should have inner and outer shame and should make the vow not to harm the life of any living being. This means they should always practice compassion. The second precept concerns not stealing, not appropriating for oneself what belongs to another, and not craving. The third precept concerns not committing sexual misconduct, not giving way to lust. The fourth precept concerns speaking the truth and the fifth abstention from alcohol.

THE PRACTICE OF TEACHING THE DHARMA

The Buddha teaches:

"The lay bodhisattva should train in giving Dharma talks. This means they should share their understanding of the Buddhad- harma with the people of their village. If there are those who

lack faith, they should try to inculcate a little faith in them. If
there are those who do not feel gratitude and do not serve their
parents, monks, and nuns, they should instruct them so that
they have the faith to love and respect their parents and have
trust in monks and nuns. They should make it possible for
those who have not yet studied the Buddhadharma to do so,
whether they are adults or children.

*"The aim of the lay bodhisattva is to bring living beings to the
practice and teach them how to transform suffering. If the lay
bodhisattva does not address the task of inspiring and bringing
the teachings of transformation to those who live in their town or
village they will be blamed by the Buddhas. It could be compared
to a doctor who has been well-trained but does not treat the people
of their town when they are sick. They just allow the sick to die.
Such a doctor will be blamed by others. Anyone who, having had
the training of a lay bodhisattva, allows their fellow townspeople
to groan with pain without trying to help, is not a lay bodhisattva.*

PRACTICING IN THE FAMILY

The Buddha explains how practicing in the family environment is not easy. When you read the Vimalakīrtinirdeśa you can remember this section. All of us who are
lay practitioners should know that the family can be a
place with many kinds of suffering. Tragedies both small
and great can occur within the family.

*"Once you are bound by the fetters of family life, if you have not
yet realized the roots of goodness it can be difficult to realize
them. If you have already realized the roots of goodness they*

*could be destroyed. You can promise to do good things but you
may never be able to do them because you just do not have the
time. Your partner calls on you or presses you to do something,
your children are crying, so you are distracted from what you
want to do. You have been fortunate to realize some wholesome
things but now you cannot continue them. When you live in a
family you have to satisfy the demands of your family members.
Your parents, partner, children, and relatives demand your
presence and countless other things. It is impossible to satisfy
all their needs. They want recognition, reward, sex, and money.
Like the great ocean that swallows up thousands of rivers yet
never looks full, their demands are never satisfied."*

In his preface to the Ānāpānānusmṛti Sutra, Master
Kang Senghui* quotes this section:

*"Love, possessions, and sensual pleasures never satisfy them,
They are like the ocean that swallows up hundreds of rivers."*

*The family can also be seen as a fire burning in a ceaseless
wind, it is very difficult to extinguish. The Buddha says that
everything in family life is frail, like a drop of dew that easily
evaporates. The binding vows we make to each other to be
faithful as long as life lasts are in reality as fragile as dewdrops.
Family life is like a drop of honey. It is very sweet but only
for a moment. Once the drop of honey is finished, other drops
come along which are often very bitter. Family life can be like a
net with many sharp thorns because the fetters of form, sound,
scent, taste, and bodily contact are like thorns. Family life*

---

* *Master Tang Hoi*, Thich Nhat Hanh, Parallax Press, 2002.

brings with it many fears and worries. We are afraid of thieves, floods, fire, the king's soldiers and so on.

This is a summary of the section that talks about the disadvantages of the family life. These teachings do not appear in the Vimalakīrtinirdeśa. If Vimalakīrti and lay bodhisattvas who like to expound deep and wonderful doctrines read this section carefully about family life, it will bring them back down to earth.

THE SIX PĀRAMITĀS

In the next part of the sutra the Buddha talks about the Six Pāramitās: generosity, precepts, inclusiveness, effort, concentration, and understanding.

GENEROSITY

"The material resources you share with others are the only real possessions that stay with you. Belongings that you keep at home for yourself are not really your belongings. When you give to others it is an investment in your future security and happiness. The possessions that you have given to others will always be there and you do not need to hold on to them. Conversely you need to guard carefully whatever you do not give away although it is not certain that you will be able to keep it even for this life, let alone for lives to come.

"When a bodhisattva practices generosity in this way the three greatest internal knots, craving, anger, and ignorance decrease

day by day. When your generosity is real, you have no attachment or greed and that is why the internal knot of craving gradually diminishes. When you give, you do so out of love, and the energy of loving kindness diminishes the energy of anger. Loving kindness and compassion erode anger and hatred. Moreover when you offer up the merit of your giving for the path of liberation, the heap of ignorance in your mind grows smaller day by day, and gradually it disappears altogether."

GENEROSITY TO RELATIVES AND FRIENDS

The Buddha also talks about the attitude of the lay bodhisattva towards their parents, children, and friends. The Buddha teaches:

"Our parents of this lifetime are not necessarily our parents of other lifetimes. The same is true for our friends. Friends are not the same when they are happy as when they are sad. Children are the same. Therefore one should not, for the sake of parents, partner, children, or friends, bring about unwholesome karma either for this lifetime or the next, even if that unwholesome karma is as insignificant as a strand of hair or a blade of grass."

THE EIGHT PRECEPTS*

The Buddha teaches that "the lay bodhisattva should observe a day practicing the Eight Precepts from time

---

* These are the Eight Precepts of the Laity practiced on Uposadha days.

to time." One should organize days of mindfulness when the Eight Precepts are practiced by oneself, one's partner and one's children.

GOOD SPIRITUAL FRIENDS

"*Lay bodhisattvas should stay close to virtuous monks. Once they have found a teacher, they should request transmission of the mindfulness trainings and practice them. Their attitude towards their teacher should be one of respect. You should not look for faults in your teacher and then show disrespect. If you see a monk who is not living the pure life of a monk, you should still show respect. You should not say: 'I only take refuge in Buddha and Dharma. As far as the Sangha is concerned, I do not take refuge in it because it is too worldly.' If you do not show respect to a monk who is not practicing the precepts, they will not have a chance to return to the path of practice. The lay bodhisattva's respect is a wholesome condition for a monastic to be determined to return to their position as a true monastic. So the lay bodhisattva is reverential towards monks and nuns.*

"*You should feel compassion for the monastic who does not keep the precepts. You should understand that the reason why that person breaks the precepts is because their internal knots are great and no one has yet helped them undo them: in fact their intention is not to break the precepts. This is why one should feel compassion and not condemn the monastic. When lay bodhisattvas enter the monastery and meet monastics they should touch the earth before they enter. They should meditate: 'This is the place where the Three Doors of Liberation: Emptiness,*

Signlessness and Aimlessness are to be practiced. This is the place where Loving kindness, Compassion, Joy, and Equanimity are to be practiced.' They should aspire that the monastic order can offer them favorable conditions for realizing the bodhisattva ideal. The lay bodhisattva should also have the aspiration to live as one who has left the home to become a monastic."

When we are attentive to these sentences of this sutra we can understand other sutras. The family life has many worldly traps and fetters that bind. The monastic life offers much freedom and ease; it is an opportunity to practice one's deepest aspiration.

TWO WAYS OF LIFE

Now the Buddha compares the life of a layperson with that of a monk.

There is a sentence worth remembering here: *"Attached to family life you can remain on this shore. Free from attachment to family life you can cross over to the other shore."*

"When lay bodhisattvas enter the monastic community they should observe the different merits of the monastics. Which ones are good scholars, which ones good Dharma teachers, which excel in the practice of the Vinaya, which are going in the direction of non-return, which in the direction of the Bodhisattva vehicle, which are practicing asceticism, which contentment, which are practicing simple living, which are diligent in sitting meditation, which are serving by manual work. All those merits

are to be seen and observed. When you see merits such as these you should bow your head in respect. If you see someone who does not have one or another of those merits, you should not despise them. When you recognize the presence of a monastic who has the mind of a bodhisattva you should try to stay close to them and learn from them the practice of the Six Pāramitās. If there are monastics who have not yet found their true direction (this means monks who have not yet decided whether to continue the śrāvaka path or follow monastics who think in the Mahāyāna way), you should intervene and help them. You should encourage that monastic to give rise to the highest mind of love (bodhicitta). In other words you should help them give rise to the Mahāyāna way of thought.

"When lay bodhisattvas see monastics competing with each other, accusing each other, not living in harmony, they should, without fear for their life, help them to reconcile. They should not distance themselves or turn their back on them. When lay bodhisattvas see a monastic in ill-health, they should do all they can to care for them and help them to regain good health."

When the Buddha had spoken the householder Ugra and the other householders prostrated to him and some of them requested monastic ordination. The Buddha asked Maitreya bodhisattva to preside over the ceremony of making the initial vow. According to the sutra, on the day of their ceremony nine thousand householders asked to receive the monastic precepts. One thousand more householders, although they did not become monks, gave rise to the highest mind of love, and they began to follow the Mahāyāna.

THE LIFE OF THE
MONASTIC BODHISATTVA

Then the householder Ugra said:

"Lord Buddha, you have spoken of the virtues and the difficulties of a lay bodhisattva. Can you now talk about the ways of training a monastic bodhisattva."

The layman Ugra was not among those who sought monastic ordination. He felt it unnecessary to ordain as a monk. On the contrary, he thought that by continuing his life as a householder he could achieve the same fruits of practice as a monastic.

Firstly, the Buddha taught that "the aim of becoming a monastic is to realize deep understanding and that is their only career." In the Sutra on the Eight Realizations of Great Beings there is the sentence "Understanding is our only career." Understanding, or enlightenment, is what we take to be our vocation. The Buddha said:

"The monastic should not expect this career of understanding to happen in the future but should realize it straight away. It is like someone whose turban is on fire. That fire has to be extinguished immediately. This is the attitude the monastic needs to have as far as their career of practice is concerned."

In India many men wear the turban. In the West it is usually the women who cover their head with a scarf. If for whatever reason the turban or the scarf were to catch fire, the hair would also catch fire. Unless urgent measures are taken to extinguish the fire the person's life is at stake. The Buddha uses this image to demonstrate how urgent it is to realize deep understanding as far as a monastic is concerned. In the Chinese version of the sutra the sentence reads: "The monastic sangha should practice as energetically as you would to put out a fire that is burning on your head."

SIMPLE LIVING

The Buddha gave careful instructions concerning the daily activities of the monastic bodhisattva. The special characteristic of this sutra is its practicality.

First of all the Buddha taught four subjects: Food, clothes, medicines, and dwelling place. The monastic bodhisattva should live simply. Do not try to have any of these four things in excess of real need. The expression used by the Buddha is "knowing enough." All we need is enough to fulfill our basic needs. We do not need anything fancy or luxurious. If we run a little short we are not upset, we have no regrets and no cravings. The monastic should know that if we have any of these four things in excess it is harmful for our life of spiritual practice. The Buddha goes on to teach separately on each subject.

1. Food

The Buddha encourages, *"the monastic bodhisattva always to keep the alms' round. The alms' round helps the monastic be in touch with the people, practice the path of liberation, and nourish humility and responsibility as monastics."*

If, having become a monk, one has one's own bank account and does not need to depend on anyone else, one will not be able to continue the monastic practice. In our own times there are many people who plan their monastic life like this. First they work in order to have some money, then they put it in the bank and withdraw it bit by bit. That kind of monastic practice cannot succeed. When the monk waits in front of a poor or rich person's house to receive the offering of food, they know that their practice affects the person who offers the food. They are aware that this person is sharing their meal with them, whether it is rice, curry, or sweet potato.

Therefore as they eat the food they feel responsible. They know that it will be very unfortunate if this donor does not have a chance to take refuge in the Three Jewels and cannot touch peace and joy, purity, clarity, and calm. If the monastic wants to have peace of mind as they eat and not to feel in two minds, they have to live in such a way as to help the donor benefit from their monastic practice.

In the sutra it says: *"If anyone gives me food to eat, I have to act in such a way as to help them dwell in the Three Refuges. Only then shall I feel at ease as I eat. As far as those who don't offer me food, either because of prejudice or miserliness, I should feel compassion towards them. If I am angry with them, if I say that they know nothing of the Three Jewels and I despise them, I lose my opportunity to develop my understanding and compassion."*

Whether receiving a bowl of rice or a potato from a poor or a rich household, monastics are able to subdue their pride. However, if they feel no gratitude while these laypeople show them great respect, they will have the opinion that although laypeople need them, they have no need of the laypeople, and consequently their pride will rapidly increase.

We have seen this happening. If laypeople pay too much respect to monks and nuns they are easily corrupted. The Buddha teaches the correct way of seeking alms: "stopping at every home in order." It means that the monastic stops in front of every house they pass before going on to the next. No house can be omitted. If the monastic decides to pass by a house because it does not offer good food, or just stops in front of it for only one minute instead of the customary three or five minutes, it is a fault.

Those of us who are monks and nuns at this present time should contemplate this teaching of the Buddha. If we depend too much on the donors it can be harmful. They may have conservative views and forbid us to follow a more progressive practice. Sometimes when laypeople make offerings they can have very strange expectations. If the monastics do not fulfill those expectations they may refuse to continue to make offerings. If monastics become a slave to their wishes it can destroy their monastic life. For example offerings may be made in exchange for monastics praying for the sick or the dead and performing funeral rites until they have no time left to do anything else, even to practice the three-month Rains' retreat. So how should the monastic proceed? If we do not apply the teachings of the Buddha to be in touch with and receive offerings from the laypeople, we shall be corrupted. We need to find a middle way. That is, we can depend on the laypeople but depend in such a way that we retain our autonomy as a monastic sangha. This is an important matter for monks and nuns to look into and discuss.

2. ROBES

This sutra discusses robes. The Buddha uses the term "faded or dull in color." Monastic robes should not be shiny or brightly colored. *"When the monastic robe is of a dull color, it will inspire confidence and respect in gods, men, and asuras."* Subdued colors have their own beauty and value.

3. MEDICINES

In the Vinayapiṭaka,* the Buddhist monastic code, the Buddha gives instructions on treating sick monastics. They are only allowed to use the medicines that were generally used by ordinary people of the time. These included medicines made from the roots, stems, leaves, and flowers of plants, urine, or cow dung. When recovering from illness and in need of a tonic, the monastic could have oil, ghee, molasses, or milk.

Through these instructions we see that the intention of the Buddha for the monastics was that they lead a simple life close to nature and help the monastic sangha not to be over-dependent on material things. This would help the monks and nuns to make progress in their spiritual life. However, in our own time we can adapt the instructions of the Buddha to be more in line with present-day society.

4. DWELLING PLACE

Then the Buddha says that "the monk should not leave his araṇya."† *Araṇya* refers to a monastery where the

---

* Teachings on the Monastic Code in the Buddhist Canon.

† This is a Sanskrit word that means forest or another secluded place.

right conditions exist for living a pure life in quiet seclusion. The Buddha stresses this because any monk or nun, even when a monastic bodhisattva, must dwell in a place that is quiet and wholesome.

It is in a pure environment that one can train in the teachings of no-self, freedom, and nonattachment. Because of the wholesome, peaceful, and joyful environment, it becomes easy to practice mindfulness since the obstacles of the outer world have been removed. The sutra says that when one practices and dwells in an *araṇya* it is very beneficial. That is why the monastic bodhisattva should never leave the *araṇya*.

"If the monastic bodhisattva has to go into town to hear the teachings, to visit his preceptor (upadhyaya) or a relation, or another monastic who is sick, they should think to themself that there are reasons why I have to go to that place, but tonight I shall return to the araṇya."

The Buddha also teaches:

"Living in a secluded place is not enough on its own to make a monk. His body may be in a quiet and secluded place, but his mind is not quiet. He is not living alone; he is living with another, and that other with whom he lives is his restless mind. Although the monk is in a place where there are only wild chattering apes and crows and no crowds of people, still there is another person in his mind."

That other person is not necessarily a person, it may be a plan or a yearning for the future. This is what the

Buddha means by the expression *"living with another"* that we find in the sutra. You can read the Sutra on Knowing the Better Way to live Alone in the book *Our Appointment with Life** to understand this teaching more clearly.

THE NOBLE EIGHTFOLD PATH AND THE SIX PĀRAMITĀS

"If you are not able to master your mind in a secluded quiet place, then you are not solid or truly alone. When in the araṇya you must practice mindfulness and the Noble Eightfold Path. If you practice like this, every minute of your life will contain all the Six Pāramitās.† The Six Pāramitās are realized concurrently in each moment of our daily life."

It is not a matter of practicing the Six Pāramitās one by one: first generosity, then precepts and so on, because keeping the precepts is in itself generosity. If our life is stable in the practice of the precepts, we are generous to others and our life is established in the Right Dharma.

"When people see that you do not commit adultery, do not drink alcohol or tell lies, they can benefit from your behavior and your

---

* Thich Nhat Hanh, *Our Appointment with Life*, Parallax Press, 2007.

† 1. The Six Pāramitās: *dāna* (generosity) 2. *śīla* (mindfulness trainings) 3. *kṣānti* (patience) 4. *vīrya* (diligence, energy) 5. *dhyāna* (meditative concentration) 6. *prajñā* (insight, understanding).

life of inner freedom; they enjoy the gift of your practice. The
Six Pāramitās are practiced all at the same time."

The Buddha then teaches that the monastic bodhisattva should practice the Three Doors of Liberation:
emptiness (*śūnyatā*), signlessness (*animitta*), and aimlessness (*apraṇihita*).

THE FOUR RELIANCES

In this sutra the Buddha teaches the four reliances, the
four principles on which we can depend to benefit from
the Dharma.

THE FIRST RELIANCE
The first reliance is: *"rely on the Dharma, not on the person."*

There are some people who have vast knowledge
about the Dharma. Due to some good fortune, they have
heard, studied, and understood intellectually a great deal
about the Dharma. However they do not have the ability
to put into practice what they have learned and their way
of life does not reflect the Dharma that they talk about.
In this situation, if we were to think: "This person lives
in an unwholesome way, how can they teach us anything about the Dharma?" we shall lose an opportunity
of learning about the Dharma from them. Although their
way of life is not admirable, it may be that the knowledge
they have about the Dharma is very precious. Therefore
we should tolerate this person in order to filter out the

precious essence of the doctrines that they have studied and understood. It may be that in the future, due to this intellectual knowledge they will wake up and begin to put into practice what they have studied. In the present they have not yet begun to practice; they study because they enjoy talking about what they have learned. They take delight in showing off and proving that they are very learned about the teachings of the Buddha. When we come across people like that we should be careful not to brush them aside saying: "They are just theorists, they have never practiced what they preach." So "reliance on the Dharma and not the person" means that we should give our attention to the Dharma and not be prejudiced about the person who teaches it.

The example for this reliance is that a diamond has fallen into a stinking and filthy rubbish bin and we will endure fumbling around in the rubbish to find the diamond. We do not throw away the diamond because of the stench and the filth of the rubbish that surrounds it.

Maybe the person teaching us the Dharma annoys us. Just listening to them for fifteen minutes is enough to make us lose our temper and want to give them a kick. Nonetheless if they have conditions to know about the Dharma, we should take the trouble to listen to them.

We need to be careful when applying the criterion of "relying on the Dharma and not the person." It is difficult for students to have confidence in teachers who do not do what they teach. As a teacher you should teach by how you act in daily life. However, if you expect your teachers to be a perfect model of all they teach, it may be very difficult to find a teacher who satisfies you. If your teacher is not perfect, you should not make the mistake of losing faith in the Buddha and his teachings.

THE SECOND RELIANCE

"The second reliance is to rely on sutras that teach the deeper meaning or the absolute truth and not to rely on sutras that teach the relative truth".

Because everyone comes from a different background, this means there are always people who need the relative truth to guide them in the spiritual practice. If someone was to force the absolute truth on them, it would not help their practice.

We should understand clearly what is meant by absolute truth sutras and relative truth sutras. In the Tripiṭaka[*] there are many sutras that do not teach in terms of the absolute truth. We cannot condemn these sutras for being unessential. These teachings were delivered by the Buddha and his senior disciples to guide those who have just entered on the spiritual path. Although such sutras do not present the deep and wonderful essence of what

---

[*] Literally "The Three Baskets (of teachings)," which are the sūtra (discourses), vinaya (ethical code of conduct), and śāstra (commentaries on the sutra).

the Buddha taught, they are able to help people out of their suffering. Although they do not teach the absolute truth, they are still teachings of the Buddha, and once we recognize why the Buddha taught them and see how they have helped us on the path, we can accept them easily. The spirit of wide acceptance is essential in Buddhism.

In some sutras the Buddha teaches us to meditate "I am of the nature to die. I cannot escape death." In other places the Buddha teaches the absolute truth of no-birth and no-death. The first teaching is a skillful means to help us transform our innate fear of death. Only when we are ready to go deeply enough into the object of our fear can we realize the teaching that there is no birth and no death.

The idea of sutras that convey the deep meaning and sutras that do not convey the deep meaning goes along with the teaching of the two kinds of truth: the relative and the absolute. The relative truth is a kind of truth, although it is not the deepest truth. It is a truth that goes part of the way but it is very important. This kind of truth is called conventional truth (*saṃvṛtisatya*). The absolute truth is sometimes called the ultimate truth (*paramārthasatya*).

Here is an example to help you understand. In your house you want to set up an altar. You would like it to be on the top story so that your other daily household activities would happen below. If you were to lie down, cook, or play in the room dedicated to spiritual practice, you would feel the space was not sacred enough. This kind of feeling—that the shrine should be at the top of the house—would be based on a relative truth. You believe that you are conducting your daily activities on a lower level and the Buddha altar is on a higher level, but as the earth turns on its axis the Buddha altar will end up underneath and you on top. Ideas of above and below are relative or conventional. As far as the ultimate truth is concerned, there is no above and no below. However, these ideas are important in our everyday life and there are times when we cannot ignore them.

Once there were a teacher and his disciple who had to take the train from Saigon to Nha Trang. According to the monastic custom the teacher should lie on the higher bed. It is not admissible for the elder to be on the low bed while the novice monk is above. Since teacher and disciple agreed to keep the convention, the novice was happy not to have to climb the ladder to the upper bunk. However the teacher felt reluctant. He was old and a little lame. What if while he was climbing the ladder, the train should jolt and he were to fall? If ever I had to go on a train with my attendant, I should say to him: "My child, please climb up and sleep on the top bunk." Since above and below are a matter of relative truth, if both teacher and disciple can see this, the disciple will have no complex about lying on the top bunk and the teacher will feel at ease lying underneath. Nevertheless, if in the same compartment there are some lay Buddhists who have not understood the absolute truth of no above and no below, the teacher and disciple would need to follow the convention, in order not to be misunderstood by the laypeople, who would think that the disciple had no respect for his teacher.

The worldly truth is sometimes called the criterion of convention and the absolute truth the criterion of the highest truth. Criterion is the word used to translate the Sanskrit word "siddhānta". There are four criteria of truth altogether and they are taught in the course on basic Buddhism.*

The Third Reliance

"The third reliance is to rely on the spirit and not on the letter."

This means we should not be caught in the literal meaning that is hidden behind the word and that there are times when we need to transcend terminology. If we are too caught in words we become their slave, and we need to be intelligent enough to go beyond the letter to discover the truth. Ideas and ideologies are only reflections of the truth and not the substance of the truth or the true nature of the thing described. If we were to go out on a sunny day into the garden, looking down at the ground we might see the shadow of a tree and we would

---

* Please see *The Heart of the Buddha's Teaching*, Parallax Press, 1998. Paperback edition, Harmony Books, 2015.

know that nearby there must be a real tree casting its shadow on the earth. We should only need to look up and we would see the tree itself. The tree has two selves. One is the shadow on the earth and the other is the tree itself that we need to raise our eyes to see. When a cloud is passing over the water, if we do not look up to the sky, we shall only see the shadow of the cloud on the water's surface. If we think that the reflection in the water is the real cloud, we are not using our intelligence. Using our intelligence, we shall know that there is a cloud in the sky. All we have to do is lift up our eyes and we will be in direct contact with the cloud.

We can say that all things have two aspects. One is the shadow or image, the other is the reality. Truth is the same. The truth of words and language is the shadow or image truth. The truth that is born from direct experience without words and ideas is the truth of the reality. The awakened ones and bodhisattvas on the way to awakening are able to experience the truth of reality. When they need to describe this truth in words and ideas, what we hear them talking about is just the shadow. If we are caught in the shadow that is all we receive. Understanding this, we can practice the principle of relying on the meaning and not on the words, and we too can attain the truth of the reality they are talking about.

Once there were two monks standing in the courtyard enjoying the view. One of the monks saw a very beautiful bird flying past and said: "Look, look at that beautiful bird!" The other monk was so busy adjusting his spectacles on his nose that when he eventually looked up, he did not see the bird. "I can't see any beautiful bird flying past," he said. To which the first monk replied: "Its true, a very beautiful bird really did just fly by." The second monk would not believe him even though the first monk did everything he could to describe the beautiful bird. The description was just words and images that could not satisfy the other monk. It is not by being in touch with an awakened being that we can obtain the substance of awakening. We have to be very bright, alert, and lucky to receive awakening from an awakened one, even if we live with that person for fifty years.

THE FOURTH RELIANCE

"The fourth reliance is reliance on wisdom, not on perception."

We should learn to be in touch with reality by means of wisdom. Perception here refers to the perceiver and the perceived. Our perception is often obscured by our craving, anger, and ignorance so when we use our perception to experience reality we distort the truth. We should find ways to be in touch with reality by means of wisdom and not use our everyday ways of perceiving. Wisdom in Sanskrit is *jñāna*; normal ways of perceiving is *vijñāna*. Wisdom is direct intuition; it does not need to go through the intermediary of reasoning and notions, and it is not impeded by craving, anger, and ignorance.

WHAT THE BODHISATTVA NEEDS TO FEAR

"The Buddha teaches that the monastic bodhisattva seeks a secluded place because they are afraid of certain things. The monastic bodhisattva begins as an ordinary person, a person who has many weaknesses and shortcomings. That is why they are afraid of town life; they are afraid of the excitement that is found in large crowds and all the accompanying afflictions. They know that they are still weak and can easily be carried away by the corruptions and unwholesome qualities that are to be found in crowded places. So they seek out a place that is calm, where there are not so many corruptions and unwholesome behaviors. In noisy, turbulent places our acquaintances may have craving, anger, ignorance, afflictions. They may consume toxins; they may have evil intentions."

They may belong to gangs of people who trick and deceive, who are violent. They may watch television programs and films that are full of violence and sex. These are the things that a bodhisattva in training should fear. They should fear watering and sowing in their consciousness seeds that are toxic. They should keep at distance those who do wrong and make good spiritual friends. They should make skillful use of their time for spiritual practice and not waste time in pursuits that take them nowhere as their life drifts away.

WHAT THE BODHISATTVA NEED NOT FEAR

The Buddha continues,

"Once the bodhisattva has learned what to fear they should learn what not to fear.

"If the monastic bodhisattva practices looking deeply into no-self they will gain the capacity of non-fear."

Once the view of a separate self is broken through, all attachments, all wrong perceptions and cravings dissolve and there is nothing more to fear.

"Someone who dwells in a pure and secluded place, is no longer caught in a separate self, has right understanding of self, and is truly dwelling in a pure and secluded place. As far as they are concerned, the afflictions cannot disturb them and thinking about the afflictions cannot shake or make them waver."

The Buddha taught that "the idea of nirvāṇa can no longer shake the monastic bodhisattva much less the idea of the afflictions." If we are afraid of the afflictions and only want to attain nirvāṇa then there is still something that can shake our solidity, and that is the desire to attain nirvāṇa as quickly as possible so as to avoid the complications of life.

The path of the monastic bodhisattva is the path of precepts, concentration, and insight. The bodhisattva should base their training in these three things, in that order. The monastic bodhisattva should practice mindfulness in order to know their teachers' intentions for them. Their teachers have wishes and expectations of their disciples. They should know their teachers' intentions and practice in accord with them. Fulfilling their teacher's expectations is the deepest way of expressing respect for the teacher.

THE INTENTION TO TRAIN AND GROW IN THE PRACTICE

The monastic bodhisattva needs to have the willingness to train and grow. Whatever someone teaches or instructs them in on the path of practice, they should respectfully receive. Even if it is only a gāthā of four lines that instructs one to practice precepts, concentration, and insight they should receive it with as much respect as they would if their own teacher had instructed them.

OBSERVING THE PRECEPTS

After this the Buddha teaches about precepts.

Precepts, concentration, and insight are the path of practice for the monastic bodhisattva. They should be practiced in all actions of body, speech, and mind.

This section of the sutra is very important. Before the development of the Mahāyāna the only precepts were those of the śrāvaka and the lay disciple. The śrāvaka precepts included the ten novice precepts, the 250 bhikṣu precepts, and the 348 bhikṣuṇī precepts. When the Mahāyāna began to develop people wanted a Mahāyāna that was wholly independent of the śrāvaka vehicle. That is why they had to create Mahāyāna precepts. It was only several hundred years later that Mahāyāna precepts took a clear form in the Mahāyāna Brahmajāla Sutra. There are two Brahmajāla sutras. One belongs to Original Buddhism and one to the Mahāyāna. It is in the latter that the Mahāyāna precepts are found.

In the Brahmajāla sutra of Original Buddhism (Dīgha Nikāya 1) the sixty-two wrong views are discussed. The subject of the Mahāyāna Brahmajāla is the bodhisattva precepts. It was not until the beginning of the fourth century CE that the bodhisattva precepts gained a firm foothold in the monasteries of China. Before precepts can be created there has to be a basis for them. Precepts must be based on a principle. We could say that the point of view on which Mahāyāna precepts were based was something that developed gradually. The Mahāyāna precepts were bodhisattva precepts that applied to both lay and monastic practitioners. The seeds of the Mahāyāna precepts and the reasoning behind them had already been laid down in the Avataṃsaka Sutra, which belongs to the first stages of the Mahāyāna and appeared before the Brahmajāla Sutra.

According to the Mahāyāna point of view there are two stages in receiving the precepts: individual and general. Individual means receiving the precepts in order to protect oneself. General means receiving for the good of all.

Precepts can be divided into three groups:

1. *Embracing us in the discipline and fine manners*

2. *Embracing the wholesome*

3. *Benefitting all living species*

When a monk or nun receives the individual precepts, first of all they receive the precepts that "embrace you in the discipline and fine manners." This is is the group of precepts that includes the ten novice precepts, and the 250 precepts of the bhikṣu and the 348 precepts of the bhikṣunī. The purpose of these precepts is to hold the monk or nun in the discipline of monastic life.

Embracing means to gather together, to receive into one's person, to bring into one's sphere of influence. The one who embraces becomes one with what they embrace. The precepts influence you and you influence the way the precepts are. The word "embracing" has a special meaning in Buddhism. In the Śrimālādevī Sutra there is the expression "embracing the Right Dharma." It means making oneself one with the Right Dharma or bringing the Right Dharma into oneself so that one becomes one with it. The Right Dharma influences us, and our duty is to preserve and develop the Right Dharma. The purpose of this first group of precepts is to prevent you from taking the wrong path and committing mistakes that make you and others suffer. Their purpose is to protect your freedom. Once you break the precepts you lose your freedom. People sometimes think that when you observe the precepts you lose your freedom, but the opposite is the truth: when you do not keep the precepts you lose your freedom.

For example when you are under the influence of alcohol you have no more freedom. Whatever your mind influenced by alcohol tells you to do, you do it. You cannot even walk straight. How can you be sovereign of yourself? It's the same when you run after sex. You are no longer free. You are like a spinning top; wherever it goes, you go. Gambling is the same. That is why precepts guarantee the freedom of the person who observes them.

The second group of precepts are those that gather together all that is wholesome. The first group is to stop us committing what is unwholesome. The second group is to help us do what is wholesome. When we practice the first group, it is in order not to create suffering. When we practice the second group, it is in order to create happiness.

As far as the Mahāyāna is concerned, to practice the precepts simply from one point of view is not enough. The Mahāyāna brings a very new way of looking at precepts. It is absolutely correct to keep the precepts in order not to create suffering but it is not sufficient. We have to do wholesome things and that is to practice the second group called "Embracing the Wholesome."

When we practice not killing, we practice embracing the discipline. If we have a chance to save someone's life but we do not take that chance, we do not observe the precepts of embracing the wholesome. A monk can say, "Since I do not kill, I keep the precepts." However, as far as the bodhisattva is concerned, if we have a chance to save someone's life and we do not take it, we break the precepts. This analysis is to help practitioners see the practice of the precepts in a wider context. It does not mean that according to the śrāvaka vehicle, people do not take every opportunity to save the lives of others.

The third group is to enable the practitioner to benefit all living species. "Living" in this context means beings that have feelings and perceptions. In former times people thought they knew which species had feelings and which did not. Scientists of our own time are not so sure which species have feelings and which do not. A Vietnamese songwriter, Trịnh Công Sơn, asked the question: "How do you know the stone does not feel?"

In summary, keeping the bodhisattva precepts is not just in order not to do wrong but also to do what is wholesome. In our heart we maintain the aspiration to realize what can give rise to peace and joy for all species that can feel and perceive.

All the bodhisattva precepts are based on these three groups called The Three Groups of Pure Precepts. The word "Pure" is not really necessary because by nature precepts are pure. In the beginning when we first receive the monastic precepts it is just for our individual protection. This means we receive the first group of precepts in order to embrace the discipline. We receive them in the presence of the sangha. For a correct transmission of the precepts to take place the sangha has to transmit them. Later on we receive the precepts for the general good. This means we have to receive the two remaining groups. The receiving for the general good includes precepts of all three groups. The receiving for individual protection includes precepts of the first group only. When we receive precepts we always begin with the first group—embracing the discipline and fine manners. At this point the monastic bodhisattva does not yet receive precepts for the universal good of all species.

In fact receiving precepts for the general good is something quite rare. In reality in only one of every fifteen monasteries or so, is it possible to receive precepts of groups two and three. The sutra tells us that receiving for individual protection is the basis of receiving precepts in the monastic tradition now as it has been in the past.

There are two ways of receiving precepts in a general sense. The first is "realization from another." It means that your precepts' body is made possible by another person. When you meet people who have the Mahāyāna precepts' body, you kneel before them and ask them to transmit the precepts to you. If they accept, they become the precepts' transmission council. In the case that you are in a place where there are no monks practicing the Mahāyāna you can realize the precepts for yourself. You turn to the Three Jewels and vow to receive the precepts of groups two and three: "I, your disciple, have received the precepts called Embracing the Discipline. Now I request the Buddha, Dharma, and Sangha to allow me to receive the groups of precepts called Embracing the Wholesome and Benefitting all Living Beings." You can also receive your precepts' body in this way.

In the past it often happened like that. In many places there were not enough right conditions for the transmission of the precepts. The important point is our mind. There is an expression "precepts of the mind." The bodhisattva relies more on their own mind than on the surrounding circumstances.

The same is true of the spirit of the Mahāyāna precepts' body. Even when the bodhisattva precepts had not yet been clearly formulated there was a clear direction and spirit for the practice of precepts. This was called "the spirit of openness" (Chinese 開 kai). In the sutra called The Section on Upāli that is the twenty-fourth section of the Ratnakūṭa Sutra, the term "Opening up the Precepts" (Chinese 開戒 kai jie) first appears. From what I have seen of this sutra I would suggest that although it may seem to be contemporaneous with the sutra called The Dharma Festival of Householder Ugra, it probably appeared a little later.

In the Vinaya we have the terms: Open up and Prevent, Keep and Transgress. "Open up" means to open, to allow to do, to make exceptions, and not to prevent. It means there are circumstances when we can do a certain thing without breaking the precepts. Under certain circumstances we could drink alcohol or not speak the truth. There are circumstances when, if we told the truth, it could lead to much suffering. Suppose someone were hiding under your bed and someone else wanted to kill them. If the murderer were to come and ask you where that person was and you were to reply, "They are under my bed," your telling the truth would lead to someone losing their life. In such a circumstance your intelligence tells you to practice "opening up" the precept. You give yourself permission not to tell the truth. There are times when a bodhisattva does not tell the truth, but one should be careful to develop deep understanding in order to know when and when not to lie.

As far as Mahāyāna thinking is concerned, it seems that the śrāvaka was constrained by the outer form of the teaching while the bodhisattva was more concerned with the content. However we can be confident that among the śrāvakas there were many who used the teachings intelligently and, by their practice of mindfulness, knew when it was necessary to speak the non-truth without having the feeling that they were breaking the precepts. The seeds of the Mahāyāna were already available in the śrāvaka disciples. We should not look down on the śrāvakas and say that they only practiced the outer form of the teachings.

PREVENTING, PROHIBITING

This is the aspect of the precepts that stops us from falling into situations where we do harm to ourselves and to others. According to the Mahāyāna, the śrāvaka precepts have the capacity only to prevent. Sometimes the Mahāyāna goes even further and says that a woman can use her beauty to lead a man into the practice. This means that beauty can be used as a skillful means without breaking the precepts.

LIVING IN THE FAMILY AND PRACTICING THE MONASTIC PRECEPTS

After the householder Ugra had asked how the lay bodhisattva and the monastic bodhisattva should live, he had another question, *"Lord Buddha, is there any way in which a lay bodhisattva like myself can learn and practice the monastic precepts?"*

The Buddha taught: *"If the lay bodhisattva can practice the five things that follow, even if he is living with his family, he can train as a monk does."*

ALL-EMBRACING UNDERSTANDING

"Firstly, the lay bodhisattva does not regret the loss of any material possession and in accord with all-embracing understanding (Sanskrit: sarvajñāna; Chinese: 一切智 yi qie zhi) he does not long for any particular reward. In accord with all-embracing

*understanding means that his mind is going in only one direc-
tion and that is the direction of all-embracing understanding.
He lives in the family but he is not concerned with making
himself rich. He has let go of all possessions and single-mindedly
dedicates all his merit to the realization of all-embracing
understanding. He is not looking for rewards within the cycle of
rebirth, since all of these are accompanied by afflictions (āsrava).*

BRAHMACARYA (THE HOLY LIFE OF CELIBACY)

*"Secondly, the lay bodhisattva practices celibacy. They no longer
think about sexual relations much less engage in them.*

PRACTICING MEDITATION IN ORDER TO HELP OTHERS

*"Thirdly, the lay bodhisattva knows how to practice looking
deeply in meditation in secluded places and how to use skillful
means to help others and does not enter into nirvāṇa for his
personal benefit.*

COMPASSION FOR ALL SPECIES

*"Fourthly, the lay bodhisattva should diligently practice the per-
fect understanding (prajñāpāramitā) and treat all living beings
with compassion in order to be able to bring them to the other
shore.*

GUARDING THE RIGHT DHARMA

"Fifthly, the lay bodhisattva guards the Right Dharma by always finding ways to teach and encourage all people to practice."

CONCLUSION

When the Buddha had finished the talk the householder Ugra stood up, touched the earth, and said: "Lord Buddha, I wish to continue to live as a lay practitioner and will do my very best to realize the five teachings that you have just given."

At that point the Buddha smiled. The Venerable Ānanda wondered what had made the Buddha happy so he stood up, touched the earth, and asked: "Lord Buddha what has made you happy today so that you just smiled?"

The Buddha replied, "I smiled because I saw how in the past the householder Ugra had made offerings to and supported the Dharma over a long period of time. Whenever a Buddha arose in the world he always practiced as a householder, making offerings and supporting the Dharma out of deep respect. Although he was always a layman, he nevertheless helped many living beings to the shore of liberation. In fact he has liberated more living beings than some monastic bodhisattvas have liberated over hundreds of kalpas. Therefore I say that the merit of one hundred thousand monastic bodhisattvas is not equal to the merit of this householder.

In this sutra we see clearly the kind of reasoning and the seeds of the ideas that are found in the Vimal-akīrtinirdeśa. We could say that the ideas expressed in The Dharma Festival of Ugra the Householder are the embryonic form of the ideas in the Vimalakīrtinirdeśa and one of the cornerstones on which that later sutra was built.

III

THE VIMALAKĪRTINIRDEŚA SUTRA

THE MAIN FEATURES
OF THE SUTRA

The Vimalakīrtinirdeśa was composed in central India and attained renown as soon as it appeared. Without the sutras that preceded it, like The Dharma Mirror, The Householder Ugra, and The Dharma Festival of the Householder Ugra, this sutra would not have been possible. The character of layman Vimalakīrti was based on Ugra the Householder. Some people have said that Ugra was Vimalakīrti in a former life.

The Vimalakīrtinirdeśa was composed in the latter half of the second century CE. We have certain proof that it appeared later than The Householder Ugra.

The Vimalakīrtinirdeśa is number 475 in the Taishō and was translated into Chinese in 406 by Kumārajīva. In all it was translated into Chinese six times. Kumārajīva's translation is the best. It is not always literal but his language is very smooth and elegant, so everyone likes to use this version. Later on Xuanzang translated it again and his version was a much more literal translation. However, it is not as flowing and easy to read as the translation of Kumārajīva. The reason why Kumārajīva was able to make such a good translation was that he understood Chinese culture well. He uses the expression filial piety, which is a very important concept in Chinese culture. The concept of filial piety is a precious jewel in Chinese culture. As far as Indian culture is concerned it is less important. Thus while translating the Vimalakīrtinirdeśa, Kumārajīva sinicized it to a certain extent by means of his skill in using words.

Forty years ago a Belgian scholar, Étienne Lamotte, translated the sutra into French. He based his translation on Master Xuanzang's version and another version in Tibetan. Before that, beginning in 1897, the sutra had been translated into English twice and once into German. The Vietnamese version that is currently available was translated from Chinese by Thích Huệ Hưng from the version of Kumārajīva. While we study the Vimalakīrtinirdeśa we shall have an opportunity to compare the versions of Xuanzang and Kumārajīva.

The original Sanskrit version is no longer extant. Nevertheless many scriptures and commentaries quote freely from the original version. This means we can still access the original version through quotations in Sanskrit in commentaries and scriptural writings that have been preserved until now.

The Vimalakīrtinirdeśa can be looked on as the manifesto of an important movement among laypeople who wanted to bring Buddhism to the people. Before that Buddhism had become a monastic religion, a spiritual path reserved for monks and nuns. The role of laypeople was to stay on the outside and just offer support by donating robes at the end of the winter retreat or food as alms.

The term *Vimalakīrtinirdeśa* contains three words. First of all there is the word *Vimala*, which means pure or unsullied. When the eighth consciousness is transformed and becomes deep understanding it is called "pure consciousness" or *vimala vijñāna*. The next word is "*kīrti*" it means fame or renown. The name Vimalakīrti means, unsullied fame or unsullied reputation. The person who has this name is worthy of renown because of their purity. Finally there is the word *nirdeśa*—it means teachings. The complete name of the sutra means *the teachings of the one whose reputation is unsullied*.

The Vimalakīrtinirdeśa is a sutra of deep meaning. Its intention is to lead people to abandon the śrāvaka path in order to undertake the bodhisattva path. The Mahāyāna movement wanted to bring into the light of day the image of the ideal person as someone who was not prejudiced, was open, and completely altruistic, in other words, the bodhisattva.

THE CHARACTERS
PRESENTED IN THE SUTRA

At the time when the Vimalakīrtinirdeśa was composed, there was a literary movement in India that was just beginning to develop. This was the development of famous epics in the form of drama, and it was very popular with the Indian people. Those who were compiling Mahāyāna sutras were influenced by this new movement in literature. All the Mahāyāna sutras that appeared during this time were presented in the form of plays. Every chapter is like a scene of a play, with its own kind of suspense, and there are all different kinds of characters: those who know about the practice and those who are worldly.

The Vimalakīrtinirdeśa therefore contains all the flavor and color of a play.

If we look at the characters in the Vimalakīrti drama, we shall see the protagonist Vimalakīrti, a lay practitioner whose role it is to commend the Mahāyāna way of thought. Vimalakīrti is a lay bodhisattva who has the ability to appear in many different forms in order to help living beings to the shore of liberation. His appearance as a lay practitioner is only one of his many ways of appearing. Although he is not a monk he is fully versed in the sutras, he is enlightened and is able to bring countless living beings to the shore of liberation. In other words, it is possible to be an authentic bodhisattva without becoming a monk and while living a normal life in the world.

In chapter two of the sutra we see that Vimalakīrti has realized the practice of *dhāraṇi,*, as well as the inclusiveness that comes with the realization that all dharmas are unborn. He has the spiritual power of fearlessness and has fully penetrated the skillful means of teaching and liberating beings. His mind is as wide as the great ocean. He observes all the fine manners taught by the Buddha and practices the bodhisattva precepts. It is not until chapter twelve, Buddha Akṣobhya, that we learn about his past lives. Before his life on earth he had his abode in the Pure Land of Akṣobhya Buddha called Wonderful Joy. This is a Pure Land in the East. Its population is somewhat smaller than that of the Pure Land of Amita Buddha in the West. In his previous lives, he had practiced diligently and made offerings to countless Buddhas and so put down many wholesome roots.

---

* The practice of being able to hold in concentration certain syllables with mystical power.

Thus we can conclude that the layman Vimalakīrti is a manifestation body whose function is to transmit the teachings of the Mahāyāna. He is not an ordinary lay practitioner who has wide knowledge about the Mahāyāna and just wants to put a spoke in the wheel of the monks who are practicing according to the śrāvaka vehicle. He is speaking not for himself alone but for many lay practitioners.

The second group of characters is the senior disciples of Buddha Śākyamuni. They stand for the teachings of the śrāvaka vehicle.

We know that the Venerable Śāriputra was an outstanding monk. He is looked on as the wisest of Buddha's disciples. In spite of this, he is portrayed in the Vimalakīrti Sutra as suffering a crushing defeat at the hands of Vimalakīrti when they engage in debate. This is something that makes monks and nuns feel quite uncomfortable when they read the sutra. They feel that their wise elder brother is being maligned.

However the debate between Vimalakīrti and the senior disciple of the Buddha is a skillful means to be able to present a comparison between the teachings of the Mahāyāna and the śrāvaka vehicle. Each of the subjects that these two characters debate is in the field of the studies and practice of the śrāvaka disciples. Although the monks are experts in the strong points of their practice, when they meet Vimalakīrti, not one of them is able to endure the onslaught of Vimalakīrti's questions.

Therefore when the Buddha was appointing some of his disciples to go and visit Vimalakīrti who was sick, everyone did their best not to be chosen and thought that to avoid having to confront Vimalakīrti was the best thing to do.

In the final chapters of the Vimalakīrtinirdeśa the compiler of the sutra makes Śāriputra ask some very foolish questions. We should always remember that Śāriputra in this sutra is just a character in a play. The more foolish he is made to look, the more brightly the light of the Mahāyāna will show itself. It is just as when in a play the robber chief appears on the stage, we have a chance to observe the ability of the courageous hero.

The last kind of role in the drama is played by the Bodhisattva Mañjuśrī and lesser bodhisattvas like Maitreya who represent the Mahāyāna. Each bodhisattva generally has a wider and greater aspiration and sphere of activity than the śrāvaka, and that is why countless living beings have confidence in them.

The most powerful scene in the sutra is the dialogue between Bodhisattva Mañjuśrī and the layman Vimalakīrti. In the meeting and exchange between these two outstanding practitioners, one of them will normally speak the language of the noumenal world while the other will speak in terms of the phenomenal. At other places in the sutra, Vimalakīrti will sometimes talk to śrāvaka monks (like Śāriputra) and sometimes talk to a great bodhisattva like Mañjuśrī. Thus his words and ideas have to change in order to be appropriate to the situation of the one he is talking to. As we read we may have the feeling that the drum and trumpet are playing different pieces of music. Vimalakīrti seems to be saying one thing at one moment and something quite different at the next. There are even people who have not understood the purpose of the sutra and have called these seeming inconsistencies the profundity and mystery of the Vimalakīrtinirdeśa.

When we read the sutra we should understand why the senior disciples of the Buddha have been presented as they are, who the layman Vimalakīrti is, and what is the aim of the sutra. If we do not know the answers to these questions, we shall feel that the sutra is maligning the Buddha's monastic disciples and making a laughingstock out of the ten senior disciples. In that case we shall only see anger and mockery directed towards the Buddha's disciples and we shall not learn anything interesting and beneficial from the sutra.

INSIGHTS INTO THE SUTRA

In order to understand the sutra clearly we shall go into each chapter one by one.

CHAPTER 1: THE BUDDHA LAND

In this first chapter called Buddha Land, the famous householder by the name of Vimalakīrti has not yet made an appearance.

Buddha land means a Pure Land that has been established by a Buddha so that he can teach the people of that land how to transform suffering. The scene that is presented here is Vaiśalī on the northern bank of the Ganges, a territory belonging to a clan called Vajjī.

Vajjī was a democratic clan. It could well have been the first democracy in the history of the human species. They voted and had a parliament. On the outskirts of the town of Vaiśālī there was a mango grove that belonged to the courtesan Āmrapālī. In the forest near that town there was a monastery called the Great Forest Monastery. Part of that monastery was a brick building with a gabled roof. This house was built as an offering to the Buddha so it could be used as a monastery. People who contributed funds to build the house included Āmrapālī and young men of the Licchavi clan. The Licchavi were well known for their intelligence. Some of the first disciples to take refuge in the Buddha belonged to the Licchavi clan. Vimalakīrti was said to belong to that clan.

At the time of the sutra, the Buddha was in Vaiśālī residing in the grove of Āmrapālī along with a sangha of eight thousand bhikṣus. Eight thousand bhikṣus already sounds like a very large crowd, but it does not compare with the number of bodhisattvas which was four times as great: thirty-two thousand. We may be wondering how the Mango Grove of Āmrapālī was big enough to hold such a large audience. We should remember that this was a very special setting. Not only were there thirty-two thousand bodhisattvas, but thirty-two thousand bodhisattvas that managed to fit into the grove. This proves that the Vimalakīrtinirdeśa has learned from the Avataṃsaka Sutra. A small mango grove of three to four hundred trees is able to contain tens of thousands of bodhisattvas. It is like the womb of Mahāmāya that was able to contain millions of bodhisattvas who came in there in order to be able to pay respect to the prince

Siddhārtha before he was born. The one contains the all and the infinitely small contains the infinitely large. This point is made later on in the sutra when the layman Vimalakīrti is sitting in his small room and hosts thirty-two thousand guests there.

Sections of the sutra that follow describe the virtuous actions and the value of all the great bodhisattvas who were present in the assembly that day. In chapter one some of the thirty-two thousand bodhisattvas are named and they include well-known bodhisattvas such as Mañjuśrī, Samantabhadra, Avalokiteśvara, and Maitreya.

Mañjuśrī is also known as Prince of the Dharma, the son of the King of the Dharma. He is the crown prince who is destined to become the next king. The Buddha is a king, not in the political sense but the king of the teachings and practice of love and understanding. That is why he is called Dharma Rāja, Dharma King. If he is king, he has to have a successor and that successor is called the Dharma Prince.

The Dharma Prince Mañjuśrī is not someone it is difficult to connect with. We should remember that we are all children of the Buddha. We are born from the lips of the Buddha because, thanks to the teachings the Buddha has given, we have been born in the spiritual dimension. The image of being born from the lips of the Buddha is a very beautiful one. It is found in the Brahman tradition. In the four castes in India, the Brahman caste is thought to be the most noble. The members of this caste are said to be born from the mouth of the god Brahma. In our case the Buddha teaches the Dharma and we receive our spiritual life from his teachings. Thus we are all spiritual children of the Buddha and we are all Dharma princes or Dharma princesses, so we should not under-estimate ourselves. You should see Mañjuśrī, Prince of the Dharma, in your heart and then you will understand the words of the Buddha. Mañjuśrī stands for the innate wisdom of the Buddha just as Avalokiteśvara represents the compassion of the Buddha. In us are both Mañjuśrī and Avalokiteśvara. When studying the sutra, when teaching the Dharma, when sitting in meditation, we do it in such a way that Dharma Prince Mañjuśrī is present.

On that day there were thirty-two thousand Bodhisattvas present including monks, nuns, laymen, and laywomen; there were ten thousand god-Brahma, ten thousand god-Brahma-Śikhin (Kings of the Form Realm, rūpadhātu) and twelve thousand god-Indra from different continents who came to hear the Buddha teach the Dharma.

We have the feeling that Maitreya Bodhisattva was a monk, because in the Householder Ugra Sutra, Maitreya was appointed by the Buddha as the one to ordain 1,200 householders as monks. We also feel that bodhisattvas Kṣitigarbha and Mañjuśrī are monks.

Besides all the śrāvakas, pratyeka buddhas and bodhisattvas there were tens of thousands of upāsaka and upāsikā (laymen and laywomen) who attended the Dharma assembly that day.

*While this beautiful serene sangha of such a tremendous size
was sitting around the Buddha, the son of a householder whose
name was Ratnākara and five hundred other sons of householders from the town of Vaiśālī, who accompanied him, came
forward. Each one of these young men prostrated before the
Buddha and offered him a jeweled parasol. Due to the virtue of
the Buddha, all these offerings were molded together to become
a large jeweled parasol that was able to cover the trichiliocosm.*

*On witnessing the spiritual power of the Buddha that enabled
this miracle to happen, everyone uttered words of praise. The
son of the householder Ratnākara came and knelt before the
Buddha and recited a gāthā of praise. After reciting the gāthā,
Ratnākara said: "We the five hundred sons of householders
have all given rise to the mind of the highest, right, and equal
awakening; we bow before you with the wish that you teach us
what are the purifying actions of the bodhisattva."*

*Buddha taught: "Son of a householder, Ratnākara, all living
beings are the Buddha land of a bodhisattva. Why? Because it is
in order to teach living beings how to transform that the bodhisattvas adopt a Buddha-field. It is in order to tame living beings,
that they adopt a Buddha-field. It is because living beings when
they enter a Buddha-field can enter into the wisdom of a bodhisattva, that the bodhisattva adopts a Buddha-field. Why? The
bodhisattva is able to realize the purification of a Buddha-field
because they want to benefit living beings, not because they want
to live their individual life with an individual liberation that is
not connected to the suffering of living beings.*

*"If someone wants to build a house or a palace, they have to
build it on the earth. It will be impossible to build it on space.*

That is why the bodhisattva has to build a Buddha-field in the world of living beings."

Now let us read sentence by sentence in chapter one.
"I vow to build a Buddha-field in the field of life and not in a place where no one lives." It means that if you want to plant a lotus you should not avoid muddy ponds, because it is only in muddy ponds that we can plant lotuses with the most beautiful, scented flowers. It is clear that the Buddha is talking about engaged Buddhism. After that the Buddha says:

The elements which purify the creation of a Buddha-field are as follows: directness, depth of insight, the mind of love or the vow to bring all beings to the shore of ultimate liberation, generosity or the vow to protect oneself and others, inclusiveness or the vow to bring peace into one's own life and into the world, effort or diligence in the practice, concentration or silencing of thinking, wisdom or understanding, the Four Immeasurable Minds (Brahma-vihāra) namely, loving kindness, compassion, joy, and equanimity, the Four Means of Conversion, which are generosity, loving speech, service to benefit others, going together on the path.

"Skillful means purify the Buddha land of a bodhisattva." This means knowing skillful ways to help living beings to liberation. *"These skillful ways are included under the Thirty-seven Wings of Awakening, namely: the Four Fields of Mindfulness, the Four Right Efforts, the Four Bases of Power, the Five Faculties, the Five Powers, the Seven Factors of Awakening, and the Noble Eightfold Path.*

"*Offering up the merit purifies the Buddha land of a bodhisattva*." Our mind offers up any meritorious action for the happiness of all.

"*Teaching the Dharma so that people do not have to undergo the eight misfortunes, practicing the precepts ourselves without criticizing the shortcomings of others, practicing the ten wholesome actions* are the elements that make one's Pure Land more and more pure, more and more happy.*"

Here is a quotation from the next section of the sutra:

"*If a bodhisattva wishes to purify a Buddha-field, they should first of all purify their own mind. Once one's own mind is pure, the Buddha-field can be pure.*

"*Hearing this Śāriputra thought to himself: the Buddha's mind is completely pure. Why then is his Pure Land, that is the sahā world where we are living, so full of impurity?*"

There is an expression used by Buddhists to describe this world, it is called the world of the five impurities. We are told what these five impurities are in the Sukhavativyūha Sutra.†

As soon as Śāriputra gave rise to this thought, the Buddha knew what was in his disciple's mind. The Buddha said: "What

---

* Not killing, not stealing, not committing sexual misconduct, not lying, not exaggerating, not speaking to cause division, not speaking cruelly, not craving, not hating, not ignorant.

† They are the cloudiness of time, views, afflictions, the idea of a living being, the idea of a lifespan.

*do you think Śāriputra? The sun and the moon give light, so
why is it that blind people are not able to see them?"*

*Śāriputra replied: "Lord Buddha it is because blind people are not
able to see. It is not anything to do with the sun and the moon."*

*Then the Buddha said: "The same is true with seeing the Pure
Land. This world is very pure. It is because your insight is still
clouded over and because your mind is not pure, that you see
everything around you as one of the five kinds of impurity."*

This is the first arrow aimed at Śāriputra. We should
not think that the Buddha is aiming this arrow. However
we should remember that our ancestral teachers who
compiled this sutra did so with the mind of the bodhisattva. The words have been put into the Buddha's mouth
by the bodhisattva who was compiling the sutra. The
characters of Vimalakīrti, Mañjuśrī and Śāriputra are all
drawn by that bodhisattva. This sutra comes from the
mind of the bodhisattva who compiled it. Śāriputra, the
most intelligent of Buddha's disciple, was not in fact as
he is portrayed here.

*When Buddha had finished speaking there was a Brahma god
whose name was Śikhin who looked over at Śāriputra and
said: "Venerable Śāriputra, do not think that world is impure.
I see this world as very pure, no less pure then the realm of the
sovereign gods."*

*Śāriputra said: "As far as I see it this world consists of hills,
mountains, valleys, thorns, rocks, and mud. How can you call
this pure?" Brahma Śikhin said: "If you see the world like that,*

it is because of your mind. If your mind were pure, you would automatically see that this world is pure."

At that point the Buddha wanted to substantiate what Brahma Śikhin had said.

He stretched out his leg and struck the earth with his toe and, automatically, the trichiliocosm became infinitely pure like the land called Adornment with the Jewels of Immeasurable Merit where the Buddha Adornment with Jewels abides. All the mud and stagnant water called the cloudiness of views, the cloudiness of afflictions, the cloudiness of living beings, the cloudiness of lifespan disappeared and Śāriputra discovered himself in a pure trichiliocosm.

This was really the Pure Land of Buddha Śākyamuni. Someone whose mind belongs to the śrāvaka vehicle, who only wants to run away from suffering and attain nirvāṇa individually, is not able to see the beauty, serenity, and purity of a Buddha land. *"Why do the Buddhas succeed in building beautiful Pure Lands like that of Amitābha? These Pure Lands are filled with lakes of the seven precious jewels, gold, and pearls, but my teacher's Pure Land is the ugly saha world." "That is because of you, it is not because of your teacher."* This idea will be fully developed later on in the sutra.

Then the Buddha said: "Look Śāriputra, do you see this Buddha-field of ours as pure?"

Śāriputra replied: "Lord Buddha it is most beautiful and pure. Never before have I seen it like this."

*The Buddha said: "Śāriputra, our Buddha-field is always pure
like this. It is because we want to bring the living beings who
are suffering to the shore of liberation that we make it appear
impure. It is the impurity of their environment that will actually become a cause for their liberation."*

What these words mean is: If, in the past, we have
described the world as full of suffering, that is just a skillful means to help beings be liberated. This way of displaying the world is not the reality of the world.

*We have to show the life of living beings with birth, sickness,
old-age, death, the suffering of attachment, desire, destruction,
and separation, so that they can wake up and follow the path of
awakening. It was never our intention to say this world is full of
the five kinds of impurity and that living beings should with all
speed find another world to live in and escape from this world.
Do not misunderstand us! Śrāvakas and pratyekabuddhas do
not misunderstand us! Do not say that our intention is simply
to lead you out of this saha world of suffering so that you can
abide in nirvāṇa! In truth this saha world is at the same time
our Pure Land and you should stay right here.*

The meaning hidden behind these words is like that.
The scene is clearly already set for opposing the śrāvaka
vehicle. We do not need to go further than chapter one;
we do not need to read the following sentences. What has
already been said is to demonstrate the engaged nature
of Mahāyāna Buddhism. Its teaching is that we have to
stay here. We have to plant lotuses in the mud. If we see

that the suffering is overwhelming, that is because of our mind. If it is our intention to run away from this world and find a better place to live, we are not a true disciple of the Buddha.

When the Buddha displayed the world as beautiful and pure, the five hundred sons of householders who had been brought along by the layman Ratnākara were able to give rise to the Unborn Dharma Eye. Eighty-four thousand people in the assembly gave rise to the mind of the highest, right, and equal enlightenment. At that point the Buddha withdrew his miraculous power and the beautiful, pure Buddha land disappeared and the sahā world manifested again as before.

Then thirty-two thousand beings, including gods and those who in the past followed the śrāvaka path, all recognized that all conditioned dharmas are impermanent and they attained the pure vision. Eight thousand monks let go of all their attachments and realized liberation.

This is the first scene of the Vimalakīrtinirdeśa. In the very first chapter, the veiwpoint of the sutra is clear: "Our Buddha land is here. Here is the Pure Land. The Pure Land is here." If it is our intention to run away from this life in order to find liberation from suffering, we are not an authentic disciple of the Buddha.

When we read this chapter we can see hidden in it teachings from the Prajñāpāramitā, Ratnakūṭa and Avataṃsaka Sutras, all of which appeared before the Vimalakīrtinirdeśa. So we can conclude that these are teachings of the Mahāyāna in its early stages. If we go back to the sutras of Original Buddhism we shall find the same teachings hidden there as well.

When Buddha struck the earth with his toe, everyone was able to see the trichiliocosm appear very pure, serene, and beautiful. People who are not accustomed to reading the Mahāyāna might well conclude that this was a miracle. If we have already read the Avataṃsaka Sutra this incident will not strike us as being at all extraordinary. It is not an objective event. It is something that is taking place within our own mind. The scenery which we call the world or the reality is only there because of our mind receiving it like that. The way we see the world is because of our mind. Therefore the toe tapping the earth is to change our way of perceiving, it is not to change the appearance of the world. Our normal way of perceiving can be compared to Śāriputra's way of perceiving here.

In *The Tale of Kiều* there is the following line:

> *There is no scenery that is sad in itself.*
> *The person is sad. How can the scenery be sad or happy?*

When you are sad there is no way that the scenery can be happy. Whether a scene appears happy or sad depends entirely on the person who observes it. Whether the world is sad or happy depends on our perceptions. So when we read this section we should understand that Buddha is not doing anything to change the reality of the world, he is changing the perception of Śāriputra and the whole assembly.

The realm of suffering and obstacles in which we live is generally called the mundane realm (*lokadhātu*). If we open our eyes wider we can enter another world, the Avataṃsaka world, where all the layers of causes and conditions, the Buddha and bodhisattvas appear. This we call the Dharma realm (*dharmadhātu*).

The Dharma realm and the mundane realm are one. It depends on our perception whether it is the Dharma or the mundane realm. A practitioner is washing saucepans or peeling carrots. As to which of the two realms they are living in, that depends on their mind. As I walk past them, I place my hand on their shoulder and ask: 'What are you doing'? This is similar to a toe tapping the earth. If they are practicing they will reply: "Thay, I am following my breathing and dwelling in the peaceful realm of mindfulness." If they are not practicing they may say: "Thay, I am washing up a saucepan or I am peeling a carrot." In that case the toe touching the earth has not produced a miracle. I only need to ask "What are you doing?" and that question could be enough for them to wake up and step out of the realm of forgetfulness, dreaming about the past, or worrying about the future, and enter the world of the wonderful present moment. Thus my question has the effect of waking someone up and bringing them out of the world of forgetfulness and sorrow into the world of all that is wonderful.

So we should not think that the Buddha tapping the earth with his toe was a miracle of a worldly kind. It was a true miracle of the kind that anyone of us in the sangha could perform.

> *It only takes a gentle breath*
> *and all kinds of miracles are there.*

By coming back to our gentle breathing we can make available a wonderful world.

In the Avataṃsaka Sutra, we come across some similar images. There was a time when the bodhisattva Vajragarbha entered samādhi and began to give a Dharma talk about the ten bodhisattva stages. When he had finished giving the talk, limitless bodhisattvas appeared in all parts of the universe and uttered words of praise: Wonderful, wonderful, Vajragarbha, all of us are also called Vajragarbha; there are countless, limitless Vajragarbhas and we are all expounding the same teaching all over the universe.

This image helps us see that when we do anything, however insignificant, whether it is a thought or something we say or a deed, that action has a profound influence at every point of the universe. When we are careful in our small actions, we are taking care of something much more significant.

---

* See Thich Nhat Hanh, *Call Me By My True Names*, Parallax Press, 1999.

The Avataṃsaka Sutra is full of this kind of miracle. If we read it carefully we shall see the significance of such miracles. It is the same as when we look into a leaf with all of our attention as a meditation; we discover that in the golden leaf that fell from the branch this morning there is the sun, the moon, the cloud, and the river. That is a miracle in itself. This kind of miracle is something we can experience every day. This miracle is not different from the miracle of countless bodhisattvas entering the womb of Mahāmāya in order to pay respect to Prince Siddhārtha. Do not think that the Mahāyāna mentions miracles too much. Buddha putting his toe on the earth was just a means to wake the sangha up and bring the audience into the wonderful world of no-birth and no-death.

CHAPTER 2: SKILLFUL MEANS

Skillful means are effective ways of helping us attain good results as we bring living beings to the shore of liberation. In Sanskrit the word is *upāya kauśalya*, in French it is *moyens habiles*. These skillful means are used by bodhisattvas to bring living beings from the shore of suffering to the shore of peace and joy. This chapter is about the life of Vimalakīrti and the skillful means he uses.

At that time in the town of Vaiśalī was a householder by the name of Vimalakīrti. He had made offerings to countless Buddhas and laid down many wholesome roots.

These lines sound very familiar. The good seeds that we have sown in the past are the energy that enables us to give rise to bodhicitta—the aspiration to realize the highest, right, and equal awakening. This aspiration is the basic condition for being a bodhisattva: someone who has the capacity to liberate all beings. This aspiration motivates us to go from finding solace in the more superficial aspects of the Dharma, so that we can penetrate the depths of the teachings. In other words it helps us to go from the śrāvaka and pratyekabuddha vehicles to the Buddha vehicle. However many unwholesome deeds someone may have committed in the past, they have also sown wholesome seeds. That is why they can become a Buddha or a bodhisattva who can take beings to the shore of liberation. This is a very basic Buddhist teaching that is developed by the Lotus Sutra.

Before going into the spiritual attainment of Vimalakīrti (e.g. his possession of the unborn eyes of the Dharma, of unobstructed eloquence, of the six supernatural powers (*abhijña*), of the practice of dhāraṇi that give the power of fearlessness, his conquering Māra and his clear penetration of all the wonderful Dharma doors), the sutra tells us that in the past *Vimalakīrti* "had made offerings to countless Buddhas and sown countless good seeds." This is something we cannot doubt, because everyone has countless past lives and during those lives, everyone has done wholesome acts, helping people and animals. The Lotus Sutra says that bringing a grain of rice to feed an animal is enough to lay down a wholesome root. To go into a stupa and respectfully bow one's head is to lay down wholesome roots. We should not just look at our weaknesses and our unwholesome actions with the result that we have an inferiority or guilt complex. Making offerings to living beings is to make offerings to the Buddha. According to Buddhist teachings, all living beings can become Buddha. That is why, if we make offerings to living beings who are undergoing hardships and misery, it is more valuable than making offerings to those who lack nothing. The Buddha is someone who lacks nothing; so to make offerings to living beings who lack the basic material necessities is more valuable than making offerings to the Buddha. When we want to make an offering we should remember this.

For instance, when lay Buddhists come to the temple they usually like to make an offering to the abbot, but the abbot may well be the most well-supplied monk in the temple. The novices may be the ones most in need. They may be the ones who need coats, warm underwear, or sandals. If you make your offering to them, it will bring about more merit.

Now let us read sentence by sentence in chapter two in order to understand the meaning of the sutra.

"Had realized all manner of skillful means." It means he had learned many ways that were effective in liberating living beings from their suffering.

"*Had fulfilled his great aspiration.*" It means he clearly understood the mind of living beings, could distinguish all the beneficial roots in people's minds, could read people's minds. These two sentences show us that Vimalakīrti was someone who specialized in looking deeply into the psychology of beings. If we cannot understand someone's mind, we cannot help him or her. This practice is to meditate on the circumstances of that person. Meditating on the circumstances of each being is looking deeply to see clearly the mind of each person, of each species of living being. When you are successful in seeing someone's mind clearly, you know what skillful means to use to help that person.

"*He had practiced Buddhism for a long time, his mind had ripened in accord with the teachings and he was unwavering in his loyalty to the Mahāyāna.*" It means he was no longer in a state of indecision. Some people were still unsure whether they should follow the śrāvaka vehicle or the Mahāyāna teachings that were still very new. Vimalakīrti had decided that he would go wholly with the Mahāyāna. We can only understand the phrase "He was unwavering in his loyalty to the Mahāyāna" when we know exactly at what point in the history of development of Mahāyāna these words were written.

"*His actions were undertaken after skillful consideration. He observed correctly all the fine manners as did the Buddha.*" It means that his actions were only undertaken in mindfulness as the result of looking deeply, and he practiced the precepts and the fine manners correctly.

"His mind was as vast as the ocean. He was praised by the Buddhas. He was venerated by disciples, Indra, Brahma, and the Wheel-turning King whenever they saw him."

This part describes the value of the basic qualities of Vimalakīrti. If someone does not yet have these fundamental qualities we should not voice the opinion that "they are a present-day Vimalakīrti."

In order to bring beings to the shore of liberation, as a skillful means he manifested as a householder in the town of Vaiśalī. He had limitless possessions and wealth simply to be able to help the impoverished on their way to liberation.

The fact that his physical form was that of a householder was only a skillful means to help those who were suffering because of great poverty. His true nature was not a householder. He was at the same time a Buddha or a bodhisattva. Although he appeared as a layperson, it was not that he was a layperson in reality.

This notion of "appearing as" is used for the first time in this sutra. Later on in the Universal Door (Samāntamukha) chapter of the Lotus Sutra, this concept of "appearing as" is used concerning the bodhisattva Avalokita. In Vietnam and China, Avalokita is usually represented in statues as a woman. Does this mean that Avalokita is a woman? In fact the male and the female are just two ways Avalokita has of appearing. The essence of

Avalokita is great compassion and great loving kindness: someone who has the capacity to hear the suffering of living beings.

In order to be able to discover the essence of Vimalakīrti, we shall need to reflect deeply. In this part of the sutra it is made very clear that his being a layperson is an appearance and a skillful means.

Because he wanted to help living beings to the shore of liberation, he used the skillful means of appearing as a householder with many material resources so as to be able to help the impoverished to the shore of liberation.

He kept the precepts purely to help to the shore of liberation those who broke the precepts.

It means that people who lived nearby and did not keep the precepts also needed to be brought to the shore of liberation and he could help them by being an example of someone who did keep the precepts purely.

The following sentences in the sutra can be summarized as follows:

He practiced patience in order to help those who were angry. He practiced diligence to help those who were indolent. He practiced the silence of meditation to help those whose minds were lost in dispersion. He practiced insight to help those who lacked understanding. Although he was a layman who wore the white robe, he practiced the way of chastity of a monk (brahmacarya). Although he lived in the family, he held himself aloof from the ups and downs of the three worlds—the desire realm (kāmadhātu), the form realm (rūpadhātu) and the formless realm (arūpadhātu).

Although he had wife and children he practiced chastity. Although he had friends and relations he was not attached to them.

These lines may sound familiar to us, because we have already read similar ideas in Ugra the Householder Sutra. It is as if the householder Ugra is an earlier form of Vimalakīrti. After he heard the Buddha teach in the Dharma assembly, Ugra vowed to remain a layman in order to practice what monks practiced. Here the layman Vimalakīrti is nothing more than a continuation of Ugra. Laypeople who wish to practice as Vimalakīrti, should apply the very traits and principles that Vimalakīrti had and not just learn the philosophical answers that he gave to questions. It is possible to practice the Buddhadharma without becoming a monk. In order to be able to live such a life to the full, the layman must practice diligently the basic principles that Vimalakīrti practiced.

If someone just learns the empty theory without putting it into practice, they create all kinds of obstacles for themselves.

Some people have not truly understood this. After they have memorized a couple of Vimalakīrti's answers to questions, they come to the monastery to debate principles of Buddhism with the monks. This is to no advantage and just creates karmic obstacles. If you are a monk and you have this experience you can smile kindly and ask: My friend, do you know how Vimalakīrti practiced being a lay bodhisattva?

Although he wore fine clothes, he had no attachment to those clothes. Although he ate and drank, he saw that he was nourished by the joy of meditation.

The joy of meditation is the happiness that comes from meditative concentration. The expression "The joy of meditative concentration is our food" is to be found in the offering verse that is used in the chanting that precedes the midday meal:

> *At the time for the midday meal*
> *I make the vow that all beings*
> *will have the joy of meditation as food*
> *and their Dharma happiness be complete.*

If he came to a place of gambling or singing and music he would use the occasion to help people to the shore of freedom.

One should remember that if one's practice has not yet reached the level of the practice of Vimalakīrti, and one frequents such places, one can be carried along by the crowd and so be of no benefit to anyone else.

He was respectful to different spiritual traditions but this never damaged his faith in Buddha's teaching.

It means he is able to dialogue with Christians, with Communists, with Taoists, but the knowledge he thus acquires never makes him lose his confidence in the Right Dharma. On the contrary, such dialogue enables his understanding of the right teachings to grow deeper every day. This is borne out of the author's own experience.

Although he was learned in worldly knowledge, he always delighted in the Buddhist teachings.

Although he watches films and reads newspapers and magazines, he continues to enjoy studying the Buddhadharma. The truth is that if we do not have much time, we should dedicate the time we have to studying the sutras. However, when we have an innate capacity for learning and a practice that is wide and deep, then any kind of reading material can help us develop our enlightened mind. Whenever I read a book, however badly it is written, however uninspiring is the material, or watch a film however bad it is, I can still see that my understanding of the Right Dharma is present. It is because while I am reading the book or watching the film, I do not lose myself in it. As I read or watch I am always looking deeply, and so I am able to understand the mind of the author.

Nevertheless, our practice has to have reached a certain level before we can do this. If it has not reached that level, we shall be adversely influenced by the negativity of what we are reading or watching. We sometimes meet people who say that they can watch bad films without being adversely affected by them, because bad films are also the Buddhadharma. Such a point of view is very dangerous because very few people have a strong enough practice not to be adversely affected by reading or watching unwholesome things.

He mastered the Right Dharma in order to be able to help important personages and unimportant people to the shore of liberation. He was involved in business affairs, and when he was successful he did not take it as a cause for rejoicing. He would present himself at crossroads or on frequented paths in order to be able to benefit beings. He would involve himself in politics in order to be able to help all people out of their suffering.

It means that he did not reject any kind of occupation. He was involved in politics but was never attached to what he was doing, he was involved in trade but never lost himself in profit or in loss.

He would enter places of sexual misconduct in order to demonstrate the harm caused by such behavior. He would enter bars to help the inebriated to regain a clear mind.

This refers to places that symbolize degradation such as houses of prostitution or bars that we normally think of as completely apart from the Right Dharma. As far as the bodhisattva is concerned, houses of prostitution and bars are also practice centers or places where the practice can be taught. When someone has the mind of the bodhisattva he can go into places with the intention to help people transform. There is a well-known saying in the Mahāyāna tradition, "Houses of prostitution, places where alcohol is used, all of them are pure practice centers." This means as far as the bodhisattva is concerned there is no place that cannot be a pure practice center.

Among householders he was considered to be the best and so he could teach Dharma doors that convinced householders. Among laymen he was considered to be the most respected, so he could help them put an end to craving. When among kṣatriyas he could approach the general or the chief officer in order to teach them the way of endurance. If he found himself among brahmans, he would help them put an end to their arrogance. If he found himself among high dignitaries or royalty, mandarins, Brahmas, Śakras, the four Wheel-turning Kings, Vimalakīrti would use skillful means to help all of them.

When we read the Lotus Sutra we see how the bodhisattva Avalokita could appear in many different ways in order to help beings. The way of thinking of the Vimalakīrtinirdeśa is to be found in the Lotus Sutra. "If Avalokita needs to, Avalokita can appear as a man or as a woman to help people and can give a Dharma talk as a man or as a woman. If necessary Avalokita can take the form of a child, a nāga, a yakṣa, a gandharva, an asura to help others."

The Vimalakīrti Sutra made its appearance during the first phase of the Mahāyāna. During that phase the Avataṃsaka Sutra appeared before the Vimalakīrti and the Lotus Sutras and the Śūraṅgamasamādhi after the Vimalakīrtinirdeśa. The Śūraṅgamasamādhi Sutra has been significantly influenced by the Vimalakīrtinird-esa. The Śūraṅgamasamādhi was translated from Sanskrit into Chinese in Vietnam in the year 255 by a monk named Kālasivi who came from India to Vietnam to teach the Dharma.

An important point of which we should be aware is that all the Mahāyāna sutras that appeared before the Lotus Sutra have a specific aim: it is to give the Mahāyāna way of thought the highest position. That is why the language of these sutras is at some times acrimonious and harsh in opposing the old tradition that is called the Dual Vehicle. When the Lotus Sutra made its appearance we see how harmonious it is, full of acceptance and inclusiveness towards the two vehicles.

The householder Vimalakīrti used these countless, measureless means to help all species of living beings' benefit.

That is why Vimalakīrti was a bodhisattva who had the capacity to appear in so many different forms in order to liberate beings. When people ask "Was Vimalakīrti a layman?" We can reply "Not necessarily." Layman was only one of the ten thousand appearances that Vimalakīrti took.

VIMALAKĪRTI'S ILLNESS
The second scene of the Vimalakīrti drama is his pretending to be sick. This sickness is also a skillful means to liberate living beings. In this scene we realize how well-known he was because when people hear about his

sickness, whether they are princes, court officials, Brahmins, etc., they all come to visit him. Thanks to these visits, Vimalakīrti has a chance to teach them all about the meaning of ill-health and the method of meditating on the true nature of one's own body.

The method of meditating on the body is not something new. In the Satipaṭṭhāna Sutta the Buddha teaches the contemplation of the body.

Vimalakīrti teaches: *"The body is impermanent, it is not a solid entity. It quickly decays. It is a storehouse of afflictions and ill-health. Do not make it a place of absolute refuge. The body is like froth on water. It is not something that can be grasped."*

All these ideas have already been expounded in the sutras of Original Buddhism. From this we can deduce that the ancestral teachers who were compiling the Vimalakīrtinirdeśa wanted to include elements that came from Original Buddhism in order to build the Mahāyāna edifice.

This shows that going back to the source is something people always want to do. We are the same. We should always remember to go back to the source. We should always use the building blocks of Original Buddhism when we present a Buddhism that is suitable for our own time.

After Vimalakīrti had taught his guests about the nature of impermanence and no-self, froth on the stream and conditioned arising as the nature of this body, he concluded: *"Thus we should feel distaste for this body and not crave for it. We should give rise to the aspiration to have the body of a Buddha in order to realize liberation."*

We should not look on this body of froth and the five skandhas as the undying Dharma body. One of the shortcomings of the Vimalakīrtinirdeśa is to see the five skandhas—body, feelings, perceptions, mental formations and consciousness as an indestructible Dharma body. It is possible that our ancestral teachers, when compiling the Mahāyāna sutras, wanted to begin with the sublime and lofty teachings and then take their audience back down to earth, so that they could read the basic practices and then take them back to the lofty and sublime. But why not begin down on the ground? Why begin with lofty ideas and then bring people down to earth? This is a question that has to be asked. We have to feel dissatisfation with this impermanent physical body in order to discover other bodies such as the Buddha body or the Dharma body. At a later point the sutra looks into where the Buddha body and Dharma body are to be found. The answer is that we have to come back to ourself and find them right here within us. The idea of feeling dissatisfaction with this body is not a lofty one and for that reason it is not mentioned again in the sutra.

The Dharma body of the Buddha is made of elements other than those that make up the fleshly body. The Dharma body is not made up of material elements such as earth, water, heat and air. The Dharma body is not foam on water but understanding and insight, liberation, generosity, observation of precepts, inclusivity, diligence and concentration. Although these elements are not material, they need material elements in order to manifest. This is the spirit in which we should look for the Dharma body.

At this point of chapter two of the sutra, there is an important sentence:

"My friends, if you wish to attain the Buddha body (this also applies to the Dharma body) and end all the sickness of living beings, you should give rise to the highest, perfect, and equal awakening."

This means bodhicitta, the mind of love. Giving rise to the mind of love is one of the practices of the Mahāyāna. If we have not given rise to that mind, we cannot possibly do the work that Vimalakīrti wanted to do, that is, to develop nonattachment to the material body in order to discover the Buddha body.

We see clearly that if we wish to realize the great work of a bodhisattva we have to give rise to the mind of love. This is made clear in the first chapter of the sutra. In the past we have put down wholesome roots (*kuśalamūla*), so we should not underestimate ourselves. Basing on the wholesome conditions that we have laid down, we should give rise to the mind of love without delay. Do not wait until tomorrow.

CHAPTER 3: HEARER DISCIPLES

Chapter three of the Vimalakīrtinirdeśa Sutra could be called Scene Three of the Vimalakīrtinirdeśa drama. In this chapter the Buddha designates a number of his disciples to go and visit the sick man, Vimalakīrti. The ten disciples who have to go and visit Vimalakīrti are the ten most outstanding disciples of Śākyamuni Buddha, called the Ten Great Disciples. Among them are numbered the following monks. The Venerable Śāriputra was the foremost in great understanding, the most intelligent of the disciples. The Venerable Mahāmaudgalyāyana was the one who was renowned for his miraculous powers. The Venerable Mahākāśyapa was the most diligent. The Venerable Subhūti had the deepest and clearest understanding of emptiness. The Venerable Pūrṇa was the most skilled in giving Dharma talks. The Venerable Kātyāyana was the most skilled in reasoning and discussing the Dharma. The Venerable Anuruddha was the most able to use his divine eyes (clairvoyance). The Venerable Upāli understood and practiced the Vinaya best. Rāhula was able to practice the esoteric practice best of all. Finally, the Venerable Ānanda was the one who had the widest learning. In spite of their great abilities they all requested not to go and visit the sick man:

Lord Buddha, I do not have the strength to go and meet Vimalakīrti and answer his questions.

Let us see how this scene evolves:

At that time Vimalakīrti thought to himself "Here I am, lying sick in bed. The Buddha is the embodiment of great love and compassion. There is every reason to think that he will feel compassion for me."

THE VENERABLE ŚĀRIPUTRA

Buddha was in the monastery when Vimalakīrti had this idea, and he immediately knew what Vimalakīrti was thinking. He straightaway told Śāriputra:

"My disciple, please go and visit Vimalakīrti." The Venerable Śāriputra replied: "Lord Buddha, I do not have the capacity to visit that gentleman. There was a time when I was practicing sitting meditation at the foot of a tree and Vimalakīrti came along. He talked about how one practices Mahāyāna meditation comparing it with śrāvaka meditation. His conclusion was that the way I was practicing was incorrect."

The aim of certain of the Mainstream Schools' Buddhism is a state of concentration called the attainment of cessation" (*nirodha samāpatti*). In this concentration the meditator puts an end to perceptions and feelings. The four *dhyānas* and four *samāpatti* (the first eight levels of concentration) do not liberate the meditator, but the ninth level known as "cessation of the thoughts and feelings" (*samjñavedayitanirodha* or *nirodha samāpatti*) is the capacity to enter nirvāṇa according to the śrāvaka vehicle. However, Vimalakīrti told Śāriputra that the attainment of cessation is not true meditative concentration. True meditative concentration is realized when the meditator is in the desire realm, the form realm, or the formless realm without the slightest agitation or dispersion. Meditation is not to transcend the desire, form, and formless realms. The attainment of cessation is not the highest meditation. If you are sitting at a busy crossroads without any agitation or dispersion, that is the highest kind of meditation.

Without leaving the attainment of cessation concentration, you are able to practice constant mindfulness whether sitting, standing, walking, or lying. Without entering the attainment of cessation (nirodha samāpatti) your sitting, standing, lying, and walking display meditative concentration. That can correctly be called meditative concentration.

While you are working at everyday tasks and your mind is able to stay with the practice, that is meditation. When your mind does not chase after an interior or an exterior object, that is true meditation. Do not think that if you collect your mind inwardly, that is meditation. Mahāyāna meditation does not have outer and inner. Mahāyāna does not speak of the destruction of the afflictions as the entrance to nirvāṇa. Dwelling in this world of afflictions without being distracted by anything is called meditation (*dhyāna*).

Śāriputra said: ."Lord Buddha when I heard him speaking like this, I did not know how to reply, and that is why I do not have the capacity to visit Vimalakīrti and ask how he is."

Śāriputra who appears here is a character in a play and not the true Śāriputra. I am confident that if you were to meet the real Śāriputra he would not reply in this inferior way. Those who practice according to Mainstream Buddhist Schools look on this sutra as maligning, because it makes their most prestigious elder brother into a laughingstock. However, when we read the sutra our mind should be open. We have to recognize that this is a role that the playwright invents in order to form the backdrop before which the Mahāyāna way of thought can stand out clearly.

In any drama we usually find a rogue and a valiant hero. If we want to create a backdrop for our hero to stand out against, a rogue has to appear on the stage. This is true in the Vimalakīrtinirdeśa. Because the playwright wishes to highlight the character of Vimalakīrti, he has to invent characters of inferior ability and he has no hesitation in using the name of the senior disciples of the Buddha to play the role of darkness before which the light can stand out. So if you are angry about the way Śāriputra is used in this sutra, rather than be angry, read with the mind of a drama critic.

THE VENERABLE MAUDGALYĀYANA

At that the Buddha turned to Maudgalyāyana and told him to go and visit the layman Vimalakīrti. The Venerable said, *"Lord Buddha, I, too, do not have the capacity to*

visit Vimalakīrti and ask after his health." When Maudgalyāyana asked not to go, he said:

*"One day when I was teaching the Dharma, Vimalakīrti came
along and said: 'This is not the right way to teach the Dharma.'
According to him the nature of the Dharma is the absolute
truth and we cannot use words and concepts to explain it. He
said that I was using notions and verbal expression and therefore the Dharma I was teaching was not the Right Dharma."*

Vimalakīrti was saying that because Maudgalyāyana
was using many notions and too many verbal expres-
sions, his Dharma talk was not a Mahāyāna Dharma talk.

At this point the Vimalakīrtinirdeśa is reflecting
the teachings of the Diamond Sutra.* Vimalakīrti says:
*"Moreover, when you teach the Dharma, it must be the real
Dharma."* The meaning of this sentence is that the nature
of the Dharma has nothing to do with words and we have
to use words so that the listener can see that although we
are using words and concepts to teach the Dharma, we
are not caught in words and ideas.

It is obvious that when we give a Dharma talk we
have to use words and ideas, but we should use them in

---

* If you are caught in the idea of the Dharma, you are also caught
in the ideas of a self, a person, a living being, and a life span. If you
are caught in the idea that something is not the Dharma, you are still
caught in the ideas of a self, a person, a living being, and a life span.
That is why you should not get caught in the idea that this is the
Dharma or that is not the Dharma. This is the hidden meaning when
the Tathāgata says, 'bhikṣus, you should know that the Dharma that I
teach is like a raft.' You should let go of the Dharma, let alone what is
not the Dharma. —Vajracchedikā Sutra.

such a way that both the speaker and the hearer are not caught in the words and notions and then it can be called the real Dharma.

Vimalakīrti says:

"The Dharma is not (the idea of) living being—it is not sullied by the idea of living being."

"The Dharma does not have (the idea of) a separate self—it is not sullied by this idea."

"The Dharma does not have (the idea of) lifespan—it is not sullied by this idea."

"The Dharma is not (the idea of) human being, of after or before. After and before are ended by the Dharma."

These four signs mentioned here in the Vimalakīrtinirdeśa are the four signs mentioned previously by the Vajracchedikā or Diamond Sutra. The four signs are Self, Human Being, Living Being and Lifespan. The Dharma that needs to be spoken is the Dharma that is not caught in the idea of living being, separate self, lifespan, and human being. If the Dharma taught is not caught in these ideas then it is not sullied by the impurities called the impurity of living beings, of separate self, of birth and death, and of human being.

If we continue to read on we shall see:

"The Dharma follows suchness without having to follow anything to a particular place."

"It abides in reality without being disturbed by the pairs of opposites (being/nonbeing, permanence/annihilation)."

"It abides in stillness because it does not depend on the six objects of senses."

"It does not come and go, and always abides in the non-cessation."

"It is in harmony with "emptiness," in accord with "signlessness," and corresponds to "aimlessness.""

"It transcends ideas of right and wrong. It is not subject to increase or decrease."

"It is not born and does not die and does not have a point of return."

"The Dharma we need to teach is the Right Dharma that is not caught in concepts and notions."

This shows that the Madhyamaka teachings* of the Eight No's have been brought into the Vimalakīrtinirdeśa. The Eight No's of the Madhaymaka are: no-birth, no-death, no-coming, no-going, no-same, no-different, no-being, no-nonbeing.

The Eight No's, as well as being present in the early Mahāyāna sutras, have already been taught by the Buddha in the Sutrapiṭaka of Original Buddhism—for example in the Sutra on Teachings to be Given to the Dying. In that sutra it says: "When conditions are right eyes are present, when conditions are not right eyes

---

* For more on the Madhyamaka teachings, see *Cracking the Walnut: Understanding the Dialectics of Nagarjuna* to be published by Parallax Press in Spring, 2023.

cease to be present. Eyes do not cease, eyes do not endure. They do not come from anywhere and do not go anywhere."

The Vimalakīrti Sutra goes further: *"In teaching the Dharma it is necessary to look deeply at the living beings who hear it in order to recognize their capacity, whether they are intelligent in listening to the Dharma or not, whether they are caught in the knowledge they already have or not."*

When we have much knowledge and points of view of our own, our true understanding is impeded. Those who study a great deal but do not put into practice what they study risk putting themselves in this dangerous situation.

Knowledge and understanding are two different things. Understanding is truly important and knowledge is less so. However if we know how to use our knowledge skillfully it can help us understand. If we do not use our knowledge wisely it will become an obstacle to our understanding.

It is like water: if it is liquid, the stream flows easily; if it is congealed as ice it will stop the flow of the stream. When we listen or study the teachings we can have intellectual ideas that come from what we already know. If we are not intelligent enough and do not make good use of our intellectual knowledge to help us have true insight or awakening, that intellectual knowledge will become an obstacle for our studies and practice. The more intellectual knowledge we have, the greater the obstacle becomes. This is not to discriminate against intellectual knowledge, but we receive and use knowledge in an intelligent way so that it can help us to understand. *Prajñā*, insight, is not intellectual knowledge. Prajñā is understanding. When you have understanding you are light and at ease and easy to approach. Someone who just has knowledge can be difficult to be with. They want to debate with us and defeat us in the debate, so we feel hesitant to come near them. In the West they say: "They know a great deal, but there is very little they understand." Vimalakīrti said:

"You should teach the Dharma with unobstructed vision and great compassion, commending the Mahāyāna, always mindful that you are repaying your gratitude to the Buddha and making possible the continuation of the Three Jewels." When the Venerable Maudgalyāyana heard Vimalakīrti's words, he pondered them and did not know how to reply. That day in the audience listening to Vimalakīrti's words there were eight hundred laypeople who gave rise to the mind of love (bodhicitta).

We are not told whether on that occasion the Venerable Maudgalyāyana gave rise to the mind of love or had already done so before that. All we know is his conclusion: *"Lord Buddha, my eloquence is not equal to that of Vimalakīrti, so I do not dare visit him to ask after his health."*

According to the tradition, Maudgalyāyana's nature was a little hot-tempered. If Vimalakīrti had come along and spoken so critically, it could have caused Maudga-lyāyana to utter a shrill cry of disagreement.

The Venerable Maudgalyāyana was a very straight-forward monk. Whatever he thought, he would say. When questioned by the wandering ascetics of the different sects he always replied to their questions by saying exactly what he felt. Later on he was murdered by the followers of another sect right in front of the entrance to the Bamboo Forest Monastery. When he was ambushed he immediately cried out for help and as soon as the monks in the monastery heard him they ran out, but by the time they arrived on the scene he had already been killed and the assassins had run out of sight.

At that time the Buddha was on his way northwards. He was almost eighty years old. The monks performed the cremation ceremony for the Venerable Maudga-lyāyana and placed the ashes in a vase, bringing it to the Buddha's hut on the Vulture Peak. The Buddha looked at the vase and saw that he had lost a prominent disciple. On the same day the Buddha heard that King Prasenajit, a very good friend, had just passed away. The Buddha asked Ānanda to go with him to find a place where they might erect a stupa for Maudgalyāyana.

From this you will see that the Maudgalyāyana por-trayed in the Vimalakīrtinirdeśa was not like the Maudg-alyāyana we know about from the lifetime of the Buddha Śākyamuni.

THE VENERABLE KĀŚYAPA

The Buddha asked the Venerable Kāśyapa to go and visit Vimalakīrti. The sutra says that Kāśyapa had once met Vimalakīrti in a poor village. The Venerable was well known for his practice of asceticism. His clothing and food were of the simplest kind and he liked to be with the poor people.

When the Venerable Makakāśyapa was practicing the alms' round in a village of poor people, Vimalakīrti came up to him and said: "Venerable Kāśyapa according to the spirit of equality you should seek alms from every house you pass. You should not pass by the houses of the rich and only stop at the houses of the poor. It is not in order to eat that you make the alms' round."

"Not in order to eat" is to talk in terms of the ultimate dimension. As far as our physical body is concerned we need to eat, but as far as the realization of nirvāṇa or enlightenment is concerned we do not need to eat. The liberation body is something all people have. It is already complete. This means that our liberation is complete, it does not need food every day in order to grow.

Our liberation body does not grow up gradually like a child. It is not because we give it something to eat every day that it will grow into a healthy young adult. That is what is meant by "It is not in order to eat, that you make the alms' round."

"It is not in order to eat that you make the alms' round" also means the alms' round is a practice in itself and is not essentially a means for obtaining food to eat. There are, however, people who think that the meaning of "not in order to eat" refers to the liberation body. Our nirvāṇa is not small or large so it does not need food. Our practice is the same. We think that the more we practice the greater our liberation will be. In fact our liberation is already there, with all its significance. It does not need to grow up gradually like a child.

"It is in order to destroy the generic sign (sāmānyalakṣaṇa) that you take the food in your fingers to eat."

There are two kinds of signs: generic and specific. Examples of generic signs would be cups or houses. These generic signs are composed of specific signs, which in the case of a house could be bricks or in the case of a cup, molecules of clay. Here Vimalakirti is saying that you need to transcend the generic sign. Vimalakirti then refers to the custom in India of eating with the fingers of the right hand.

"It is by not receiving that you receive the food that is offered."

When you receive the food offering you receive it in the spirit of not receiving. We could say that this way of talking is a little casuistic. When we receive something it is so that the person who is making the offering can also receive. The person who makes the offering is happy, has merit. The person who gives, receives wholesome fruits. So in the matter of receiving alms one transcends the ideas of receiving, that is of the person who receives, the person who gives, and the object that is given. These three ideas disappear and one is no longer caught in the ideas of giving and receiving. Later on the patriarchs taught the emptiness of the three things: the person who makes the offering, the person who receives it, and the gift that is given. All three become one. The gāthā we practice as we hold our bowl is:

> *This is the bowl of the Tathāgata*
> *that is held in my hands.*
> *I vow to be able to realize*
> *the emptiness of giver, receiver, and gift.*

So when we extend our hand to receive, we smile, because we see that the person who gives, the person who receives, and the gift are all one.

"As you enter the village you should see it as empty."

The monks stayed in the forest, in deserted caves. When entering the village, you should not be caught in the idea that this is a place. The Chinese character for "village," 聚 *ju* means the place where people gather together to live. Your perception of a village is an idea which you need to remove.

"You should look at forms as though you were blind."

This means that when you see forms and colors you are not caught in them. It may be the sight of curry, of white rice, or a beautiful donor. All these forms, although they are visible to your eyes, are not objects of attachment for your mind. If you can do that, you can be called someone who has the demeanor of one who makes the alms' round.

"You hear sounds as if they were echoes; you are aware of scents as if they were the wind. You taste without discriminating tastes. You touch objects as if you are realizing the truth. You know all the signs of phenomena are like a magic show; by nature they are not self nor are they other. They have not been born and they do not die."

A monastic on the alms' round is confronted at all times by a stream of perceptions—there are sights, sounds, and objects of touch. That is why you have to look deeply in order to transcend all notions about the form, sound, scent, taste, touch, and mental impression. If the monastic who is making the alms' round is able to do this, they are worthy of making the alms' round.

Making the alms' round is not primarily in order to have something to eat, it is a practice in itself. While monastics hold their bowl and walk from house to house, they dwell in meditative concentration. When their eyes are in contact with forms, their ears with sounds, and their mind is in touch with mental objects, they look deeply to see the true nature of all phenomena.

"Venerable Kāśyapa, if possible, without transcending the eight wrong actions, realize the eight liberations; if possible, use the

appearance of the eight wrong actions in order to penetrate
the Right Dharma. If possible, by eating one meal, give to all
species of living being and at the same time make an offering
to all the Buddhas and the holy ones. If you do that, you make
the alms' round and eat the midday meal according to the Right
Dharma."

Why did Vimalakīrti say to the Venerable Kāśyapa
that he did not need to give up the eight wrong actions,
but could use them to penetrate the Right Dharma? It is
because we have an idea that if we want liberation we
shall have to rid ourselves of all that is wrong in order to
achieve what is right. If we are able to transcend the idea
of right and wrong and see that what is right is made up
of what is wrong, then we are making the alms' round
in accord with the Right Dharma, we are sitting to eat
our meal in accord with the Right Dharma, and making
a pure offering to the Dharma body in accord with the
Right Dharma. It is like when a skillful gardener sees a
compost pile with all kinds of rotting matter, they feel no
disgust, irritation, or fear. They can use all the rotting
matter to make green manure and fertilize their roses.
The do not discriminate against the garbage in favor of
the flowers.

*Kāśyapa said: "Lord Buddha, when I heard Vimalakīrti speak,
I saw things that I had not seen. I felt great respect for all the
bodhisattvas. I felt that this householder had such eloquence
and wisdom that anyone who heard him could give rise to a
mind of the highest, right, and equal awakening. From that*

time until now I have not used the the sravaka and pratyekabuddha vehicles to instruct people. Lord Buddha, for this reason
I do not have the capacity to ask Vimalakīrti after his health."

We have to commend the Venerable Kāśyapa for being able to understand Vimalakīrti's words. The Venerables Śāriputra and Maudgalyāyana, on the other hand, were not able to glean anything from Vimalakīrti's words to them. The sutra only remarks on the benefit that other people received from listening to the dialogue between Vimalakīrti and the monks. It says nothing about whether they themselves benefitted anything.

THE VENERABLE SUBHŪTI

Next is the turn of the Venerable Subhūti. Subhūti was famous for his understanding of emptiness as taught in the Prajñāpāramitā Sutras. He too was told by the Buddha to visit Vimalakīrti and ask after his health, and he also declined to go. The reason was that one day when he was making the alms' round in the affluent quarter of Vaiśalī, he had come to stand in front of the house of Vimalakīrti to request alms. He had walked into a nest of fire ants. After Vimalakīrti had taken hold of Subhūti's bowl and placed rice and curry in it, he held on to the bowl while he gave Subhūti a Dharma talk.

"Venerable Subhūti, as far as the food of equality is concerned,
all phenomena are equal. Since all phenomena are equal, then
food is equal. If you make the alms' round in this spirit, you are
worthy to receive alms."

This means that as a monk or a nun makes the alms' round they should be able to see the equal nature of all phenomena. Equal nature in Sanskrit is *samatā*.

"Besides, even though you still have thoughts of attachment, hatred, ignorance, craving for sensual pleasures, anger, and confusion, you do not need to feel disgust for them or want to run away from them, nor do you identify yourself with them. You do not think that infatuation and ignorance are entirely different from liberation. You see that in the five crimes of immediate retribution there is the seed of liberation, that in bondage there is liberation, and in liberation there is bondage. You do not see the four noble truths but still you are not ignorant of the four noble truths as is the ordinary person. Practicing like this, you are worthy to receive and eat the food of the donor."*

In reading this section of the sutra, the principle of nonduality is clearly evident. We have to see flowers in refuse and refuse in flowers. We have to see the afflictions in the awakening and the awakening in the afflictions. We have to see that the sheet of paper is made from elements that are not the sheet of paper, like the sun, the clouds and the forest. Although those elements are not the paper, the paper would not be possible without them. Looking at "right" we see that "right" is made of things that are not "right." This means that we do not reject anything. The good gardener does not reject any

---

* Matricide, patricide, killing an arhat, maliciously causing a Buddha to bleed, splitting the sangha.

organic rotting matter. Similarly the good practitioner does not run away from afflictions and knows how to turn afflictions into awakening. "The afflictions are the awakening, the Buddhadharma is worldly Dharma," are sentences we often hear repeated in discussion on the Dharma. They come from the nondual way of thought.

"Lord Buddha, when I heard these words of Vimalakīrti I was unsure of what he could be talking about."

This is a criticism directed against Subhūti that is difficult to believe. In fact Subhūti was someone who had penetrated deeply the *prajñāpāramitā* teachings on emptiness. However the idea here is that Subhūti had only penetrated a narrow view of emptiness and had not yet understood the "emptiness" of the Mahāyāna. According to the Vimalakīrtinirdeśa the Venerable Sub-hūti is still a śrāvaka monk who has not yet reached the Mahāyāna. Someone who has penetrated the teachings on emptiness has reached a deep level of practice and yet the sutra belittles the Venerable Subhūti to the extent of saying that *he felt light-headed and had no idea how to reply. All he wanted to do was withdraw. He did not even dare ask for his bowl to take back with him.*

At that point Vimalakīrti said: "Venerable Subhūti please take your bowl. Do not be afraid. What do you think? If the Buddha were to manifest a magical body and ask you what I have asked you, would you be afraid?" " I replied that I would not." Then the householder Vimalakīrti said: "All phenomena are a magical

appearance. You should not be afraid. Why? Because all spoken
words are a magical appearance, and since the wise ones are
not caught in words, they are not afraid." The Venerable Subhūti
was afraid so Vimalakīrti had to calm him: "I also am like that.
I am only a magical appearance. Do not be afraid of me."

So the character of Vimalakīrti is portrayed as someone who has compassion. When I read this sentence, I
feel more sympathy with the compiler of the sutra, and
for the first time I feel sympathy with Vimalakīrti.

THE VENERABLE PŪRṆA

This section is about the monk whose full name was
Pūrṇamaitrāyaṇīputra, He was one of the monks who
were most skilled in giving Dharma talks. Pūrṇa means
fulfillment and maitrāyaṇa means kind, friendly. Mai-
trāyaṇī (loving, kind friendly) was his mother's name.
His name means Fulfillment as the Son of Loving Kindness. When the Buddha told Pūrṇa to go and visit Vimalakīrti and ask after his sickness, he said:

> "Lord Buddha, I do not have the capacity to go and visit him
> and ask after his health. Once I was sitting in the forest with a
> group of newly ordained bhikṣus. I was talking to them about
> the Dharma. Vimalakīrti came along and said: "Venerable
> Pūrṇa, do be careful. Do not put food that has gone bad into
> a bowl made of precious gems. Make sure you have pene-
> trated the psychology of these monks before teaching them the
> Dharma… Understand their aspirations… Do not confuse
> beryl with ordinary glass."

What Vimalakīrti meant was: maybe what these monks need is the highest teachings of the Mahāyāna and it would be a great pity if all you were giving them was the teachings of the śrāvaka vehicle. Sometimes the capacity of the minds of people is as wide as space and they are waiting to hear teachings of great breadth while all you are giving them is your teachings that are still narrow. That is letting them down.

This is very severe criticism, especially when Pūrṇa was considered to be the best teacher of the Dharma among Śākyamuni's disciples.

"If you are not able to see the capacities and roots of living beings, do not teach the Dharma to them—that would be a great pity for them. Those monks do not have any wounds in their hearts, but you teach the Dharma to them in such a way that they receive wounds. It is as if there is a healthy cow, you come along and give it medicine, and it becomes lame. That is a shame for the cow."

"Do not put the great ocean into a buffalo's footprint; do not make the light of the sun equal to the light of the glowworm."

What Vimalakīrti means is that their mind can receive the great ocean of the Right Dharma and you take something small like a buffalo's footprint in the hope that you can fit the whole ocean into it. How could that be possible? They have a great yearning, their aspiration is very high. How can you satisfy it with a little Dharma from the śrāvaka vehicle?

*At that point Vimalakīrti entered meditative concentration
(samādhi) and used a miraculous power to make it possible
for the newly ordained bhikṣus to see their former lives. They
had laid down wholesome roots in the presence of five hundred
Buddhas in their former lives. They had given rise to the mind
of the highest, right, and equal awakening. When they remem-
bered having given rise to the mind of love in former lives, they
came and prostrated at the feet of Vimalakīrti and he gave
them a Dharma talk that turned them in the direction of the
highest, right, and equal enlightenment.*

This meant they had the capacity to receive the
Mahāyāna.

*Pūrṇa said: "Lord Buddha, at that time I acknowledged that
śrāvakas like myself should not give Dharma talks!"*

These words are a very heavy canon to fire at the disciple of Śākyamuni Buddha!

THE VENERABLE MAHĀKĀTYĀYANA

We now go on to the Mahākātyāyana scene. This monk
was well-known for his capacity to make commentaries
on the Buddha's teachings. His reasoning was very solid
and strong.

*The Venerable Mahākātyāyana said: "Lord Buddha, it hap-
pened that day that the Buddha gave teachings to the bhikṣus.
After he had spoken, he went to rest. It was my responsibility
to give a further explanation of what the Buddha had taught
to the monks. That day the Dharma talk had been on suffering, no-self, emptiness, and nirvāṇa. While I was explaining*

to the monks, Vimalakīrti appeared and said: 'Venerable, do
not teach like that. You must not talk about the true nature of
dharmas with a mind which is caught in birth and death. For
in truth no dharma is born and no dharma dies. This is the
meaning of impermanence.'"

According to the simplest and most basic explanation, impermanence is birth and death at every moment.
That is the śrāvaka point of view. Vimalakīrti says:
"dharmas have never been from the beginning and will never
cease to be." That is the Mahāyāna view. Birth and death
are outer appearances and the basis of all phenomena
is unborn and undying. It is the same for water and
waves. You see waves rising and falling, being born and
dying. As far as the ocean water is concerned, it does
not rise and fall, it is not born and does not die. When
you understand that, you can explain the real meaning of impermanence. If you have not yet understood,
the explanation you give belongs to the small Dharma.
Vimalakīrti continued:

"The five aggregates are completely empty of a separate self and,
as a result, are without birth—this is the meaning of suffering. All dharmas are ultimately nonbeing—this is the meaning
of emptiness. The self and the nonself are not two different
things—this is the meaning of no-self. Phenomena have never
been to begin with, and hence will never cease to be—this is the
meaning of nirvāṇa."

Vimalakīrti means: You can only understand suffering when you have penetrated the teachings of true

emptiness. You monks who say that life is suffering, that life is like this, and life is like that, will not arrive at any insight if you have not yet realized the insight into the transcendent understanding of True Emptiness. When you see that self and no-self are two aspects of reality, that self is no-self and no-self is self, only then will you really understand no-self. When you are able to see that being is emptiness itself and emptiness is being itself, which means that wonderful being is true emptiness and true emptiness is nothing other than wonderful being, only then will you understand emptiness as the Buddha meant it.

If you want to talk about nirvāṇa and cessation, you should know the truth that all phenomena are all lying in their nirvāṇa nature already. All phenomena have never been born and have never died. In the light of that you will understand what nirvāṇa truly is. Nirvāṇa does not lie in the future. Nirvāṇa lies in the present because all dharmas are abiding in nirvāṇa. All dharmas have the nature of nirvāṇa inherent in them.

This is the difference between the Mahāyāna way of thought and the sutras that are in terms of the conventional truth. In the sutras of conventional meaning, dharmas are subject to birth and death. If you teach about nirvāṇa in terms of birth and death, that is not the real nirvāṇa. It is just the nirvāṇa of the sutras of conventional meaning. This is taught very clearly in the Śrīmālasiṃhanādasūtra (Lion's Roar of Queen Śrīmālā

Sutra). In this sutra the queen teaches: *The Dharmakāya which still has the afflictions is called the Tathāgatagarbha. Birth and death are possible in the Tathāgatagarbha. Death is the disappearance of the feelings and the organs of sense. Birth is their arising. Without the Tathāgatagarbha there would be no distaste for suffering and aspiration for nirvāṇa.* Here we see how samsāra and nirvāṇa can be the same thing.

In this section, the Vimalakīrtinirdeśa mentions only five principles: impermanence, suffering, emptiness, no-self, and nirvāṇa. Nevertheless, it is very important. It reflects the five ways of understanding these principles in the conventional sutras in comparison with the way these five teachings were understood in the Mahāyāna. We could stop here and discuss these differences for a very long time but we want to go on and read the next scene of the sutra.

THE VENERABLE ANURUDDHA

The Pali version of this monk's name means "In accord with the mind." Anuruddha is regarded as the monk who had the divine eyes. These eyes are able to see what is happening far away. They can see into the whole trichiliocosm.

The Venerable Anuruddha said to the Buddha: "One day as I practiced slow walking meditation, there was a Brahma by the name of Śubhavyūha and a number of other Brahmas who lit up brightly the path on which I was walking. They came

and prostrated and then asked: "Anuruddha, how far are you
able to see with the divine eyes? I replied: "My divine eyes are
able to see into the three great chiliocosms that are taught by
Buddha Śākyamuni. I see them as clearly as if they were a
mango that I was looking at in my hand. I can see clearly every
detail of the trichiliocosm." At that point Vimalakīrti appeared
and said to me: 'Venerable Anuruddha are your divine eyes
a conditioned appearance or an unconditioned appearance?
If they are conditioned and just depend on signs, they are no
different from the five miracles of the non-Buddhists. If they are
not dependent on signs, they are unconditioned and according
to reason they are not able to see.'"

Vimalakīrti questioned the Venerable Anuruddha as
to whether his divine eyes were conditioned or unconditioned. If they are conditioned, how can they be different
from the five miracles of the non-Buddhists?* They are
not of any significance. If you say that they are not conditioned how are you able to see anything with them?
As an unconditioned phenomenon what is left to see or
not to see?

"Lord Buddha when I heard this I was reduced to silence. When
the Brahma gods heard Vimalakīrti say this, they were aston-
ished, prostrated, and asked him: "Householder is there some-
one in the world who has the divine eyes?" The householder

---

* The five miracles shared by the non-Buddhists are the first five
abhijña: 1. magical powers (*iddhi-vidha*), like passing through a
wall; 2. divine ear (*dibba-sota*); 3. penetration of the minds of others
(*ceto-pariya-ñāna*); 4. remembrance of former existences (*pubbe-*
nivāsānussati); 5. divine eye (*dibba-cakkhu*).

Vimalakīrti replied: "The Buddha has the true divine eyes,
because he always abides in samādhi and is therefore able to
see all the Buddha worlds. It is not only when he uses the divine
eyes that he sees them."

"At that point the Brahmā Śubhavyūha along with his retinue
of five hundred Brahmas all gave rise to the highest, right, and
equal enlightenment. They prostrated at the feet of Vimalakīrti
and immediately disappeared from sight. That is why I do not
have the capacity to go and ask him after his health."

THE VENERABLE UPĀLI

This scene is about the Venerable Upāli who was the
foremost in understanding the Vinaya. When the
Buddha asked him to go and enquire after Vimalakīrti's
health, he recounted how one day two bhikṣus who had
transgressed the precepts came to ask his advice. He was
instructing them on the nature of their offense and the
way to confess it, and Vimalakīrti came and put a spoke
in his wheel.

Vimalakīrti said: "Venerable Upāli do not instruct the monks
thus. The more you instruct them, the more troubled they
become. Why? Because the offence is not to be found inside or
outside (the offender) or somewhere between inside and outside.
Buddha has said that when the mind is defiled, living beings
are defiled. When the mind is pure, living beings are pure. If
you cannot find the mind inside, outside, or somewhere between
inside and outside, how can you find the fault? All phenomena
in their true nature of suchness are not defiled or pure. Ven-
erable Upāli, when your mind is liberated what offense can it

commit? The mind of all living beings has always been pure and that is why you cannot find where the fault is. When your mind manifests mindfulness it is pure, but when mindfulness does not manifest it is impure. When your mind is caught in the idea of a separate self it is impure, but if it is not caught in this idea it is pure. Therefore the notions of pure and impure, offense and no offense are just ideas and we cannot understand or grasp them when we have not yet grasped the truth that mind in its true nature transcends these ideas."

This section of the sutra contains the idea: "The mind is in its origin pure and clear." This idea is already latent in the sutras of Original Buddhism and later on, in the Mahāyāna, led to new concepts such as that of the Tathāgatagarbha (Tathāgata store).

Vimalakīrti concluded: "We can only understand the Vinaya and master insight into the precepts, transgressions, and their retribution when we are aware that all dharmas are constantly being born and dying. They are like a magical appearance, a flash of lightning. Dharmas do not arise without relying on each other, they are objects of wrong view, (which means that our perceptions and our cognition of them are incorrect). When we understand that, we shall have a deep understanding of unwholesome karma, merit, transgressing or not transgressing the precepts. In short, if we do not have insight into the suchness of all phenomena, whatever we say about unwholesome karma and transgressing the precepts is incorrect. I see that you have not yet mastered this insight that is found in the Mahāyāna sutras." After the two bhikṣus heard Vimalakīrti they praised him saying: "Vimalakīrti is truly wise. The Venerable Upāli cannot equal him."

Vimalakīrti certainly robs all the senior disciples of the Buddha of their prestige.

THE VENERABLE RĀHULA

The next of the Buddha's monastic disciples told to go and visit Vimalakīrti is Rāhula. He told the Buddha why he could not go and enquire after Vimalakīrti's health.

On one occasion a large gathering of young Licchavi came to where I was. They said: "Venerable Rāhula, you are the son of the World-Honored One and you renounced becoming a Wheel-turning King in order to become a monk. What are the advantages and the benefits of becoming a monk?"

They were wanting to become monks, but their minds were not wholly made up and still they had not received their parents' permission. They saw that Rāhula was still a young monk so they came to ask him about the monastic life: How do you live? Are you happy? How do you serve people?

While I was explaining to them the advantages and merit of leaving the home, Vimalakīrti came along and said: "Venerable Rāhula, you should not talk about the advantages and merit that come from the monastic life. Why? Because the monastic life is precisely to leave behind advantages and merit."

Leaving the home is for leaving the home; it is not done because there is an advantage involved or because it brings merit.

Vimalakīrti continued: "As far as conditioned dharmas are concerned, one may speak of them as having advantages and merit. But someone who leaves the home enters the realm of the unconditioned, and in the realm of the unconditioned there are no advantages and merit".

Out in the world people talk about conditioned dharmas as having benefits and leading to merit, but leaving the home is something unconditioned. In leaving the home you have let go of everything, so you cannot talk about advantage or disadvantage in the matter.*

"When you become a monk you no longer see the difference between 'leaving the family' and 'staying in the family.' When you are able to leave behind the sixty-two wrong views of non-Buddhists and are able to dwell in nirvāṇa, when you can master all the afflictions and the different kinds of māra, when you can unify in concentration your mind and senses, then you have truly left the home."

Having said this, Vimalakīrti turned to the young men and said: "You have heard the Right Dharma, now you should leave the home, because to meet the Buddha is a very rare opportunity."

The young men thought that this was indeed true so they replied, "Householder, we really want to become monks and that is why we have been questioning the Venerable Rāhula

---

* The Chinese expression 出家 or Sanskrit *parivrāja* means literally "leaving the family" it is used to mean becoming a monk; so there is a play on these words in this part of the sutra, "becoming a monk" and "leaving behind."

about the monastic life, but our parents have not given us their permission." Vimalakīrti replied: "So there is no need for you to become monks. It is enough for you to give rise to the mind of the highest enlightenment, because that is the essence of leaving the home." When they heard this thirty-two Licchavi, sons of householders, gave rise to the mind of highest enlightenment."

Although Vimalakīrti encouraged the young men to undertake the monastic life, he said that all they needed to do was to give rise to the mind of highest enlightenment. This means they should become monks in their hearts and minds only. So even if their parents did not give permission they were still monks in essence.

The Venerable Ānanda

Next it was Ānanda's turn to be told by the Buddha to go and visit Vimalakīrti and ask after his health. Ānanda was the Buddha's attendant. It would be out of place for him to decline to do his teacher's bidding. However he said:

"Once the Buddha was indisposed and could not eat solid food, so I went out to ask for some milk. I was standing before the house of a Brahmin when I saw Vimalakīrti approaching. He asked: Venerable Ānanda, it is still very early and the dew is on the grass, why are you standing here?" Ānanda answered frankly: "I have come to request milk for the Buddha who is unwell." Vimalakīrti immediately replied: "Venerable, do not speak like that! Do not say that a Buddha is unwell. The Buddha body is as enduring as diamond. If you say the Buddha is sick you are maligning the Buddha. The Wheel-turning King does not fall sick, much less the Tathāgata whose merit is much greater. If

you go into the villages and spread such rumors then the members of the various sects will look down on the Buddha. They will malign the Buddha saying: "The Buddha is sick and is unable to cure himself so how can he cure the sickness of others? How can you call him the King of the Dharma? Go back to the monastery, don't spread any more rumors!"

"Lord Buddha, I felt very ashamed. The Buddha had clearly instructed me to go into the village and request milk. I could not have misheard. While I was hesitating whether I should bring milk back for the Buddha or not, there was a voice that came down from the sky: "It is true, the Buddha does not need milk. However since he is pretending to appear on this earth, he also has to pretend to appear sick like everyone else in order to be able to help beings. There is nothing wrong with the fact that you have come to find milk for the Buddha. You should take milk back with you."

"Lord Buddha, it is because Vimalakīrti's wisdom and eloquence is of such magnitude that I do not dare go and ask him after his health."

In this chapter Ānanda is represented as being as meek as a lamb and with no capacity to engage in dialogue with Vimalakīrti. In fact the Venerable Ānanda was learned and intelligent, not at all like he is represented here.

CHAPTER 4: BODHISATTVAS

Chapter 4 is on the bodhisattvas. In this chapter the Buddha assigns a number of bodhisattvas to go and visit Vimalakīrti and ask after his health. Some of these bodhisattvas including the future Buddha, bodhisattva Maitreya, have not yet reached the highest level of practice.

BODHISATTVA MAITREYA

Maitreya, the future Buddha, is sometimes known by the name Ajita (invincible). The Buddha asked Maitreya to go and ask Vimalakīrti after his health. The bodhisattva asked to not go.

We should know that Maitreya Bodhisattva had been a bodhisattva in his last lifetime before becoming Buddha. In his next lifetime, he will become the Buddha who is the successor of Śākyamuni. His Pure Land will be this sahā world. Buddhists in Asia, aware that Maitreya is the future Buddha, choose New Year's Day to be his feast day. Maitreya is our future happiness. His name is a good one, for Maitreya means the Buddha of Love.

When he asked to be allowed not to go, Maitreya said:

"Lord Buddha, the story begins when I was still in the Tuṣita heaven. That day I was talking about the stage of non-regression to a number of kings in heaven. When he heard this, Vimalakīrti came up to see what was going on."*

---

* This heaven has two parts. One part is called the inner palace. It is the place where the Buddhas and Bodhisattva Maitreya dwell along with their retinues. The other part is called the Outer Palace. It is the place where men and gods dwell. The Tuṣita heaven belongs to the Desire Realm and is the fourth heaven which can be reached by meditative concentration.

"After he had come up to greet us, he gave his opinion: 'Venerable Bodhisattva, I have heard it said that the Lord Buddha has predicted that in your next life time you will attain the fruit of the highest, right, and equal enlightenment. So what is meant by 'next lifetime'? Is it a past, present, or future lifetime?'

"After that Vimalakīrti started discoursing on the Mahāyāna principle. He said: 'Reality lies outside of ideas concerning the past, the present, and the future. The past has already gone, the future has not yet come, and we are not able to grasp the present. As soon as we see the present, it has already become the past. So did Buddha predict that you would become Buddha in your past life, your present life, or a future life?' He quoted a sentence from a discourse of the Buddha: 'O monks, in this very moment you are being born, aging, and dying at every instant. If this is true, what is exactly the time when you become Buddha?' Vimalakīrti added: 'The essence of reality is nirvāṇa. It is permanent, happy, self, and pure. Thus the bodhisattva does not need to become Buddha. The bodhisattva has become Buddha for countless lifetimes already. In his true nature he is already Buddha. As far as I see it, it is not correct to talk in terms of becoming Buddha in the future.'"

From the point of view of the ultimate dimension, suchness, and true nature, there is no past, present, and future. There is no matter of having attained, have not yet attained, and shall attain. Therefore it is not correct to talk about becoming Buddha in the future or becoming Buddha in the next lifetime. It is like when we talk about the wave and the water. It is not the ocean that goes up and down, is high or is low. As far as the wave is concerned we can say high or low, going up and going down. Here Vimalakīrti talks about the ultimate dimension in order to raise objection to people talking about Maitreya becoming Buddha in the future.

Let us read a few lines from the sutra:

"How can there be a prediction of the birth of suchness or a prediction of the death of suchness?"

"Suchness" here means the nature of reality. How can the true nature be born or die? So as far as suchness is concerned it is very strange to talk about a prediction that someone will become Buddha, because all living beings belong to suchness, all phenomena lie within suchness, and Bodhisattva Maitreya also belongs to suchness. If Bodhisattva Maitreya also belongs to suchness, if Bodhisattva Maitreya is already suchness, then why talk about realizing or not realizing, predicting or not predicting. It means that Vimalakīrti just wants to talk in terms of the absolute and does not allow anyone to mention the relative anymore. All Buddhas, all living beings are abiding in nirvāṇa so do not talk about attaining nirvāṇa in order to be enlightened. If you talk about realizing the path you have to talk about *bodhi*, because bodhi means awakening or enlightenment.

This section of the sutra talks about the nature of bodhi. The translation of Master Xuanzang is clearer so later on we shall compare the translation of Master Xuanzang with that of Master Kumārajīva.

"Bodhisattva Maitreya, You should give teachings that will help the sons of the gods who are here today not to be caught in this idea of bodhi."

"What is bodhi? Bodhi is something we cannot grasp with our body nor with our mind. Why? Because the nature of bodhi is extinction (nirvāṇa)."

Nirvāṇa is the extinction of all ideas and all afflictions. From the standpoint of extinction of ideas, we cannot talk about birth, death, being, nonbeing, same, different, coming, going, because nirvāṇa is not any of these signs or these ideas. That is what is meant by bodhi. Even if you wanted to speak about bodhi, you would not be able to do so because in speaking you would have to use signs, perceptions, and ideas. The Chinese version of Kumārajīva says *What cannot be perceived is bodhi.* This sentence's meaning is not very clear.

The translation of Xuanzang is as follows: *Bodhi needs nothing to be added to it; no object is the cause of its increase or decrease.* This is quite correct as far as Vimalakīrti's way of thought is concerned, so Xuanzang's translation is clearer and more coherent.

As far as the true nature is concerned, bodhi belongs to the extinction of ideas and cannot be described by words or ideas. *Bodhi has no increase.* It is not possible that yesterday our bodhi was 70 percent and today, because of our practice, it is 80 percent. That is not bodhi. This is also the meaning of the Prajñāpāramitā Sutras—neither produced nor destroyed, neither increasing nor decreasing, neither defiled nor immaculate. The sutra tells us first that bodhi has nothing to do with signs, because it is the extinction of all ideas. Secondly, bodhi is not something that grows greater or smaller.

If we continue to read the translation of Kumārajīva: *Bodhi cannot be practiced,* because it cannot be the object of memory or of thought.* Bodhi does not come from our practice because it is not subject to increase or decrease.

In the version translated by Xuanzang this section reads: *Bodhi is the non-functioning of all reasoning and reflection.*

It means bodhi is not a matter of practicing or not practicing. Practice and no practice belong to the realm of reasoning and ideas. All that we can discuss, all that we can think about has nothing to do with bodhi. This means bodhi is not hard work. Hard work lies in the realm of reasoning and ideas.

The next sentence in Kumārajīva's version is: *Bodhi is cutting off all attachment to views.* It is similar in the translation of Xuanzang: *Bodhi is cutting off forever because all our views are eternally cut off.* Views here means the ideas of birth, death, increase, decrease, coming, going, etc. Once these have been cut off, there is bodhi.

The next sentence of Kumārajīva is: *Letting go is bodhi because all wrong perceptions are let go of.* Xuanzang

---

* The word 行 here is to be translated as "practice," not as 現行 "manifest."

translates: *Bodhi is letting go because all grasping and attainment are let go of.*

The next sentence of Kumārajīva is not clear. It says: *Bodhi is obstacles and the end of all aims.* Probably the word "without" is missing before "obstacles." In the Tibetan version it says: *Bodhi is where there is no obstruction.* In the version of Xuanzang it reads: *Bodhi is without fetters because it is eternally free from agitation and turbulence.*

So we can translate the sentence to mean *Bodhi is without obstacles because it is not hindered by aims.* This means that because we have goals, plans, and aspirations, our mind is disturbed and bodhi cannot manifest. This non-obstruction is a help in the sense that we do not have yearnings, calculations, and strategies in our mind even if it is a strategy to arrive quickly at enlightenment.

The next sentence in Kumārajīva's translation is *Bodhi is not invaded.* It means not invaded by craving. This sentence can be explained, but its meaning is not immediately clear. The version of Xuanzang reads *Bodhi is peace because all the discriminations of our mind have been eternally put to rest.* This sentence is about the silence of bodhi, because all discriminating notions are absent.

In Xuanzang's version there follows the sentence: *Bodhi is without disharmony because in it all attachment to ideas and all disputation have been laid aside forever.* Where there is bodhi there are no disputes, because bodhi transcends all views.

Bodhi is peaceful abiding because it dwells in the realm of the Dharma (Xuanzang). Bodhi dwells in the Dharma realm rather than the mundane world (*lokadhātu*). The Dharma realm is the realm of the truth of the Dharma. This is the ultimate truth.

We do not need to review all these terms. All we need to know is that here Vimalakīrti is telling the gods of the Tuṣita heaven that we cannot describe the nature of bodhi in terms of words and ideas. If we talk about the realization of enlightenment using the conventional language, people could misunderstand, and Vimalakīrti made his appearance in the Tuṣita heaven in order to prevent the gods there from misunderstanding. That is what is meant by the sentence *"The reason I had to come here was because if I did not, Bodhisattva Maitreya might unskillfully lead the gods to misunderstand the meaning of bodhi and that would be a shame for the Tathāgata."*

Maitreya said *"Lord Buddha, when the gods had heard Vimalakīrti speak, two hundred of them gave rise to the Dharma patience which is not born and does not die."*

Patience means the ability to tolerate great happiness. It is not just suffering that we have to tolerate. Sometimes happiness is so great that we have to tolerate it. If not, the five skandhas that make our life possible will fall apart. According to tradition, Queen Mahāmāya could not tolerate the enormous happiness she had when she gave birth to Siddhārtha and for that reason she died and was reborn in a heavenly realm. There are people who win the lottery and when they hear the news they have a heart attack. The practice that the gods realized was that of tolerance or patience (*kṣānti*) of the Dharma, a happiness that is so great that it is called "unborn," in other words nirvāṇa. Nirvāṇa is not born, does not die, is not defiled, not pure, not subject to increase or decrease, does not come, does not go, is not one, is not many. It would take a long time to repeat all the opposites that are negated by nirvāṇa, so the sutra just uses the word unborn as an abbreviation for them all.

"Lord Buddha, because of that I am not able to visit Vimalakīrti and ask him after his health." This is how bodhisattva Maitreya refused to comply with the Buddha's request.

THE YOUNG BOY PRABHĀVYŪHA

At this point the Buddha turned to look at a young boy of about fourteen or fifteen, whose name was Prabhāvyūha (Adornment with Light). In the Mahāyāna sutras all young boys and girls are very talented. They are all bodhisattvas. If we say that these characters are not really children we lose a great deal of the richness of the Mahāyāna. In the Mahāyāna, women, children, and laypeople are very adept. If we say that these Mahāyāna characters are not really women, children or laypeople, we lose what is good in the Mahāyāna.

When Buddha told the young boy Prabhāvyūha to go and visit Vimalakīrti and ask after his health, the young boy said: "Lord Buddha, I am not able to go and ask Vimal-akīrti after his health. One day I was just leaving the city of Vaiśalī and I met Vimalakīrti coming in. I asked him: 'Sir, where are you coming from?' He said: 'I am coming from the seat of enlightenment (bodhimaṇḍa).'"

This means the place where the Buddhas sit to attain enlightenment, the Diamond or Vajra Throne. Master Xuanzang translates *bodhimaṇḍa* as "the wonderful enlightenment," which means "I come from a place of deep and wonderful enlightenment."

"At that point I asked: 'What is the seat of enlightenment?' and Vimalakīrti gave a number of definitions:

'The direct mind is the seat of enlightenment.' The direct mind is the mind that is upright, honest, and does not falsify anything.

'Accomplishment is the seat of enlightenment because we accomplish everything we undertake.

'The deep mind is the seat of enlightenment because it realizes great merit.

'The mind of love (bodhicitta) is the seat of enlightenment because it makes no mistakes.

'Generosity is the seat of enlightenment because when giving one expects no reward.

'Observing the precepts, patience and inclusiveness, right effort, meditative concentration and insight are the seat of enlightenment.

' *Loving kindness, compassion, joy, and equanimity are the seat
of enlightenment.*

'*The four means of conversion are the seat of enlightenment.*

'*Great learning is the seat of enlightenment.*

'*Mastery of the mind is the seat of enlightenment.*

'*The thirty-seven wings of enlightenment are the seat of
enlightenment.*

'*The teaching of conditioned co-arising is the seat of
enlightenment.*'"

You know all these definitions, because they are very
important practices in both Original Buddhism and the
Mahāyāna.

'*The afflictions are the seat of enlightenment.*' This means
that we practice in the world where there are afflictions
without trying to run away from them. It is because there
are afflictions in our own mind and around us that we
undertake the practice of mindfulness in order to transform them.

'*All phenomena are the seat of enlightenment.*' We do
not run away from, and are not afraid of, forms, sounds,
odors, tastes, tactile contact, and objects of mind. We
stay right in the world of sense objects in order to
practice.

'*The Three Realms are the seat of enlightenment. All the
Māras are the seat of enlightenment.*' We are not afraid of
the Three Realms or of the Māras.

'The lion's roar is the seat of enlightenment, the ten powers, the four fearlessnesses, the eighteen attributes of a Buddha are the seat of enlightenment.' The "ten powers" are the ten powers of understanding that a Buddha has.[*] The "four fearlessnesses" are the four kinds of fearlessness belonging to the Buddhas.[†] The "eighteen attributes" of a Buddha are not found in a pratyekabuddha or a śrāvaka.[‡]

---

[*] That Buddha has the power to understand: 1. What is correct and what is incorrect. 2. The causes and results that make up the karmic retribution of living beings in the three times. 3. All the samadhis that lead to liberation. 4. The high or low faculties of living beings. 5. The different desires of living beings. 6. All the different realms of living beings. 7. The coming and going of ordinary people, of the holy ones, of the mundane and the supramundane. 8. The nature of suffering, happiness, long life, or short life. 9. The births, deaths and previous lives of living beings and the Nirvāṇa without any more bondage of the holy ones. 10. That one has oneself put an end to karmic retribution and habit energy; there is no more birth and death or taint of afflictions.

[†] When the Buddha gives a Dharma talk his fearlessness arises from four things: 1. Omniscience—an understanding of all mundane and supramundane phenomena. 2. Ending bondage: knowing clearly the karmic births and deaths of all beings 3. Obstacles to the path: uses māra-dharma to teach Buddhadharma. 4. The end of suffering: teaches Dharma doors that will put an end to the afflictions.

[‡] 1. Faultless bodily action. 2. Faultless speech action. 3. Faultless mind action. 4. No dispersion. 5. Always in meditative concentration. 6. Omniscience. 7. Uninterrupted aspiration. 8. Uninterrupted diligence. 9. Uninterrupted mindfulness. 10. Uninterrupted insight. 11. Uninterrupted liberation. 12. Uninterrupted liberation by insight. 13. All bodily action executed in accord with understanding. 14. All speech action executed in accord with understanding. 15. All mind action executed in accord with understanding. 16. Unobstructed understanding of future lives. 17. Unobstructed understanding of past lives. 18. Unobstructed understanding of present lives.

'If the bodhisattva practices the pāramitas to teach living beings,
then their every action, word and thought, at any time and in
any place are a seat of enlightenment.'

"When Vimalakīrti had finished speaking, five hundred gods
and men who were present in the audience all gave rise to the
mind of the highest, right, and equal enlightenment. Therefore I
do not have the capacity to go and ask him after his health."

In the section on the young boy Prabhāvyūha, the
sutra is concerned with the principle (理) rather than
the action (事). The sutra takes what is phenomenal and
explains it in terms of the noumenal and takes what is
cause and explains it in terms of the result. This is what
is meant by gathering together all the actions and direct-
ing them to the principle.

When we come to the section on Bodhisattva
Jagatīṃdhara (Earth Supporting Bodhisattva), there is
another kind of offering up. It is offering up the self for
the other. It means to bring our whole person to offer to
others.

BODHISATTVA JAGATĪṂDHARA

*One day the bodhisattva was in his meditation hut when Māra
the Villain* brought twelve thousand very beautiful goddesses,
accompanied by music, to pay respect to the bodhisattva.
Because the bodhisattva's vision was not yet unobstructed, he
mistook Māra for Indra, the king of the gods. He stood up and
said: "Welcome Indra, I am glad you have come. Even though
your merit has made it possible to enjoy the five pleasures of life,*

you should look on them as impermanent. You should see that your lifespan, possessions, and merit are all impermanent, so that you can realize a deeper kind of happiness."

Māra said: "Venerable sir, I have brought you these twelve thousand goddesses to be your housemaids. Since you are unmarried, you have no one to help you in the house."

Māra had just finished speaking and Vimalakīrti appeared and said: "Bodhisattva, be careful! This is not King Indra, this is Māra. Be careful."

Māra said: "How come you are always coming along and putting a spoke in the wheel?"

Vimalakīrti said: "Māra, do not offer all these goddesses to the bodhisattva. Offer them to me. I really need their help."

At that, Māra thought Vimalakīrti had come along to make trouble so he decided to become invisible. However he could not disappear because the spiritual power of Vimalakīrti was so great.

We should remember that in the sutras, especially those of the Southern School, Māra the Villain often appears with the intention of disturbing the Buddha. Sometimes he appears as a snake in order to instill fear in the Buddha. Sometimes he appears as a politician to tempt the Buddha into politics. Every time Māra appears, Buddha recognizes him and says: "Māra, I know it is

---

* Māraḥ Pāpīyān, the king of the māras of the desire realm.

you," and Māra disappears. This is something very real, because Māra is within our own mind and can appear many times during the day in different guises. The day before the Buddha realized enlightenment, Māra appeared and said: "What makes you so sure you will be enlightened tomorrow?" Buddha smiled, placed his fingers on the earth and established mindfulness. When he was fully mindful, he lifted up his eyes and Māra disappeared immediately.

Often when wrong thinking arises in our mind, Māra shows himself. When we know that our thinking is wrong thinking, it automatically ceases. When we look with the eyes of mindfulness, wrong thinking disappears straightaway. This is a wonderful method of Buddhism called "Acknowledge wrong, and wrong ceases." If we are not mindful, how are we to know if Māra is teasing us or it is a serious threat? All of us have been confronted by Māra many times during the day. If we are not mindful, it is difficult to protect our own body and mind and that of other people.

To return to the tale told by bodhisattva Jagatīṃdhara:

Since Māra was not able to disappear, he reluctantly resigned himself to give the twelve thousand goddesses to Vimalakīrti. At that point, Vimalakīrti had official authority over them all. He said: "Sisters, you should give rise to the mind of highest enlightenment. Do not run after the five sense pleasures anymore. You should practice the spiritual path, the path of true happiness. The path I shall show you is the path of Dharma

*happiness; the happiness of the Right Dharma; the happiness
that is in accord with the Right Dharma."*

"The Goddesses asked 'What is Dharma happiness?' Vimalakīrti replied: "To have confidence in the Buddha is happiness.
To make offerings to the Three Jewels is happiness. To cook
for those who come to hear the Dharma is happiness. To let
go of the five objects of sensual desire is happiness. To see the
danger of the five skandhas is happiness. To do what is of benefit to living beings is happiness. To act in accordance with the
teachings of, and make offerings to, the ones who are worthy
of respect is happiness. To cultivate the roots of goodness is
happiness. To practice mindfulness and concentration is happiness. To cut off the afflictions is happiness.' When Vimalakīrti
gave these criteria for happiness it gladdened the hearts of the
goddesses."*

After he had given the goddesses to Vimalakīrti,
Māra began to regret what he had done. When the time
came for him to go back to his heavenly realm all alone
he felt so sad.

"So he suggested to Vimalakīrti that he return the goddesses to
him and said: 'Follow me back home!' The Goddesses replied,
'But you gave us to Vimalakīrti, how can we follow after you?
Here we have learned about a new kind of happiness, happiness
in accord with the Right Dharma. We do not want to return
and drown in infatuation for the five objects of sense pleasure
anymore.' Māra insisted: 'Layman Vimalakīrti, please give me
back these goddesses. Surely a bodhisattva does not keep anything for himself? If you are a real bodhisattva you will give me
back the goddesses.'"

"Vimalakīrti said, 'Although you have given them to me I have no desire to hold onto them. Sisters, if you want to go back with Māra, then go. When you have gone back you can continue to practice Dharma happiness in your own environment.'

"Then Vimalakīrti taught the goddesses how they could continue to practice happiness according to the Right Dharma in Māra's heavenly realm.

"After the twelve thousand goddesses had received the practice which would liberate them, Māra disappeared and no one could see any trace of him."

When he had told this, the bodhisattva Jagatīmdhara added: "Lord Buddha, I have seen the supremacy of the spiritual power, the wisdom and eloquence of Vimalakīrti and that is why I am not able to go and ask him after his health."

BODHISATTVA SUDATTA

Another bodhisattva we need to hear about is Sudatta. Sudatta is the son of a very rich family, so he is called "son of a householder." When refusing to go and ask after the health of Vimalakīrti, Sudatta said:

"There was a day when I orgainzed a large offering for poor people. It lasted for seven days. Offerings were given to all kinds of people, śramaṇas, brahmins, monks of all sects, to the poor, the destitute, and to beggars.

"While this offering was going on, Vimalakīrti came along and said: 'Only the Dharma is of lasting benefit. Son of a house-holder, you should organize a Dharma offering.'

"I asked, 'What is a Dharma offering?' Vimalakīrti said, 'The
Dharma is offered to all living beings. It is not offered just to
certain people as you are doing here. Dharma is offered to all at
the same time, not some people receiving first and others receiving later as in your present offering. While you are bringing
relief you are only bringing relief to a certain number of people.
You have left aside so many people who are worthy to receive
relief but who are not receiving it. The Dharma brings relief to
all living beings, all at the same time, leaving no one out. The
relief work I am talking about is done by loving kindness, compassion, joy and equanimity, by the Six Pāramitās, the Three
Doors of Liberation: emptiness, signlessness and aimlessness,
by the four Saṃgrahavastuni (Four Means of Conversion):
generosity, loving speech, benefitting others, going along with
others. When you practice generosity by your realization of the
practice for the sake of all living beings, that is the true meaning
of generosity. It is sharing in the ultimate sense. Sharing in this
way we are benefitting all living beings at one and the same
time. We do not omit a single being from the embrace of great
compassion in our heart. If you are able to do that, then you
are really worthy to organize a great offering meal.'"

When he heard Vimalakīrti speak he was very
pleased because he saw that the spirit of generosity in
the Mahāyāna goes beyond space and time.

"I took off my pearl necklace, knelt down, and offered it to the
layman Vimalakīrti. The layman refused the offering and said:
'What would be the point of my receiving this valuable necklace?' I replied: 'Please accept it because you have brought me
inestimable happiness.' He accepted the necklace and divided it

in two. One part he gave to the poorest person who was there that day. The other half he offered to a Buddha called Duṣprasahā Tathāgata.* This Buddha was also present in the assembly that day."

This part of the Vimalakīrti Sutra reminds us of the Lotus Sutra. In the chapter called Universal Door, after the Buddha has talked about the wonderful power of the vows of Avalokita, the bodhisattva Akṣayomati, was very inspired. He removed his very precious pearl necklace and offered it to Avalokita Bodhisattva. Avalokita refused to accept it. However the Buddha encouraged him to accept it, so he did so and divided it into two parts. One half he offered to Buddha Prabhūtaratna who represents the ultimate dimension. The other half he offered to Buddha Śākyamuni who represents the historical dimension. The Vimalakīrtinirdeśa arose prior to the Lotus Sutra, and scenes from the former influenced the compilers of the latter.

"When Vimalakīrti had made the offering he said: 'The reason why I did this was to demonstrate equality. The highest being in this assembly is a Buddha, the lowliest is the desperately poor man.'" In other words this was something that the son of the householder could learn from. It was the practice of generosity according to the Mahāyāna: all giving should be based on compassion and equanimity.

---

* His name means "Difficult to attain," because his Pure Land is so far away from the sahā world.

If the son of a householder had asked Vimalakīrti: "What about those who lie between the two poles of highest and lowliest? Should they not also be offered what they need to live?" We do not know what he would have replied.

The son of a householder Sudatta finished the story by saying: *"Lord Buddha I do not have the ability to visit him and ask after his health."*

CHAPTER 5: MAÑJUŚRĪ ASKS AFTER THE SICKNESS

After his senior disciples and bodhisattvas who had only recently realized the practice and whose spiritual power was not yet solid and deep, had said clearly that they could not go to Vimalakīrti and ask after his health, Buddha turned to Mañjuśrī Bodhisattva and said:

"Bodhisattva, please go and visit Vimalakīrti and ask after his health." Mañjuśrī Bodhisattva obeyed. He said: "The layman Vimalakīrti is a special person. Few can equal him in wisdom and eloquence. Although I am very much aware of that, I am still ready to obey the Lord Buddha's request and go and ask after his health."

Mañjuśrī Bodhisattva is known as the Dharma Prince, which means the spiritual son of the Buddha, the first-born of the Buddha. This bodhisattva is the symbol of great understanding. If the one who represents great understanding were not able to accept the request to visit Vimalakīrti, it would be difficult to imagine who could.

Mañjuśrī's reply shows that while being wise, he was free of the complexes of superiority and inferiority. He knew himself and he knew others. The true understanding is that which is not caught in the knowledge you presently possess and never boasts that your understanding is absolute or supreme. True understanding recognizes the value and the ability of your interlocutor and does not despise them.

When Mañjuśrī undertook to go and visit Vimalakīrti, all the bodhisattvas, śrāvaka disciples, gods Indra, Brahma, and the Four Heavenly Kings felt very happy. They thought that being present at a conversation between these two famous personalities would be very exciting. It was a once-in-a-lifetime opportunity and none of them wanted to miss it.

We have already seen that the Vimalakīrtinirdeśa is presented as a drama. This is the fifth scene of the play. It is a very important scene where there is an exciting contest in understanding between Mañjuśrī Bodhisattva and Vimalakīrti, both very well-known figures in Buddhism and the two protagonists of this drama. Everyone wanted to witness it. Just like when two world champions face each other in the ring, everyone is bursting to go and see, so they are willing to pay anything for a ticket to be able to witness a unique contest in history.

*Then Mañjuśrī bodhisattva, with all the bodhisattvas, great
disciples, and gods and men, having paid respect to the Buddha
went into the town of Vaiśalī.* It is like when everyone goes
downtown to a great music festival.

*At that time the layman Vimalakīrti knew that Mañjuśrī
bodhisattva was bringing a huge crowd to visit him. He
used his spiritual power to make all the furniture in his room
disappear so that all that was left was the bed on which he
was lying.*

This is something we could also do. If we knew
an hour beforehand that a large crowd was coming to
visit us, it would be no trouble to move the furniture
out of the room. If so many people were coming, how
could there be enough tables and chairs for them all
to sit down? So the best thing is to move them out
of the way. From the point of view of the symbolism,
this action means: the absence of something makes its
presence possible. Without absence, presence is not
possible. So this removal of furniture is interpreted
as meaning "if you want to present the wonderful
presence of things you have to present the truth of
emptiness."

Later on Vimalakīrti will borrow from another
Buddha realm thousands of large lion thrones. If he did
not clear all the furniture out of his house, how would
he be able to bring in more than thirty thousand lion
thrones for his guests to sit on?

When the party of visitors arrived they saw the empty room with just Vimalakīrti lying on his bed, maybe from time to time letting out a pretense groan, because he was not really sick, he was just appearing to be sick. Pretense here means manifesting himself like that in order to be able to bring beings to the shore of liberation.

When Mañjuśrī walked into the room he was welcomed by Vimalakīrti who said: "Welcome! Mañjuśrī has come, how precious! Your coming does not have the sign of coming, your seeing does not have the sign of seeing."

He does not waste time in delivering his first blow: The coming that is not coming: that is the true coming. The seeing that is not seeing: that is the true seeing.

Mañjuśrī bodhisattva replied: "You are right, layman! That which has come is not coming. That which has gone is not going." Here he is beginning to teach the principle of no-coming, no-going, one of the basic principles of the true nature as presented in Mahāyāna Buddhism.

The true nature in Sanskrit is *tathatā*. The true nature of all phenomena is not to arrive and not to depart, not one, not many, not born, not dying. The study of the true nature lies in the sphere of the Prajñāpāramitā teachings, that is the teachings on emptiness. On the other hand there is the study of the appearance that is the phenomenological aspect. This lies in the sphere of the Manifestation–only school also known as Consciousness-only school. It is also called

Dharmalakṣaṇa which means things as they appear or the appearance of things.

The provenance of the Manifestation-only school* is the appearance or phenomenological aspect. The provenance of the Prajñāparamitā school is the true nature of things or the noumenological aspect. We begin our studies and practice with the phenomenological and gradually we penetrate the true nature of reality. In Chinese it is called 從相入性, which we can translate into English as "beginning with phenomena you arrive at noumena."

When these two special personalities meet they immediately go into the noumenological aspect. When Vimalakīrti says: *"Your coming does not have the sign of coming, your seeing does not have the sign of seeing,"* Mañjuśrī knew that in this case he could not possibly talk in phenomenological terms, he would have to go straight into the noumenological. So he answered: *"You're quite right, layman. What has come does not come. What has gone does not go. Why is this so? This is because when one comes, one does not come from anywhere; when one goes, one does not go anywhere."*

This is the principle of no-coming, no-going. This teaching is also given in the sutras of Source Buddhism. When conditions are sufficient, eyes manifest and we

---

* The School which began in India with the teachings of Vasubandhu and Asanga in the fourth or fifth century CE and was brought to China by Xuanzang.

see eyes. When conditions are not sufficient, eyes are unmanifest and we do not see them. Eyes do not come from anywhere and will not go anywhere. Our body of flesh and blood is the same. When conditions are sufficient, our body manifests. When conditions are not sufficient our body is unmanifest. Our body does not come from somewhere in space and, after it disintegrates, it does not go somewhere in space.

An eternal question in philosophy is "Where do we come from and where shall we go?" The answer according to the Buddha is very simple: "We come from nowhere and there is nowhere we shall go to. We manifest when enough conditions come together. We go into hiding when those conditions are no longer sufficient."

Mañjuśrī did not really want to talk about noumena when he had only just arrived so he said: "*Let's not talk about that now. Let me inquire after your health first.*" Since one person is appearing to be sick, the other has to appear to ask after his health. It is all a matter of appearance.

"*What is up? Are you taking medicine? Are your improving? The Buddha is asking after you.*" When we meet each other, we have to ask first of all "How do you do?" Although you see that the other person is in good health, as strong as an elephant, you still have to ask, "How are you?" It is all meaningless, but in social intercourse, however meaningless the questions are, you still have to ask them. If we ask them, they seem superfluous but if we do not ask them, we feel something is missing. So although this is a meeting between two great intellectuals, in greeting each other they still need to go through the social courtesies.

After their social courtesies, the bodhisattva began the more serious talk. *"What is the cause of your sickness? How long have you been unwell? What needs to be done to regain your health?"*

At this point Vimalakīrti begins to give a Dharma talk: *"My sickness comes from the ignorance associated with craving."*

Obviously, this diagnosis is not for Vimalakīrti alone but for all living beings. The cause of sickness is ignorance. Ignorance is lack of understanding, or a surfeit of understanding when we store up too much knowledge, especially knowledge that contains prejudices, is incorrect, bars our way ahead, and brings about a state of stagnation. If we are wise, our knowledge will benefit our understanding. If we are not wise, it will become something that obstructs and blocks the free-flowing of our mind.

The sickness of living beings originates in ignorance. Craving is the result of ignorance. Craving here means attachment, clinging on to, and yearning for things that are not worthy of our craving. These things could be destroying us but we still crave them. Therefore suffering arises. That is sickness. In the twelve links of interdependent arising, ignorance is the link that is generally listed first of all. Craving is the cause of grasping, which is to hold tight on to something, usually an idea. Craving and grasping are the sickness of living beings.

"Because beings are sick, I am sick." This is one of the famous quotes from the Vimalakīrtinirdeśa. It is talking about the teaching of conditioned arising and interbeing. This is correct. If society is sick, then we will be sick, too. It is very difficult to avoid being sick when society is sick, unless we have a great deal of freedom, a very strong aspiration, and we can erect ramparts and moats to resist the sickness. The ramparts and moats for practitioners are precepts, concentration, insight, and sangha.

When we live in a society that is beset by violence and hatred, where strong brotherhood and sisterhood are lacking, everything we hear, see, and feel can become a channel for bringing disease into our bodies and minds. Sooner or later we shall be infected. We too will carry in us the violence, hatred, suspicion, and depression of the society. If we know how to practice, and use precepts, concentration, and insight as our armor, if we know how to use the sangha as our nourishment, we can avoid being infected. "If the environment is sick, we shall be sick" is the principle of interbeing portrayed by the Avataṃsaka Sutra.

"If living beings are no longer sick, my sickness will automatically be cured." In the first Dharma talk during a retreat given for veterans in North America, I used this idea. Thanks to that I was able to begin to help them

undo the knots of their suffering from the start of the retreat. American veterans have many complexes. They came to Vietnam to make war and returned home traumatized. They suffered defeat so the American people showed them no gratitude. People who took the side of the "hawks" showed no gratitude and people who had opposed the war sided with the hawks in showing no gratitude to the veterans. Because of this the veterans suffered greatly when they returned home. Neither the hawks nor those who opposed the war wanted to know anything about them and their suffering. Neither side offered to try to understand, embrace, and show them compassion. When they returned to their native land, they suffered constant illness of body and mind. They nearly all need psychiatric treatment. They all suffered and made their wives, children, and the surrounding society suffer.

When for the first time I walked into the room where the talks were to be given, I felt an atmosphere that was heavy and stifling and I said: "Your suffering is the suffering of those who are not veterans. If people who are not veterans knew how to practice then you too would be healed. Because they lack understanding, compassion and tolerance, you continue to be sick. If they practiced, if they had compassion and understanding, then you would be healed." I spoke as simply as I could and they understood straightaway. I did not use the Buddhist terminology of the Vimalakīrtinirdeśa, which says: *"If the bodhisattva wants to be healed he must act to heal living beings. When living beings are healed, the bodhisattva is healed."*

Vimalakīrti said: *"You asked me, Bodhisattva Mañjuśrī, 'Where does your sickness come from?' My reply is: The reason why the bodhisattva is sick is because of his compassion."* The bodhisattva feels the pain of living beings as their own pain because they have seen the truth of interbeing, that because you are sick I am sick. Even though you are in your ivory tower, in your sangha, and observing your precepts, you still feel the pain of your society. To be a true bodhisattva you must experience sickness. But you know that in order for the sickness of living beings to be healed you have to heal your sickness first. A bodhisattva learns the art of healing so that they can heal themselves and so help living beings and the planet to heal. What is more, the bodhisattva does not leave the healing process to start too late. Even before the sickness is too serious they know that every step and every breath can heal. At any moment one can fall sick. At any moment one can be healed. So we can say: "because living beings are sick, I am sick," but we should also say: "Because I am healed, living beings are healed." We cannot say: "I am sick because living beings are sick" and leave the situation at that. The great aspiration of the bodhisattva is that for as long as living beings suffer, they will stay in the world of living beings to help them heal. They are not afraid of birth, sickness, old age, and death and will ride on these waves in order to rescue beings who are drowning.

In this exchange of courtesies, Mañjuśrī asks: *"Layman, how come your house has been emptied of its contents and no one was seen helping you?"*

Vimalakīrti replied: *"The realms of the Buddhas are all empty. It is not just my house that is empty."*

One way that we have to adorn and build our Pure Land is with emptiness. Without emptiness, nothing is possible. Emptiness is the nature of everything. Emptiness is a precious jewel which we use to adorn our Buddha land. Only when there is true emptiness, can there be wonderful reality.

Then Mañjuśrī Bodhisattva asked: *"What do you need to bring about emptiness?"*

Vimalakīrti: *"Things are already empty, so what more do you need? You use emptiness to bring about emptiness."*

Mañjuśrī: *"What is emptiness made of?"*

Vimalakīrti: *"Emptiness is made of emptiness. If its nature is emptiness why do we need to make it empty? Its nature is without discrimination and that is why it is empty."*

This section in the translation of Master Xuanzang reads:

"Is it possible to use our discriminatory mind in order to see emptiness clearly?"

"The mind's capacity to discriminate is also empty."

"Why is that?"

*"Since the nature of emptiness cannot be grasped by discrimina-
tion, that is why it is truly emptiness."*

To put it more clearly, we cannot use our discriminatory mind to penetrate the nature of emptiness. Our
discriminatory mind is a phenomenon and as with all
other phenomena, its nature is emptiness.

*"So where can we find emptiness? Upon what basis can we
establish emptiness?"*

The answer is that "emptiness is found in the sixty-
two kinds of wrong view" that are mentioned in the
Brahmajāla Sutta (DN1). These wrong views were all
theories expounded by the non-Buddhist sects during
and before the lifetime of the Buddha. According to
Vimalakīrti, the truth about emptiness can be found in
these sixty-two views. Right in the wrong views we can
find what is not wrong. It means that if we are able to
look deeply into the sixty-two wrong views and "transcend them, we shall be able to penetrate the nature of
emptiness." It is equivalent to asking: Where do we find
the flower? The answer is: We find it in the garbage can.
If we know how to make use of the garbage, we can grow
beautiful flowers.

"Where can you find the sixty-two views?" asked Manjushri.

"They can be found in the liberation of the Buddhas."

"And where can the liberation of the Buddhas be found?" asked Manjushri.

"It can be found in the mental formations of living beings," replied Vimalakīrti.

Thanks to meditating and practicing deeply the liberating Dharma of the Buddha, we can see the substance of the sixty-two wrong views. Both the liberating practices of Buddhism and the wrong views need each other. The Buddhadharma is like the flower and the wrong views are like the garbage. If you do not know the Buddhadharma, how can you see that wrong views are wrong views? If you cannot see that wrong views are wrong views, how can you know the Buddhadharma? The same is true with doubt and enlightenment. If there is no doubt, there is no enlightenment. If we do not give rise to challenging questions about the Buddhadharma, then our understanding of the Buddhadharma will not deepen. Similarly, if there are not afflictions, there will not be awakening. In the opposite way, if there is no awakening, how can we know that something is an affliction? That is why we say "the afflictions are the awakening." Someone who has many afflictions and knows how to look deeply into them will arrive at awakening.

The mental formations of living beings are the most fertile earth for us to sow the flowers of the Buddhadharma. If there were no afflictions and no suffering, how could there be earth to plant the flowers of liberation?

The sutra teaches that we should discover the Buddhad-harma in the mental formations of living beings.

"So when you (Mañjuśrī) ask me (Vimalakīrti) why I do not have attendants, I want you to know that all kinds of māra and those who hold wrong views are my attendants. Why? Because all the kinds of māra delight in the realm of birth and death, and the realm of birth and death is the environment for the bodhisattva. Those who hold wrong views delight in wrong views, and the bodhisattva knows how to remain unmoved by such views."

Why do I not seek out the kind and holy monks and nuns to be my attendants? Because they are not of any use to me. When Māra and the holders of wrong views are my attendants, my mind becomes brighter and more skillful every day. They are fertile earth made of a great deal of rotting garbage that I can use to plant many beau-tiful flowers.

The various kinds of Māra and holders of wrong views are attached to the cycle of saṃsāra. But the bodhisattva is one who by nature refuses to abandon those who are caught in this cycle. Bodhisattvas stay in the midst of birth and death in order to liberate others from birth and death. That is why, thanks to having Māra as an attendant and living with Māra, I have become a bodhisattva.

This is easy enough to say but it is not so easy to do. If we live with Māra and we do not have the mind of love, we do not observe our precepts, and we do not have insight, after a while we shall no longer be a bodhisattva, we shall become Māra as well. That is why it is one hundred times more difficult to be a lay bodhisattva than it is to be a monastic bodhisattva. In a pool of mud it takes a lotus to stand out in relief. In a garden blooming with flowers, we only have to be a bud in order to offer something beautiful to life.

We can summarize this scene of the sutra under the following headings:

1. *Vimalakīrti empties his house. It means that emptiness is the source of being. True emptiness is the root of wonderful being.*

2. *The discussion on the principle of no-coming, no-going.*

3. *Seeing that illness and asking after illness are just a guise or appearance.*

4. *The discussion on the principle that all things inter-are.*

5. *The discussion on the nature of emptiness, and the nonduality of awakening and the afflictions.*

6. *Elucidation of the environment in which a bodhisattva acts. The bodhisattva is a flower that can only spring up in places where there is a great deal of garbage or suffering. If we look for a bodhisattva in a place where there are virtually no afflictions, it will be unlikely that we shall find a true bodhisattva.*

Mañjuśrī bodhisattva asked: *"Householder what kind of sickness do you have?"* This is asking about the nature of the sickness.

"My sickness has no form. It is signless. It is invisible. This sickness is not connected to the body because the body does not have a visible sign. It is not connected to the mind because the mind is like a magic show." My sickness is not of the body nor is it of the mind.

"Living beings fall sick because the four elements are not in harmony, but my sickness is not like that. The reason for my sickness is because living beings are sick, I am sick."

Mañjuśrī asks: *"If one bodhisattva wants to comfort another who is in ill-health, what would be the correct way to comfort him?"*

"The bodhisattva should say that the body is impermanent, but you should not feel disgust with it because of that and develop aversion for the body. You can say that the body suffers, but you do not encourage the other to abandon this body in order to enter the peace of nirvāṇa. You say that this body has no self, but you invite the other to go to realms of suffering in order to bring living beings to the shore of liberation."

This means that the bodhisattva accepts the truth of impermanence but does not reject the things that are impermanent. They accept that there is suffering and do not run away from suffering. They accept the truth of no-self but use their person to enter life and liberate living beings. They use the conventional reality of self in the sense that there is a liberator and a liberated being. The bodhisattva does not proclaim: "Since there is no self, there is no need to liberate anyone from suffering." If we explain no-self in these terms we have not yet understood the reality of no-self. We have just understood a theory.

"You should say that this body is empty and silent (空寂). ("Empty and silent" here means free from all signs.) But do not say that you have to leave the world in order to find the peace of nirvāṇa."

"You should say that one should confess one's past mistake, but should not be caught in the idea of the past. You should remember the times when you have been ill in order to have compassion with those who are ill now."

This means if we have never been sick ourself, we shall not see or understand the suffering of someone who is sick. If we do not know how to manage our own suffering, we shall never see that others are suffering, and we shall not feel compassion for them and help them. Sickness is a necessary means in our teaching and helping living beings. That is why Vimalakīrti needed to appear to be sick. Therefore the sentence *"this body is impermanent, but you should not feel disgust with it because of that and develop aversion for the body"* describes the attitude of a bodhisattva. Although they accept impermanence, they are not averse to a body that is impermanent.

We remember towards the beginning of the sutra in the chapter on Skillful Means, when Vimalakīrti appears to be sick and allows friends to come and visit him, he encourages them: "*You should feel disgust for this body. Do not cling to it nor regret its impermanence. Remember to yearn to become Buddha.*" But here he says the opposite: "*Do not feel disgust for the body.*"

By reading the sutra carefully we shall understand the reason for this change in attitude. In the first instance he was teaching the Dharma to a group of people who are infatuated with their bodies and their wishes were for worldly comforts. All they wanted was to look after and pamper their own impermanent bodies. That is why Vimalakīrti said: "*Do not cling to this body. Feel disgust for this body.*" His aim was to help them give rise to the mind of love and become bodhisattvas and discover the Buddha body. In the second instance, he is talking to a great bodhisattva. He did not need to encourage one who was already a bodhisattva to give up the attitude of a small mind in order to enter the Mahāyāna.

In short, although the truth is that things are impermanent and nonself and we can suffer because of this, we do not become passive and negative and just seek personal comforts in order to ignore the suffering of living beings. A bodhisattva should always give rise to diligence, vowing to be a king of doctors to heal all beings. That is the essence of this section of the sutra.

Mañjuśrī asked: *"Householder, when a bodhisattva is sick, how should they master their mind?"*

Vimalakīrti replied: *"A bodhisattva who is sick should consider this: sickness comes from the afflictions (kleśa) and wrong perceptions that we have accumulated in the past. The root of these afflictions and wrong perceptions is the idea of a separate self."* The idea of a separate self means the illusory idea about a self that is independent from all else and eternal.

This is also the view of Original Buddhism. Original Buddhism also maintains: our afflictions and suffering come from wrong perceptions, and those wrong perceptions are based in the idea of a separate self. We think that only we suffer. We think that we suffer because of the people around us. The truth is that one person's suffering is everyone's suffering. Suffering does not belong to a separate self. If we heal suffering we have to do so by understanding that there is no self. We heal ourselves, and others help us heal. In the same way, they heal themselves and we have to help them heal.

All wrong perceptions come from the wrong perception about self, and the method of healing has to come from our *looking deeply into the nature of all dharmas (dharmasaṃjña).*[*]

According to Mainstream School's Buddhism, there is no personal self, but there are dharmas. There is no "I"

---

[*] Here *dharma* refers to elements that make up something.

but there are elements that make up an "I." "I" am made of elements that are not myself, so although there is no "I," there are elements that make up the "I." This is the view of the Sarvāstivāda school.

"The bodhisattva should reflect: the body is made of an assembly of many dharmas, it is a process of birth and death. When it is born it is the dharmas that are born. When it dies it is the dharmas that die." So here dharmasaṃjña means looking deeply into dharmas to help us uproot the idea of a separate "me."

The Mahāyāna holds a different view: dharmas, that is, the elements that make up an illusory idea of a self, are also empty. Therefore, according to the Mahāyāna, the personal self is empty and dharmas are also empty. That is why when the bodhisattva is sick, they have to put an end to their wrong perceptions of dharmas.

In the beginning, the bodhisattva uses the reflection on dharmas in order to put an end to the idea of a personal self. But then, because they are caught in a wrong idea of dharmas, they have to practice to let go of that idea. The idea that dharmas are separate selves is upside down. Therefore someone who is not caught in the idea of a personal self but is still caught in the wrong idea of dharmas is still sick. The sickness must be cured from the root by removing both ideas.

"The bodhisattva should reflect: In the body there is no self. If sickness comes, it is because of attachment to self. Therefore one should not wrongly give rise to attachment to self but should

understand that this attachment is the root of the sickness.
Thus the bodhisattva should remove all ideas of self by estab-
lishing themselves in the meditation on dharmas: various dhar-
mas have come together to form this body. When it arises it is
because the dharmas arise, and when it ceases it is because the
dharmas cease. They form a continuum without recognizing
each other. When they arise, they do not think, "I have arisen,"
and when they cease, they do not think, "I have ceased." (After
looking deeply in this way) the sick bodhisattva needs to remove
the idea of dharmas. They tell themselves: 'This idea of dhar-
mas too is a form of upside-down thinking, and upside-down
thinking is a serious sickness. I need to remove it.'"

How we can understand this section? Some practitioners are very afraid of dharmas. They believe that
because dharmas are impermanent and without a self,
they make me suffer, so I should distance myself and
escape from them. That place of escape is called nirvāṇa.
In nirvāṇa dharmas are not to be found. Form, sound,
smell, taste, touch, and objects of mind are all my ene-
mies. They are the root of suffering and misery. If I want
to be liberated I have to find an escape from them.

Mahayanists do not agree with this. In the Ratnakūṭa
Sutra there is an example that makes this easy to understand: Someone picks up a stone and throws it at a dog.
The dog feels pain and anger and runs up to the stone,
barking in revenge. Out of ignorance the dog thinks that
the cause of its suffering is the stone, while in fact the
cause is the person who threw the stone. When we suffer
it is the same. We suffer because of our wrong views and

ignorance. Therefore we always blame what we see, hear, smell, taste or think about as the cause of our suffering.

The intelligent practice is to put an end to our wrong ideas and transform our perceptions. It is not to hate things around us, saying that they are the cause of our pain.

If while living with the sangha we suffer a great deal, we generally say that our suffering is made by other members of the sangha. Actually the sangha is not the real root of our suffering. The root of our suffering comes from our way of looking, understanding, and interacting with the sangha. The same is true when we live in society. Our suffering comes because we have not understood the nature of society and we do not know how to organize our own life in order to have peace, joy, and liberation. We hate society and we seek refuge in the monastery. If while in the monastery we continue to feel rancor towards society we shall not suffer any less for being in the monastery. The monastery is a place for us to transform. It is not a place to escape from society. A true monastery is a place that gives us an opportunity and the ability to return to society, be able to live peacefully in society, and contribute to its transformation.

According to the Mahāyāna, it is unthinkable that we shall be able to find a nirvāṇa that is apart from the phenomenal world.

"How can the bodhisattvas remove the upside-down view of dharmas?"

"They have to practice letting go of the idea of a self and what belongs to a self." The way of practice starts again from the beginning. Self is "I" and what belongs to self is "mine."

In order to understand this section of the sutra more clearly and be able to apply it in life more easily, we need to elaborate on "I" and "mine."

The view of a separate self appears in different guises. The most common guise is the idea that this body is me. This means the physical body, one of five skandhas.

"This body is me" means I identify myself with this body. Being caught in a self means to identify oneself with the five skandhas: body, feelings, perceptions, mental formations, and consciousness: I am this body, I am this feeling, I am this perception, I am this mental formation, I am this consciousness. Identifying myself with one of the five skandhas or all of the five skandhas is called "being caught in self."

Apart from the physical body, there are four other skandhas: feelings, perceptions, mental formations, and consciousness. Here we are only talking about the physical body to represent all five skandhas.

The second way of being caught in a self is "this body is mine." It is not me but it belongs to me. This is called being caught in what belongs to self. It means I am something different from the five skandhas and the five skandhas are something different from me but they belong to me. When we are caught in the idea "this body is me", we are caught in the idea that we are one of the skandhas. But when we are caught in "this body is mine," we see "I" and the skandhas as two separate entities and the skandhas as my possessions: in the same way as we see "my house" as one of my possessions.

The third way of being caught is "this body is in me" or "I am in this body." We think that there is an I or a soul and in this I or soul there is a body. Or, we think that in this body there is an I or a soul. In this third guise, we do not say "this body is me" or "this body is mine," but that "in me there is the body," or "in the body there is me." This wrong view, which is called "the view of existing in each other" (執相在) is more subtle.

The fourth way of being caught is "the universe is myself; I am the universe." The universe is something enduring and eternal, so I am also enduring and eternal. This is a way of being caught in self that is common in Brahmanism and expounded in the Upaniṣads. It does not belong to Buddhism. Nonetheless many Buddhists are caught in just this view and say that it is a Buddhist principle.

Above we have just talked about the way of looking that is wrong and how the teachings need to negate what is not true. There is also a positive way of teaching. For example we teach that all things inter-are, all things depend on each other. Generally Buddhist teachings help us see what is not rather than what is. We can only realize what is true when we can see what is not true. This is the method of Buddhism known as the "Via Negativa." We negate what is not true rather than state what is true.

By reminding ourselves of and removing what is not true, we come closer to the truth. If we take as an example the durian fruit, how are we to talk about the durian? Only by eating it can we really know what it is. If we need to talk about durian, we can say it is not jackfruit, it is not mango, it is not banana, and so on. The more we say about what it is not, the more the other person's wrong ideas about durian will diminish. As we remove the things that are not durian, we slowly come to know durian better and we come closer to the true nature of durian. Even if we have not experienced directly that true nature, at least we know that it is not something we already know about.

The way the Buddha taught is the Middle Way between extremes. The Middle Way transcends the ideas of eternalism and of nihilism. Eternalism means a thing is always like that, eternal and unchanging. Nihilism means nothingness, nothing exists.

When we are caught in an idea of self, it is eternalism. Then Buddha tells us not to be an eternalist so we become a nihilist. To be caught in nihilism is worse than being caught in eternalism. It is as if, when someone says jackfruit is not durian, mango is not durian, and so on, we say durian does not exist. We say "Since durian is not something I already know, it does not exist." In fact durian does exist and we can only be in touch with durian by eating it for ourselves. That is called realization.

So what is nirvāṇa, reality, emptiness, suchness? We can only answer that they are not this, they are not that. We have to experience them for ourselves. We have to penetrate their nature in order to be able to see and understand them. Buddha removes what is not nirvāṇa, reality, emptiness, in order to bring us nearer to their reality. We have to taste it for ourselves, penetrate it for ourselves, experience it directly in order to wake up. There is a sentence in the Dharmapada that reads: "Light up your own torch to shine light on your path," which means the same thing.

We have to leave behind the ideas of me and mine. We have to leave behind the idea that there is something inside and something outside, that the self is inside, and the nonself is outside. We feel that myself is my feelings, my perceptions, my mental formations, and my consciousness, and everything else is not myself.

We need to go deeper to see the nature of what is called samatā (平等性), 'sameness." Vimalakīrti says *"What is sameness? It is the sameness of self and nirvāṇa. Why? Because self and nirvana are both empty. Why are they empty? Because they are both mere designation they are empty."*

What do we mean by the sameness of self, and what do we mean by the sameness of nirvāṇa? When we say there is no self but there is nirvāṇa, we lose sameness.

Nirvāṇa is just an idea and self is also just another idea, so the two are the same.

We should not say that the self does not exist but nirvāṇa does, because nirvāṇa cannot be explained in terms of being or nonbeing. To say "nirvāṇa is not" is wrong, but to say "nirvāṇa is" is also not correct. So how can we experience nirvāṇa? We have to go into the idea of self and discover the nature of self in order to see the nature of nirvāṇa.

Self is just an idea, but that idea is of the nature of no-self. It means that our idea of a self is made up of elements that are not self. There has to be a reason for us to be caught in a self. Grasping to self (*ātmagraha*) is like a flower or a cloud; all are made possible because of elements other than themselves. A dream is the same. Although there is no solid object there for us to touch, it is still made up of everything that is not a dream. A dream comes about because of physiological, psychological, and sociological elements as well as from our unconscious yearnings and wrong perceptions. If we go deeply into the substance of a dream, we shall also discover the substance of the universe.

Why is there the idea of self? Because there are all the causes and conditions that give rise to it. If we see the empty nature of self, we see the substance of nirvāṇa. Therefore although in life we do not meet a tortoise with fur or a hare with horns, they are ideas that have a basis. If we meditate on the nature of a tortoise with fur, we can discover the nature of the universe. It is the same for Father Christmas. How could he really exist? Nevertheless we have an idea about Father Christmas. Father Christmas arises from psychological and socio-logical elements, and the needs of children and of adults. Looking into the idea of Father Christmas we can see the basis of the universe. The idea of Father Christmas is like the idea of a tortoise with fur or a hare with horns, or the Vietnamese Kitchen God. Many cultures have fig-ures equivalent to Father Christmas.

As soon as we open our mouths to say something we have already taken a sword, which cuts it into two parts. For example when we say "table" we have already made a distinction that this is the table and everything else is not the table. In the same way, when we say nir-vāṇa, we have already recognized that there are things that are not nirvāṇa. Self is the same. *"That is why we talk of the sameness of self and nirvāṇa. They are both empty. Because they are mere designation, they are empty."* Language is just words we use to give things names, to point out something, it is not the reality of the thing being pointed to.

All dharmas, whether a table, a flower, or nirvāṇa, are ideas of table, flower, and nirvāṇa. All these ideas are like a trademark called appellation. Appellations and ideas are methods used to point to dharmas. However, appellations and ideas do not help us to touch the nature of dharmas. The reason is that names and appellations cut reality into pieces, separate one thing from another, remove the nature of sameness and equality of all things.

It takes intelligence to be able to use appellations and ideas without being caught in them. An intelligent person hears names and concepts but is not caught in them. If both the one who is teaching the Dharma and the one who is listening to the Dharma know how to use names and concepts, they will have a very deep communication. If both of them are caught in names and concepts, communication will become difficult and the teaching will not achieve its purpose.

We use language to give phenomena names. The name goes along with the idea of is and is not. Take the table for example: this word contains the idea that there are things that are tables and things that are not tables. That is why in the Tiantai school, truth is presented under three different headings (*sanguan*, 三觀, "threefold contemplation"): empty, appellation, and middle way. This teaching comes from the Mahāprajñāpāramitā-śāstra of Nagarjuna, where there is the following gāthā:

> *All dharmas that arise from causes and conditions*
> *I call them empty.*
> *They can be called designations,*
> *and they can be the middle way.*

This gāthā means that Nagarjuna refers to dharmas arising from causes and conditions as empty. Those dharmas can also be called mere designations (appellation), where the designation is "table" or "flower," etc. Those dharmas are empty, but it does not mean that they are not there. They are there in the form of ideas and names and we have to deal with them by means of the names we give them. This method of dealing with things is called "mere designation." It means that when we use the word "table," table is a dharma (object of mind). The table exists but exists in the form of a name. If we are intelligent we can relate the table with its nature of emptiness.

Another name for emptiness is "Middle Way." We can call all dharmas "mere designation," and we can also call them "Middle Way." The Middle Way takes pairs of opposites and realizes that they are extremes and they do not describe reality. Being and nonbeing are two extremes, two opposites, and there is a middle way, which is interbeing. When we talk on a superficial level, dharmas can be called "nonbeing," "being," or "not nonbeing," and "not being." But on a deeper level all dharmas are empty of a separate self. It looks as if there are three aspects of a dharma, three ways of talking about a dharma (emptiness, mere designation, and middle way). In fact mere designation and middle way are contemplations that are doors to emptiness. So really there is only one aspect, namely emptiness, which includes the two others.

We cannot say that the Middle Way is being or nonbeing, is birth or death, is coming or going, pure or impure. These are all words. Words or language are what is meant by mere designation in the teaching on the threefold contemplation of the Tiantai school. The seeds of that teaching can be found in this section of the Vimalakīrtinirdeśa on the emptiness of language.

After the mention of the emptiness of language, we come to a mention of the nonattainment of the object of perception.

"As long as there is grasping to the object of perception, there is sickness.... How should we understand this object of perception that we grasp to? We should understand that it cannot be attained. If there is no attainment, there is no grasping. How can one end grasping? By removing two wrong views. What are these views? The views of a subject that is inside, and the object that is outside. If these two are removed, there is no attainment."

No attainment is talked of here as a method of practice. It means "no inside" and "no outside." It means we do not need to search for anything outside of ourselves anymore. We do not need to attain anything anymore since everything is already sufficient and everything is already available. Nirvāṇa is already there. All objects of mind are dwelling in nirvāṇa. We do not need to run after nirvāṇa anymore. It does not lie in time and is not determined by space. Therefore the bodhisattva feels secure and at home in the world of birth, old age, sickness, death, and the afflictions. That is because the bodhisattva has realized that all dharmas dwell in nirvāṇa.

This section of the sutra continues: *"In this way, the sick bodhisattvas master their thinking in order to end the suffering of old age, sickness, and death. That is the enlightenment (bodhi) of a bodhisattva."*

Birth, old age, sickness, and death are the world of awakening for the bodhisattvas, because the nature of birth, old age, sickness and death are enlightenment (bodhi) or nirvāṇa or awakening. Therefore the bodhisattva can dwell peacefully in the world of birth, death, and the afflictions and still be free and at ease.

The sutra continues on the subject of fetters and liberation. *For the bodhisattva it is a fetter to be infatuated by the taste of meditative concentration (dhyāna).*

There are practitioners who see liberation in terms of an escape from birth and death for oneself alone. But what is meant by the liberation of a bodhisattva? What is meant by fetters, and what is meant by liberation? If we crave the peace and silence of sitting meditation and make sitting meditation a hiding place because we are afraid of the life of the world, we are still caught in fetters. We are not liberated, nor are we yet an authentic bodhisattva. These words are a way of denouncing certain arhats or those who are practicing to become arhats and are looking for peace and quiet for themselves alone.

A liberated bodhisattva has recourse to skillful means. This means that a liberated bodhisattva has the capacity and the means to help living beings be liberated. If not, then that person is caught in fetters and is not someone who has been liberated. Therefore this idea is completely contrary to the idea of those who look for the quiescence of nirvāṇa.

"What is meant by saying that wisdom without skillful means is a fetter? It means that with the mind full of pity and concern, a bodhisattva adorns themselves and a Buddha land, leads numerous living beings there, and ripens them with the practice of emptiness, signlessness, and aimlessness. If they use wisdom not shaped by skillful means to liberate these beings, it is a fetter.

This is a translation of Kumārajīva. In the translation of Xuanzang the meaning of this section may be clearer. We can paraphrase Xuanzang's translation as follows:

If a bodhisattva knows how to adorn a Pure Land and within that Pure Land knows how to help and establish living beings on the path of liberation, that bodhisattva is liberated. If a bodhisattva does not know how to adorn themselves and their environment and does not know how to use skillful means to help living beings, they are caught in fetters.

A bodhisattva should know how to make life beautiful. If you say: "The practice of Buddhism does not need beauty, the Buddhist center does not need a flower garden, the floors do not need to be swept; in my practice I can eat in a way that is not beautiful, sleep in a way that is not beautiful; this life is just a temporary affair while there is another kind of life that will last forever and that is what I need," that is fetter. An authentic bodhisattva knows that part of the practice is making the practice center a place that has an ambience of purity and beauty. The bodhisattva will plant flowers and take care of the plants, making the people who come to practice happy. Such is a bodhisattva who adorns a Pure Land and is liberated.

In the next section, the practice of offering up the merit is mentioned:

When the bodhisattva removes wrong views and the afflictions,
they offer up these roots of goodness which they have cultivated
to the highest right enlightenment. If we long for anything less
we are a bodhisattva still caught in fetters.

Everything we do today, whether it is walking meditation, sitting meditation, mastering our afflictions, or cultivating a field of merit, if we do not offer them up for the highest and equal awakening, we are not liberated. We have to offer it up for all living beings, which means we have the deep aspiration for all living beings and ourselves to realize the highest fruit of enlightenment. That is what helps us to be a liberated bodhisattva.

> *All the merit I have accomplished,*
> *all the merit I accomplish in time to come,*
> *I offer up for all living beings everywhere,*
> *so that we can all realize the fruit of Buddhahood.*[*]

---

[*] Traditional Chinese sharing the merit gāthā.

Such is the vow of the liberated bodhisattva. If you say "Today I have accomplished a certain amount of merit, I wish it to go towards my being able to dwell peacefully in the Pure Land of Amitabha or the nirvāṇa of peace and quiet," then you are not yet a liberated bodhisattva.

If we read on we shall see what is meant by contemplation of the body. Contemplation of the body is a classical method of Buddhist meditation that is also called "Contemplation of the body in the body." Here contemplating the body is described as follows:

The land where bodhisattvas practice the establishments
of mindfulness without seeking to remove the body, feelings,
mind, and objects of mind, is the Buddha land of a
bodhisattva.

We have to contemplate that the body is impermanent, painful, empty, and nonself. However, although the body is impermanent, painful, and nonself, we do not feel disgusted with the body and think that we should like to abandon it. Nor do we want to abandon its impermanence, nonself, pain, and emptiness. That is authentic liberation. Although the body is sick, we are not disgusted by it and we do not run away from it into the world of cessation (*nirodha*), that is real liberation, that is the true understanding of skillful means. Skillful means is the ability to make use of impermanence, pain, emptiness, nonself, sickness, and so on in order to make them a path of awakening.

All the sections of the sutra that follow are on the subject of the Middle Way. To be in the world of birth and death and not to be made impure by it is the Middle Way. To dwell in nirvāṇa but not to withdraw into the world of cessation is the practice of the bodhisattva. Nirvāṇa is here in the world of birth and death. We can dwell peacefully here and not need to run away to another realm.

If we continue to read to the end of this chapter, we shall see another path of practice. It is the Middle Way that is called the way of "non-indifference." Non-indifference means not abandoning this life in order to find peace and quiet for ourselves. For example:

To practice the four limitless minds without the desire to be reborn in the world of brahma is the practice of the bodhisattva. To practice the dhyānas, the meditative attainments, liberation, and the various samadhis, but not in order to be reborn in the form and formless realms is the practice of the bodhisattva. While following the Noble Eightfold Path, to still enjoy the innumerable paths of highest awakening is the practice of the bodhisattva. While cultivating stopping (śamatha) and looking deeply (vipaśyanā) and not falling into absolute quiescence, that is the practice of the bodhisattva. While manifesting as a śrāvaka or pratyekabuddha and not abandoning the Dharma of the highest awakening, that is the path of the bodhisattva. While dwelling in the absolutely pure nature of dharmas but continuing to manifest according to conditions in the world of saṃsāra, that is the practice of the bodhisattva."

CHAPTER 6: THE INCONCEIVABLE LIBERATION

The inconceivable is what we cannot imagine, cannot conceive, cannot explain or describe. In this chapter, what is inconceivable is liberation. In Sanskrit it is *acintya vimokṣa*, "the inconceivable liberation." These are skillful methods used to liberate living beings from their suffering, and it is difficult to imagine or conceive of them.

In this chapter, as in the following one, Śāriputra is used as the figure who represents the śrāvaka vehicle. Śāriputra was a high monk. He was enlightened and was one of the most intelligent of the Buddha's disciples. He was the eldest brother of all the monks. He was not shaken by praise or mockery. In this sutra Śāriputra is put forward as the representative of the śrāvaka (hearer disciple) vehicle and compared unfavorably with the representative of the bodhisattva vehicle, with the intention to prove that the śrāvaka vehicle is inferior to the bodhisattva vehicle. We who are reading the sutra and who already know about Śāriputra and his huge contribution to the sangha of Buddha Śākyamuni, cannot help but feel that the Śāriputra presented here has nothing to do with the Śāriputra we know about.

If we look deeper we see that the sutra is just making use of Śāriputra in order to make a comparison between two different emphases in Buddhist practice. The aim is not to scorn the practice of Śāriputra as being lowly and mean. We, the monastic and lay heirs of Śāriputra, should not allow this use of Śāriputra to hurt our pride.

At the beginning of the chapter, Śāriputra is portrayed as observing that although so many bodhisattvas, śrāvakas, and gods have come to visit Vimalakīrti, the house still seems empty so there is no reason to have to stand, why not bring in chairs to sit on.

At that time Śāriputra thought to himself: "There is not even a chair in this house. So where are these bodhisattvas and hearer disciples going to sit?"

Vimalakīrti is able to read the mind of Śāriputra and says: *"Venerable monk, did you come here to sit down or to seek the Dharma?"*

Śāriputra replied: *"Naturally, I came to seek the Dharma."* This was a very kind reply.

Vimalakīrti said: *"What is meant by seeking the Dharma?"*

Taking that as his starting point, he gave a Dharma talk on seeking the Dharma. He said: *"We should not use the five skandhas to seek the Dharma."*

On reading this we may well think: What other than our body, feelings, perceptions, mental formations, and consciousness can we possibly use to seek the Dharma?

Vimalakīrti continues:

"One who seeks the Dharma does not seek it through clinging to the Buddha, Dharma, and Sangha. They do not seek the Dharma by recognizing suffering, removing its origin, realizing its end, and practicing the path. Why? Because the True Dharma is free from theorizing and cannot be expressed in words. To repeat: 'suffering must be recognized, its origin has to be destroyed, its end has to be realized, the path has to be practiced,' is theorizing. It is not the Dharma.

"Therefore Śāriputra, if you are looking for the Dharma, you should not be looking for anything."

This means when someone comes to the Dharma, without an idea about the Dharma, then they are truly seeking the Dharma.

Earlier we heard Mañjuśrī say: *"Because I have not arrived I have arrived. Because I have not departed I have departed."* This kind of speaking is only effective for those who are on the same frequency or the same level as Vimalakīrti. It is not conventional language. Here the meaning is: as long as we still want to abandon something in order to seek something else in its place, for example we want to abandon the world of defilements and replace it with the Buddha, Dharma, and Sangha, that is not the attitude of an authentic seeker of the Dharma. In that kind of seeking there is still a state of discrimination, a rejection of compost and a longing for flowers, because we are ignorant of the fact that only out of compost can we have flowers.

There is nothing very different in this way of reasoning from what we read in the last chapter. If we are seeking the Dharma and we want to leave suffering behind and chase after what we call "not suffering" ("Dharma happiness"), that is not the attitude of nonduality, and not the highest way of seeking the Dharma.

Vimalakīrti added: *"The Dharma has no goal of activity. If one actively pursues the Dharma, one is pursuing a goal and this is not seeking the Dharma."*

It is not because we are always active or because we try so hard that we have the Dharma. The Dharma is always there in its true nature. It is not because we make a great effort in the practice that the Dharma increases. In its true nature the Dharma is already sufficient within us.

"The Dharma cannot be grasped or let go of." We cannot hold tightly on to the Dharma nor can we throw it away.

"The Dharma does not have a place of abode." It means that the Dharma does not have a location in space or in time. It does not have an outer appearance.

"The Dharma is unconditioned." This means the Dharma is not brought about by causes and conditions. It cannot be produced.

All phenomena, like flowers, books, etc. are conditioned (*saṃskṛta*). It means that they only come about due to the coming together of many causes and conditions. The true Dharma is not created by the coming together of causes and conditions. It is always available. We just need to practice in order to be in touch with it. That is why it is called the unconditioned Dharma. The person who seeks the Dharma at the highest level should do so with the mind of nonduality and nonattainment.

There is a special characteristic of the Vimalakīrti-nirdeśa. Sometimes it talks in phenomenological terms, sometimes in ontological terms. The drum is playing one melody and the trumpet another. If we are not attentive, it will seem that the sutra is not talking sense. At one moment it talks in terms of the wave and at another in terms of the ocean water. This going back and forth between the ultimate and historical dimensions does not help us to see the connection between the two. From the start to the finish, the sutra seems to be in two different languages or on two different frequencies.

If we examine this we may also see that this is a method that can keep us awake. If we only see waves and never see the water, our life is wasted. The language of the sutra seems to contradict itself. However, it is an opportunity for the reader to stop looking at reality in terms of phenomenological language and to begin to speak and look in terms of the ontological. If you are a wave and all you know about yourself is that you are a wave, you miss the very important point that as well as being a wave you are the water. Only when you know that you are water, will you transcend ups and downs, coming and going, great and small, success and failure.

The reader, however, can feel uncomfortable when at one moment the sutra is talking about the outer form of things and at another about the ontological nature of things. If we are able to read with a mind that is more inclusive and more understanding we shall be able see the wonderful depth of the sutra.

Vimalakīrti first gave Śāriputra a teaching on how to seek the Dharma, implying that Śāriputra's attitude in seeking the Dharma was immature and not part of the Great Vehicle. In this Dharma talk he wanted to show everyone that bringing beings to the other shore is something that cannot be conceived of by ideas or described in words.

Then he turned to Mañjuśrī and asked: *"Mañjuśrī you have been to all the universes. You have visited innumerable places. In what Buddha land have you seen the most lion seats?"*

Mañjuśrī replied: *"There is a world called Merudhvajā. In that world there is a Buddha by the name of Merupradīparāja who is manifesting now. His body is of enormous dimension. The living beings in that world are also very large and the lion seats in that realm are the most beautiful and comfortable you could find in all the universes."*

When Vimalakīrti heard this he used his miraculous powers. As a result of this, the Buddha Merupradīparāja transported to the sahā* world and brought into the tiny

---

* Sahā refers to the land where we human beings are living. It is a world where we have to endure difficulties.

hut of Vimalakīrti thirty-two thousand enormous lion seats, so that the whole assembly would have a place to sit. If you were to use your fleshly eyes to count you would see thirty-two thousand guests in Vimalakīrti's hut that day.

"For the room was broad and spacious enough to hold all these thirty-two thousand lion seats without being crowded in the slightest. The cities of Vaiśalī and Jambudvipa and the other of the four continents seemed in no way cramped but all appeared just as usual."

This section has clearly been influenced by the teaching of the Avataṃsaka Sutra, that the one is in the all and the all lies in the one. The infinitely small can contain the infinitely large. For example, a mustard seed can contain the sun, the moon, and the four great oceans.

In response to the invitation of Vimalakīrti all the great bodhisattvas mahāsattvas sat on the lion seats. However those who had only recently become bodhisattvas and the hearer disciples, including the Venerable Śāriputra were unable to climb onto the seats. The seats were very high and their bodies were too short. Imagine that you were tiny children two or three years old and the bodhisattvas were adults forty or fifty years old who had no difficulty in sitting on a chair, but you have to try clambering up and every time you fail to arrive on the seat. Clearly the sutra is insulting the Venerable Śāriputra and all the hearer disciples. They are not of a stature to sit and dialogue with the bodhisattvas. Although Vimalakīrti knew that, he still drew people's attention to it by saying,

"Venerable Śāriputra, please be seated on the lion seat."

The venerable monk replied: "Layman, this seat is far too high. We are not able to climb on to it." Thus the Vimalakīrtinird-eśa insults Śāriputra.

Then Vimalakīrti said: "Venerable monk you should prostrate before the Tathāgata Merupradīparāja and then you will be able to sit on the seats."

All the hearer disciples who were present that day joined their palms and recited Namo Merupradīparāja Buddhaya and immediately their bodies increased in stature and they were able to sit on the lion seats without any difficulty.

At that point Vimalakīrti started to talk about the wonderful inconceivable ways that were aimed at liberating living beings, which are called *acintya vimokṣa* (inconceivable liberation). He said:

"Śāriputra, when bodhisattvas dwell in this liberation, they can take something as tall and broad as Mount Meru and put it inside a mustard seed without enlarging one or shrinking the other, and Mount Meru will still have its original shape. They would be able to take all the waters of the four great oceans and place them within one pore of the skin. In doing this they would not cause the creatures of the deep to feel disturbed or lacking in space.

"Venerable Śāriputra, bodhisattvas who dwell in the inconceivable ways of liberation can hold the trichiliocosm in their hand as quickly as a potter places a lump of clay on the potter's wheel without any of the beings in the trichiliocosm knowing about it. What is more, Śāriputra, if there are living beings who need a long period of time in order to be liberated, the bodhisattvas can make seven days into a kalpa and the living beings will feel that they have lived for a kalpa."

If beings want a long time, the bodhisattvas can give them a long time and turn seven days into a kalpa so that those living beings will see that they have practiced for a long time and they will be able to realize enlightenment. Those living beings lack self-confidence and think that in order to succeed in the practice they need a long time.

"Or if there are beings who do not want to live in this world for a long time and they are qualified to enter enlightenment, the bodhisattvas can squeeze a kalpa into seven days so that to those beings it seems like only seven days."

If there are living beings who do not want to practice a long time, they want their practice to ripen quickly and they think that in a very short time they can be enlightened, the bodhisattvas can shorten one kalpa into seven days for those people to practice.

There is nothing new in this. In the concluding paragraph of the Satipaṭṭhāna Sutta, the Buddha teaches: "A bhikṣu who practices the four establishments of mindfulness for seven years can arrive at liberation." The Buddha also saw that people would suffer if they felt the time would last too long, and therefore he said: "If the bhikṣu practices the four establishments of mindfulness for seven months, then he could also reach liberation." Then the Buddha added: "If someone practices the four establishments of mindfulness for one month, they could also reach liberation." The compassion of the Buddha goes as far as this. Then the Buddha continued: "If anyone practices the four establishments for two weeks, they can also be liberated".

If we read this section of the Satipaṭṭhāna Sutta in the spirit of the Mahāyāna, we shall understand the great compassionate mind of the bodhisattvas. In the later history of Buddhism terms such as "sudden enlightenment" were used. The kind of people who have very wide minds reach enlightenment as soon as they hear deep teachings and these people are called "sudden enlightenment bodhisattvas." Those who listen to less deep teachings have a correspondingly lesser realization, but over time they come to realize the deep teachings. They are called "gradual enlightenment bodhisattvas."

As far as the ultimate reality is concerned, we are already enlightened. There is nothing we need to yearn for. We only need to wake up and see that we have all that we need. The concept of nonattainment is the idea that we do not need to go looking for enlightenment somewhere else. Sudden enlightenment means we do not need to build up merit bit by bit in order to be liberated. Everything needed for liberation is available in our

true nature. This is what is taught in the Vimalakīrtnird-
eśa and other sutras like it.

In the following section the sutra speaks of wind
and fire.

"Śāriputra, the bodhisattvas who dwell in the inconceivable lib-
eration can suck into their mouths all the winds from the ten
directions without doing any harm to themselves or breaking
down any trees. Or, when the worlds in the ten directions come
to the end of a kalpa and everything is destroyed by fire, they
can take all those fires and hold them in their belly. Though the
fires go on burning as before, they suffer no harm."

This morning as I practiced walking meditation in the
cold morning air, I could see myself breathing out clouds.
That is a miracle! A steamy breath of water vapor does
not have to be large to be called a cloud. As far as human
beings are concerned a cloud should be large but as far
as bacteria in the air are concerned the water vapor that
we breathe out is a cloud. Great or small is just an idea
in our mind.

In a poem I wrote, there is the line "In a breath, I
breathe out ten thousand galaxies". This is very true
because when we breathe out, every atom in our breath
is a galaxy. Every atom has a nucleus and around it are
the electrons that are circulating at a speed of three hundred thousand kilometers a second. From the point of
view of nuclear physics, every atom is a galaxy. As far as
the universe is concerned the planet Earth is like a speck
of dust. As far as the Avataṃsaka Sutra sees it, every

time we exhale, in our out-breath is a Milky Way and every drop of vapor in it is a star.

Although we are living a miracle at every moment, we keep looking for miracles somewhere else. The fact that we are still alive today, can open our eyes and see the blue sky, can place our feet on the oak leaves that have just fallen, listen to the early morning song of the breeze in the forest leaves, is a miracle! If we do not live with mindfulness we live as someone unable to see, hear, or be aware of what is there. When we live in mindfulness we receive everything that is wonderful in this present moment and the miracle is happening at every moment.

This morning the sound of the red autumn leaves on the tree as they danced in the wind was wonderful, like the rain falling. Every oak leaf contains the trichiliocosm. Even so, we tread on the leaf without knowing it. The universe and life itself belong to people who are awake. If you are not awake you cannot receive any of the wonders of the universe. The French have a saying: "Le monde apartient à ceux qui l'écoutent." The world belongs to those who listen to it.

If we can live for twenty-four hours, being in touch with the universe with our eyes, ears, body, mind, and mindfulness, our life will not have been wasted. We only need one day to taste the Pure Land in this very life.

Please do not live your life as something transient and passing with no true meaning. Even if you know you only have two or three days to live, do not see today as having no lasting import. A day is an eternity. A day is an eon and we should live our twenty-four hours deeply. Stop living your days just to have them over and done with. Make your Pure Land real right here and now.

"*Śāriputra, bodhisattvas who dwell in the inconceivable libera-tion can use their miraculous power to appear as a Buddha, a pratyekabuddha, a hearer disciple, the god Indra, a Brahma king, a Wheel-turning King in order to help beings to the shore of liberation.*"

A bodhisattva can appear as a Buddha, because *bodhi-sattva* means a being who awakens themselves and others. If you know how to use your conscious breathing in order to be awake, you can play the role of Buddha. When we are awake, whether we are hugging a child or drinking a cup of tea, we are playing the role of Buddha to help people be liberated. This is something we can do. This is a miracle we can realize. If we do not do it, it is because we do not want to or because we have the complex we cannot.

All sounds, whether great or small in all the ten direc-tions—like the fallen leaves, the song of the birds, the acorns cracking as they break under our footsteps—are all describing the Buddhadharma to us. They are recit-ing the Lotus Sutra, the Vimalakīrtinirdeśa, the Pra-jñāpāramitā. They are teaching impermanence, no-self, and nirvāṇa. They are the radio stations of suchness. If we do not turn on our radio set we shall not be able to hear these Dharma talks.

This is made clear by the Sukhāvatīvyūha Sutra. Whenever the wind blows through the rows of trees in the Land of Great Happiness, they give rise to a wonderful sound and if you listen to it, you hear the Dharma being taught. The truth is we do not need to go to a world that lies far away to the west in order to hear these sounds. We only need to stay in our world with mindfulness and all that we hear in the wind blowing and the birds singing becomes a teaching of the Dharma.

"Every flower bud, every pebble, every leaf is chanting the Lotus Sutra." That is one of the lines in the poem "Calling."* It is wonderful and it depends on us whether we see it or not.

After Vimalakīrti has finished talking about the inconceivable liberation, Venerable Kāśyapa, who was the monk to convene the sangha after the Buddha passed into nirvāṇa, said to Śāriputra:

"It is like someone displaying painted images before a blind man who cannot see them. In the same way, when we hearer disciples hear this doctrine of the inconceivable liberation we are all incapable of understanding it. If wise people hear it there will be none who do not set their minds on attaining the highest enlightenment. But what of us who are forever cut off at the root, who with regards to these Mahāyāna teachings are like rotten seeds?"

---

* In Thich Nhat Hanh, *Call Me By My True Names*, Parallax Press, 1999.

Here the hearer disciples are depicted as making a confession. Kāśyapa says that he has followed a minor teaching and has not known the Great Vehicle, which is of such great significance. "We are just rotten seeds that are of no benefit to the world."

In this section Vimalakīrti is not playing the role of the one who forces the hearer disciples to admit their mistake of following the little vehicle. They are portrayed as admitting their mistake of themselves. Maybe out of compassion the ancestral teachers who compiled this sutra used very sharp words in their way of presenting the disciples of the Buddha. Later on in the sutra we see sentences that are much more condemning: *"As far as profane people are concerned, they still need to be born and die and travel in saṃsāra. Still they can hope for liberation. As far as hearer disciples are concerned there is no such hope."* It means that profane people are profane in the present moment but in the future they will be able to encounter the right teachings of the Mahāyāna and thereby have the chance to become bodhisattvas. All hearer disciples can hope for is their personal liberation so that they can enter the great nothingness and extinction of all desire. That is why they are like rotten seeds. They are not good for anything. Therefore Vimalakīrti prefers profane people to the hearer disciples like the venerable Śāriputra and Mahāmaudgālyayana.

This section means that if you practice, you should practice according to the Mahāyāna. Either practice to become a bodhisattva or do not practice at all. Wait until you encounter the Mahāyāna before you practice. Do not practice the half measures of the minor teachings allowing yourself to become a rotten seed, which in time to come will not be able to grow into a mighty tree.

In the next section after Venerable Kāśyapa confesses his weakness, Vimalakīrti gives a teaching about the role of those who make our lives difficult:

"Venerable Kāśyapa, you should know that the māras who try to destroy the buddhas and all the great works of awakening performed by the bodhisattvas, are themselves manifestations of bodhisattvas. If there were no māras, if there were not difficulties, if there were not challenges then no-one would be able to accomplish the great work of awakening, which is to take all beings to the shore of liberation."

People who make us suffer or make our life difficult are those who help us in our practice and training most of all. Devadatta* for example, is a great bodhisattva. We should not look at the inconceivable liberation with a restricted vision. We have to see that all these obstacles on our path are just the manifestations of great bodhisattvas who want to help us make progress on our path of practice so that we can fully realize our great aspiration.

---

* The cousin of Śākyamuni Buddha who out of jealousy tried to kill the latter.

CHAPTER 7: MEDITATION ON
LIVING BEINGS

At the beginning of this chapter, Mañjuśrī asks Vimalakīrti: *"How do you look at living beings?"*

Vimalakīrti replied:

"As magicians look on the beings they conjure up, so the bodhi-
sattva looks on living beings. As the wise view the moon in
water or a face or form seen in a mirror, as a mirage in the dry
season, as the echo that follows the cry, as clouds in the sky, as
foam on the water, bubbles on the water, as a thing no firmer
than the trunk of the banana tree, lasting no longer than a flash
of lightning, thus does the bodhisattva regard living beings."
When we look at living beings we should see them like that in
order not to be caught in our perceptions about them.

Mañjuśrī asked: *"If bodhisattvas look on beings in this*
way, how can they treat them with loving kindness?"

"They treat them with a loving kindness that is undualis-
tic; for internal and external have no place in it."

"What do you mean when you speak of compassion?"

Vimalakīrti replied: *"I mean that whatever benefits*
the bodhisattvas gain, they share them with all other living
beings.

Mañjuśrī: *"What do you mean by joy?"*

Vimalakīrti: *"Any way the bodhisattvas can aid or enrich*
others they view as a benefit for others and never feel regret
(about having helped others)."

Mañjuśrī: *"What do you mean by equanimity?"*

Vimalakīrti: *"Whatever blessings or fortunes the bodhi-sattvas bestow, they expect nothing in return."*

Equanimity is the ability to let go. It is the ability to act without needing anyone to know that we are acting, to be worthy of the gratitude of others but not expecting anyone to show gratitude. We do not need our name to be on the list of donors. Joy is the joy of our practice that fills our heart to the brim as well as the hearts of living beings. It allows all regret and all guilt from the past to disappear. Compassion and loving kindness are practices that alleviate suffering and bring happiness to living beings. They have to be practiced in the spirit of joy and equanimity.

Mañjuśrī asked: *"If bodhisattvas fear the cycle of birth and death, what should they rely on?"* This is the same as the question that Subhūti asks in the Vajracchedikā Sutra: "When the bodhisattvas give rise to the mind of love, what should they rely on?" In the sutra the Buddha answered: "They should not rely on anything whether it be form, sound, smell, taste, touch, or object of mind."

Here Vimalakīrti replies: *"Bodhisattvas fearing the cycle of birth and death should rely on the power of the Tathāgatha's great heart."* It means that all our actions should be based on the one motivation: to liberate beings from their suffering. Only with such an aspiration do we not become rotten seeds. Without that aspiration whatever we do we shall become a rotten seed. That aspiration is called "bodhicitta," the mind of love.

Mañjuśrī: "*If they hope to rely on the power of the Tathāgatha's great heart, what should they do?*"

Vimalakīrti: "*If they hope to rely on the power of the Tathāgatha's great heart, they should dedicate themselves to the vow to save and liberate all beings.*"

Mañjuśrī: "*If they hope to save living beings, what must they free beings from?*"

Vimalakīrti: "*If they hope to save living beings, they must free them from the afflictions.*"

Mañjuśrī: "*If they hope to free them from the afflictions, how should they proceed?*"

Vimalakīrti: "*They should proceed by the method of Right Mindfulness.*"

Mañjuśrī: "*How does one proceed by the method of Right Mindfulness?*"

Vimalakīrti: "*One proceeds on the basis of no birth and no death.*"

Mañjuśrī: "*What is the root of desire and greed?*"

Vimalakīrti: "*False constructions of the mind are the root (abhūtaparikalpa).*"

This sentence is orthodox Buddhism. False constructions of the mind are our ignorance and our wrong perceptions. These are the root of craving. Because we cannot see the nature of things clearly, we run after them and become infatuated with them. Because we do not know how to look deeply, we do not know how to use the microscope of meditation, we have an internal formation of attraction and attachment.

Mañjuśrī: *"What is the root of false constructions of the mind?"*

Vimalakīrti: *"Upside-down thinking (viparyasa) is the root."* In other words, it is wrong perception. Viparyasa means "upside-down" (倒想). We do not see things as they are.

Mañjuśrī: *"What is the root of upside-down thinking?"*

Vimalakīrti: *"No standpoint (apratiṣṭhāna) is the root of upside-down thinking."*

Mañjuśrī: *"What is the root of having no standpoint?"*

Vimalakīrti: *"What has no standpoint cannot have roots."* Master Xuanzang's translation is clearer: *"Your question does not make sense. How can no standpoint have a base since no standpoint means there is no object in which to abide. Clearly no standpoint cannot have a base so how can you ask such a question?"*

At this point Vimalakīrti says: *"Mañjuśrī, it is from the root of no standpoint that all dharmas take their stand."* Authentic bodhisattvas practice everything and put into effect all great undertakings, but all this rests on one thing—the no standpoint, which means they are not caught in anything.

At this juncture there is a change of scene. A goddess appears. Where the goddess came from we are not told. We have already been told that Vimalakīrti has no attendants. He was able to change his hut into a place devoid of any furniture by magic. Now a goddess appears. Where could she have come from? Did he borrow one of Māra's goddesses? This however is not an ordinary goddess because she is able to answer the questions of Kāśyapa and Śāriputra very eloquently.

At that time a goddess appeared in Vimalakīrti's room and, seeing these great beings who were teaching the Dharma, she made herself visible. She scattered flowers that fell on to the bodies of the bodhisattvas and the senior disciples of the Buddha as a sign of welcome. When the flowers fell on the bodhisattvas they fell to the ground. But when they touched the hearer disciples they did not fall but clung fast to their robes. When the senior disciples of the Buddha saw that the flowers had not fallen they used their hands to brush them off, but the flowers refused to fall and clung obstinately to their robes.

Seeing this the goddess asked Śāriputra: "Why do you need to brush off the flowers?"

'These flowers are not in accord with the Buddha's teachings. As a monk I do not adorn myself with flowers, and that is why I am brushing them off."

"Venerable monk, do not say that these flowers are not in accord with the Dharma. These flowers do not discriminate. It is you who discriminates. Because your mind discriminates between what is the Dharma and what is not the Dharma, the flowers attach themselves to you. If someone who has left the household life makes such distinctions, that is not in accord with the Dharma. One must be without discrimination to be in accord with the Dharma. Look at the bodhisattvas—the flowers do not stick to them because they have already cut off all discriminating thoughts."

This means that authentic lay bodhisattvas can wear a pearl necklace or a fancy garment, oil their body and hair with fragrant oils, and doing these will not do any harm to them as bodhisattvas. There are people who do not wear jewelry or smart clothes, do not style their hair, but in their minds they have so many prejudices. The degree of liberation that they have could be very small compared with the lay bodhisattvas who adorn themselves. It is like a man looking at a beautiful woman with a very pure mind. It does no harm whatsoever to look in that way. Someone else might not dare to look and every time he sees a woman he looks down at the ground. That person is still caught in attachment. The flowers did not attach themselves to the bodhisattvas because they had ended the discriminatory way of looking at things. The monks, though they were senior disciples of the Buddha, were still afraid of birth, death, form, sound, smell, taste, and touch, and that is why they were limited by birth, death, form, etc. Someone who has left behind all fear and discrimination cannot be affected by the five sense pleasures. Similarly if you are afraid of the food tasting good, good food is still an obstacle for you. On the other hand, if you are not afraid of good-tasting food, then whether it tastes good or not, it will not be an obstacle.

These points have been made many times in this book. Before we had the story of the man throwing a stone at the dog. The root of the dog's pain was not the stone but the man who threw it. The root of our suffering is not our five skandhas, not the flowers that fall on to our robes. The root is our mind being attached.

Śāriputra was surprised at seeing the goddess: *"Have you been here a long time?"* It means that Śāriputra knew the goddess had not just arrived.

"The time that I have been in this house is as long as the length of time you have been liberated."

In the version of Master Xuanzang, it says: *"Goddess, have you been in this house for a long time?"*

The goddess: *"Has the elder Śāriputra been in liberation for a long time?"*

This means something like, the liberation in which Śāriputra dwells has no beginning and no end. This question of the goddess means: can the essence of Śāriputra's liberation be calculated in terms of time? Is it possible to say that his liberation has been there for five, ten, or a hundred years? At that point, Śāriputra was silent and could not reply.

The goddess said: *"Venerable monk, you have great wisdom, why are you silent"?*
She meant: "You are the most intelligent among the senior disciples of the Buddha so why are you silent when I ask you this question?"

In the translation by Xuanzang this section reads: *"The Venerable is a great disciple of great wisdom and eloquence. Why does he not reply to this simple question?"*

At that point the Venerable Śāriputra says: *"How can liberation be described in words? How can I respond to your* question in these terms?" Śāriputra is using the language that the Buddha used. As far as nirvāṇa and liberation are concerned, words cannot be used to describe them. Conditioned dharmas can be talked about. Unconditioned dharmas cannot be described in terms of language.

The goddess said, "*Venerable monk, language and words are all marks of liberation. Why? Because liberation is not internal, not external, and not both internal and external. Words likewise are not internal, not external, and not both internal and external. Therefore Śāriputra you can speak of liberation without doing away with words. Why? Because all dharmas are marked by liberation.*" It is because we are caught in them that language and words harm us. If our mind has truly penetrated the matter, we can use language and words freely without being restricted by them. This means we can talk as long as we are not caught in words and language.

Śāriputra asked: "*Doesn't liberation mean putting aside craving, anger, and ignorance?*" In other words can craving, anger, and ignorance also be liberation? This question is meant to show us that the character of Śāriputra in the drama has not got the message. The goddess already said that all dharmas are liberation, and naturally all dharmas include craving, anger, and ignorance. Nevertheless Śāriputra's view in this sutra is still dualistic: liberation is one thing, and craving, anger, and delusion are something else. He still sees flowers as flowers and garbage as garbage and has not seen that flowers are only possible because of garbage. The sutra repeats this idea many times.

The goddess said: *"The Buddha, when addressing people who are proud, asserts that one must put aside craving, anger, and ignorance in order to attain liberation. For those who are not proud, the Buddha asserts that the nature of craving, anger, and ignorance is liberation itself."* It means we can find liberation within craving, anger, and ignorance. If there is no craving, anger, and ignorance, how can we attain liberation? Liberation has to be liberation from something.

The Venerable Śāriputra said: *"Excellent! Excellent! What have you practiced, what have you attained to give you this eloquence?"*

The goddess replied: *"It is because I have not attained anything that I have this eloquence. Those who think they have attained or realized something still have pride."* Here the sutra explains more about nonattainment and non-realization. The Sutra in Forty-Two Chapters, which is a sutra still influenced strongly by Source Buddhism, also has Mahāyāna terminology that was added to it during its several hundred years of development. In it is the sentence: "My practice is the cultivation of non-cultivation, the practice of non-practice, and the realization of non-realization." It means my way is to cultivate non-cultivation, practice non-practice, and realize non-realization. The Sutra in Forty-Two Chapters appeared in Vietnam at the beginning of the second century of the Common Era.*

At this point Śāriputra asks the goddess another feather-brained question: *"Do you belong to the the śrāvaka, the pratyekabuddha† or the bodhisattva vehicle?"* We should remember always that the Śāriputra represented in this play is made out to be as feather-brained as possible. The more feather-brained he is, the more brightly the contrast to the Mahāyāna shines out.

Goddess: *"Because I teach the śrāvaka vehicle, I am a śrāvaka. Because I have understood on my own the principle of causes and conditions, I use the pratyekabuddha vehicle to liberate beings. Because I use the Dharma of great compassion to liberate living beings, I practice the Mahāyāna.*

"When someone enters a forest of magnolia champaca, they will only smell the fragrance of the champaca flowers and they will not smell anything else. In the same way, when someone enters this room, they smell only the fragrance of the Great Vehicle and take no delight in smelling the fragrance of the śrāvaka and pratyekabuddha vehicles."

Champaca is an Indian species of the magnolia genus. The tree is very tall and the flowers are incredibly fragrant. It can also be found in South America. Going into

---

* We know this because Master Tăng Hội, who was born at the beginning of the second century, mentions this sutra.

† Someone who does not need a teacher or a sangha in order to be enlightened to the fact that all things are caused and conditioned.

a grove with these trees, the only scent we smell is that of its flowers; all other scents are masked.

"Venerable Śāriputra, I have been in this house twelve years and I have never heard the Dharma of the śrāvaka vehicle or pratyekabuddha vehicle being taught. I have only heard the teachings of the Dharma of great loving kindness and great compassion of the bodhisattvas and the inconceivable teachings of the buddhas." This means that the goddess only finds significance in the Mahāyāna teachings. Once she had tasted first class food, all other foods had become bland.

"Since you are so accomplished how come you continue to bear the body of a woman? Why do you not turn yourself into a male form?"

Here Śāriputra is portrayed as someone very conservative and simple-minded. The goddess replied: *"Venerable monk, for these last twelve years I have looked for the female form of mine but I have not found it, so what is there to change? If a magician were to conjure up a phantom woman and then someone asked her why she did not change out of her female body, would that be a sensible question?"*

"No," said Śāriputra, *"the magical creation of a woman has no real form so what is there to change?"*

"All dharmas are just the same. They have no real form so how can you ask why they do not change their form?" This means the goddess does do not discriminate between male and female and that is why she is not restricted by the idea of a female form.

It's not enough for her to bait Śāriputra in this way, she goes further and uses her miraculous power to change Śāriputra into a woman, a "Bhikṣuṇī Śāriputra" and she changes herself into a man.

The Venerable Śāriputra feels very insulted. Why had he suddenly become a woman? What a disgrace! He thought to himself he should use some spiritual power to turn back into a male. However the miraculous power of the goddess was stronger than his and even though he used all his might he was unable to change back into a man.

Seeing this the goddess who is now in a male form makes another joking remark: *"Venerable Śāriputra, why do you not change this female body of yours into a male body?"*

The reply of Śāriputra is rather feeble: *"I have no idea how I became this woman."*

The goddess said: *"Venerable Śāriputra, if you were able to change your female form into a male form, all women would be able to do the same. In fact you are not a woman. You are just manifesting as a woman. All women are like that. Although they are manifesting as women they are not in fact women. Therefore the Buddha has said that all dharmas are not male or female."* Dharmas are not born and do not die, do not increase or decrease, they are not pure or impure, so how can we be caught in the idea of "male" or "female"?

Having spoken, the goddess smiled and withdrew her spiritual power and Śāriputra resumed his male form. Then she asked: *"Where has your female form gone?"*

Śāriputra replies: *"The form and shape of my female body is not made and is not made different."* Śāriputra has become enlightened.

The goddess nodded her head: *"Excellent, excellent, Venerable Śāriputra! All dharmas are like that. They are not made and are not made different. This was taught by the Buddha."* This section shows us how Śāriputra gradually arrives at the nondualistic understanding, which is not caught in views.

Then the goddess asked: *"Śāriputra, have you attained arhatship?"*

The same question is asked in the Vajracchedikā sutra where Subhūti is asked: "Subhūti, what do you think? Does an arhat have the thought, 'I have obtained the fruit of an arhat?'" Subhūti replied, "No, Bhagavān. Why? There is truly no dharma which may be called an arhat. Bhagavān, if an arhat has the thought, 'I have attained the Arhat Path,' then this is a person attached to a self, a person, a being, and a lifespan. Bhagavān, I do not have the thought, 'I am an arhat free of desire.' If I were thinking this way, then the Bhagavān would not speak of 'Subhūti, the one who dwells in peace.' It is because there is truly nothing dwelled in, that he speaks of 'Subhūti, the one who dwells in peace.'"

We all hope that Śāriputra will give a good answer. He says: "*I have attained arhatship because there is nothing to attain.*" The goddess replied: "*Quite so. It is true of all buddhas and bodhisattvas that nonattainment is the real attainment.*"

In reading these paragraphs the mind of those who composed this sutra is clear to see. Questions are put to give a chance to answer in such a way as proclaims the teachings of the Mahāyāna.

At this point Vimalakīrti intervenes with some words intended to comfort Śāriputra: "*Do you know that this goddess has made offerings to ninety-two thousand million buddhas? She has practiced over many lifetimes. She has the perfected spiritual power of aspiration and has become a bodhisattva of no-regression.*" Vimalakīrti means that Śāriputra does not need to have a complex or be downcast, because the goddess is like a Buddha.

In the Lotus Sutra Śāriputra plays a principal role and Buddha predicts to him directly that he will become a buddha in the future. The Lotus Sutra is much kinder in its approach. It is a harmonizing force and much in accord with the true teachings of the Buddha. It is also true that the Lotus Sutra borrows many ideas from the Vimalakīrtinirdeśa. One example is when the goddess says: "*Because I teach the śrāvaka vehicle, I am a śrāvaka. Because I have understood on my own the principle of causes and conditions, I use the pratyekabuddha vehicle to liberate beings.*"

This idea planted a seed which later became the idea in the Louts Sutra that says "All three vehicles have the

Buddha nature (會三歸一)." The śrāvaka and pratyeka-buddha vehicles are beneficial. They can take us on a stretch of our journey. They are not rotten seeds.

CHAPTER 8: THE DESTINY OF A BUDDHA

This chapter is also called "The Family of the Tathāgata." There are many kinds of family. There is the family in which we have many ties and which keep us very busy as we take care of it. That is our worldly family. The family of the Awakened Ones is a favorable condition for our practice. In this chapter the word "family" stands for the sangha and our good spiritual friends who are able to support us and guide us on our path of practice. This family of bodhisattvas who are practicing the way of inconceivable liberation is very large.

This chapter begins with a rather bizarre paragraph when Bodhisattva Mañjuśrī asks Vimalakīrti: *"What is the destiny of the bodhisattva according to the Buddhadharma?"*

The answer could shock us. *"The bodhisattva goes to an unwholesome destiny and that is the destiny of the Buddha."*

Prof. E. Lamotte* translates the Sanskrit word *agati*, "a destiny not to be gone to," into French as "déviation," meaning "off the path." We translate it here as "unwholesome destiny."

---

* *L'Enseignement de Vimalakīrti*, Université Catholique de Louvain, 1987.

Vimalakīrti: "The bodhisattvas go to the destiny of those who commit the five heinous crimes of immediate retribution. They arrive in the hell of incessant suffering but feel no anguish or anger. They are free of offense and defilement.

"They go to the destiny (which results) from attachment and desire, but they are free. They go to the destiny (which results from) anger and aversion but have no anger and aversion toward living beings. They go to the destiny (which results from) delusion but use wisdom to master their mind.

"They go to the destiny (which results from) breaking the precepts but establish themselves in the practice of the pure precepts and see the danger of committing the slightest fault.

"They go to the destiny (which results from) indolence and laziness but are committed to the practice of right diligence and seek all wholesome roots.

They go to the destiny (which results from) arrogance in order to serve as a bridge and support for living beings."

This means that if bodhisattvas are motivated by the mind of love with the aspiration to reach complete enlightenment and liberate all beings from suffering, wherever they go, wherever they stay, they remain themselves and never lose themselves. When you see bodhisattvas who are able to sit in a wine bar and joke with prostitutes without losing themselves, you know they are on the right path.

In short when the mind of love is real, our environment cannot dictate to us and we do not lose our true self or our spiritual self. Other people see us doing certain things and they think we have fallen from the spiritual life, but in fact we are still a bodhisattva and we are still on the right path of practice.

The eighth-century Indian Buddhist monk Śāntideva was influenced by the Vimalakīrtinirdeśa. In his poem the Bodhicaryāvatāra, there is a famous verse that runs:

Whatever the suffering of the world may be,
may it all ripen in myself.
By the pure actions of bodhisattvas
may the world be happy.

In these words we can see clearly the influence of the above section of the Vimalakīrtinirdeśa. The bodhisattva is not afraid of the suffering of the lower realms and is willing to go there to help all beings. If our practice is still weak we need to remind ourselves of the suffering that results from wrong action, to deter us from doing what causes ourselves and others to suffer. As a bodhisattva we do not do wrong actions but still we are willing to undergo the suffering that people incur as a result of wrong actions.

If this section of the sutra is misunderstood it is very dangerous. Someone who drinks a large quantity of alcohol and lives a dissolute life of debauchery could misinterpret these words to their own advantage, saying: "I am a bodhisattva and I can do these things. You cannot, because you have not reached my level!" Arguing in this way they allow themselves the liberty to do whatever they like. This has happened in a few monasteries. In the end the matter leaks out and the practice community is ruined.

If you want to practice and you take these words as your guide without understanding their real meaning it is extremely dangerous. To be caught in the outer form of the teachings is dangerous enough but to believe that one can be liberated without practicing the mindfulness trainings is much more so.

After this Vimalakīrti asks Mañjuśrī: *"What is the Tathāgata seed?"* This means which seeds in our con-sciousness when watered will lead to one practicing as a Tathāgata?

The bodhisattva replied: *"The body is the seed. Crav-ing, grasping, attachment, hatred, and delusion are the seeds. The four upside-down views* are the seeds. In sum the sixty-two wrong views† and all the afflictions are seeds of the Tathāgata."*

We have this mortal body, which is a seed of the Tathāgata. Sometimes we say that our body is the root of unwholesome actions. In the *Sutra on the Eight Reali-zations of Great Beings,*‡ it is said that the body is a forest

---

* Viewing the impermanent as permanent, the no-self as self, the defiled as pure, suffering as happiness.

† The sixty-two wrong views are described in the first sutta of the Dīgha Nikāya (Brahmajāla Sutta, Net of Views).

‡ Thich Nhat Hanh et al., *Chanting from the Heart*, Parallax Press, 2007.

of unwholesome actions. Here we see the opposite. This is easy enough to understand because without this body how could we practice and help others to practice? If we know how to practice, then that forest of unwholesome actions becomes a seed of the Tathāgata.

If we do not have ignorance, craving, or grasping, we can never realize wisdom and put an end to craving in order to be liberated. Understanding comes from the transformation of ignorance. If we do not have garbage like this we cannot grow the flower of enlightenment.

Awakening is made out of afflictions. Without afflictions there is no awakening. If there is no compost, there can be no flowers. That is why Buddhism has the teaching that the afflictions are the awakening (*bodhi*). In the same way we can say the right-hand side is the left-hand side, because as long as there is a right-hand side there will be a left-hand side and vice versa.

Mañjuśrī: "The lotus does not grow on the upland plains; the lotus grows in the mud and mire of a damp low-lying place. In the same way the Buddhadharma cannot grow in a person who has perceived the unconditioned and is determined to attain the highest upright restraint. It is only when living beings are in the midst of the mire of the afflictions that the Buddhadharma is born in them. If you plant seeds in the sky they will never grow. Only when you plant them in well-manured soil can they sprout and flourish. In the same way, the Buddhadharma will not grow in a person who has perceived the unconditioned and is determined to attain the highest upright restraint."

If someone who looks upon this body as impure, as the root of wrongdoing, if they see that this life is full of the impurities of wrongdoings and is tired of it, they will want to go in search of liberation. They will want to abandon this body, this society, and this life. Then even if they enter nirvāṇa, that nirvāṇa would not be liberation. That nirvāṇa would only be a temporary escape because they are escaping from the seeds that make a Tathāgata, the seeds of loving kindness and compassion.

The attitude of wanting to escape from one's own person, one's society, one's world full of impurities, trickery, and suffering is not a Buddhist attitude. It is an attitude that rots the seeds of a Tathāgata. The seeds of a Tathāgata are love and understanding. Love and understanding have to be practiced in the midst of this world of suffering.

Next Mañjuśrī says: *"If we do not go into the great ocean we shall not find the priceless pearls. If we do not go into the ocean of the afflictions we shall not give rise to the understanding of all things (sarvajñāna)."* So life is full of afflictions, this body is full of unwholesome actions, and if we do not go into them we cannot reach the highest fruit of awakening.

Then Vimalakīrti says: *"Mañjuśrī, ordinary people who do not practice are grateful to the Buddhadharma, but the śrāvaka is not. Why do I say this? Because when these ordinary people hear the Buddhadharma, they can set their mind on attaining the supreme path, determined that the*

Three Jewels will never be lost. But the śrāvakas who have overcome the five lower internal knots* may hear the Buddhadharma and yet not be capable of giving rise to the aspiration for highest enlightenment."

For those who have entered nirvāṇa the seeds of Tathāgata have no chance to sprout. They have completed their task and are of no more benefit to anyone. The arhat who enters nirvāṇa—complete extinction—cannot be of benefit to anyone.

As far as the Mahāyāna is concerned, living beings who are drifting on the ocean of birth and death, people who do not practice and drift and sink in their suffering, are those who have a future. This is because if they give rise to the mind of love and begin to practice according to the Mahāyāna, there will be a day when the seed of awakening in them sprouts, blooms a flower, and gives fruits. Then they will become fully enlightened ones.

This section has been put together so as to describe in a rather extreme way something which is very important: if we try to escape suffering we shall lose some of the most precious things we have.

After this a bodhisattva by the name of Sarvarūpasaṃdarśana stands up and asks Vimalakīrti, in what environment a bodhisattva should live?

---

* The knots of viewing my body as myself, being caught in rules and rituals, doubt about the teachings, attachment to pleasure, and ill-will. For meditation practices on the internal knots see *Blooming of a Lotus*, Thich Nhat Hanh, Beacon Press 2022.

Sarvarūpasaṃdarśana: *"Layman, who are your father and mother, wife and children, your relatives, servants, workers, and friends? Where is your entourage, your elephants, horses, and carriages?"*

Vimalakīrti answered in the following poem:

> *"The insight that brings us to the other shore*
> *(prajñāpāramitā) is the bodhisattvas' pure mother.*
> *Skillful means are their father.*
> *The guides and teachers of the world are born from these.*
> *Dharma happiness is their wife.*
> *Loving kindness and compassion are their daughters.*
> *The Dharma and the truth are their sons.*
> *The meditation on emptiness and tranquility are their house.*
> *Their disciples are the afflictions and the dust of the world, who do what the bodhisattvas tell them.*
> *The thirty-seven wings of awakening*
> *(bodhipakṣyadharma)* are their good friends.*
> *Through them they gain right awakening.*
> *The Six Pāramitās† are their fellow practitioners.*
> *The Four Means of Conversion‡ are the singing girls.*

---

* All the basic practices taught by the Buddha, including the Four Foundations of Mindfulness and the Noble Eightfold Path.

† The generosity, practice of mindfulness trainings, patience, diligence, meditative concentration and wisdom that take us to the other shore.

‡ Generosity, loving speech, beneficial conduct, and accompanying others.

*The songs they sing are the teaching of the Dharma,
such is their music.
Their elephants and horses are the six supranormal
powers.*

*Their chariot is the Mahāyāna.
Their whip and rod are the one-pointed mind as they
travel the Eightfold Path.†
They are clothed in the garments of shame before self
and shame before others.
Their couch is the four meditations‡ where the pure
way of life is born.
Their food is the sweet nectar of the Dharma, their
drink the taste of liberation.
They bathe in purification of the mind, annointing
themselves with the perfumed oil of the precepts."*

Someone who does not have shame before self and
shame before others is very foolish. In the sutras it is
often said that someone who has shame is adorned with
the most precious and beautiful jewelry. When we feel
ashamed and know that we could do better, we make
effort in the practice. When we make mistakes and can

---

* Magical power, the divine ear, knowing others' minds, the divine
eye, recollecting past lives, destruction of the āsavas.

† Right view, right thinking, right speech, right action, right livelihood,
right diligence, right mindfulness, right concentration.

‡ The first concentration has thinking and is filled with joy and happiness; the second has no thinking and is filled with joy and happiness;
the third has no joy but the happiness of equanimity; and the fourth
has equanimity in pleasure or pain.

accept that we have made that mistake, we shall not do it again. If someone else is practicing better than we are, we feel happy and vow to follow in their footsteps. All this is what is meant by shame. Without this mental formation we cannot make ourselves beautiful within and therefore adorn our life with all that is precious. After a couple more paragraphs, the poem continues:

> "If the bodhisattvas live during a time of armed conflict,
>   they give rise to the mind of compassion,
>   transforming those who are fighting,
>   and causing them to dwell in a land without contention.
>   If there are great wars,
>   the bodhisattvas make the strength on both sides equal.
>   They manifest their spiritual authority
>   and subdue people so that peace is restored."

During the war in Vietnam I read and memorized very carefully this part of the poem, and I often quoted these lines in Dharma talks. When we are living in a situation of war we must allow it to water our seeds of compassion and our motivation always to do everything we can to bring the war to an end. If we are vegetarian and say we want to help beings but do not do anything to stop one side killing the other, we are not a descendant of the Buddha or a bodhisattva. We teach people not to want conflict, not to contribute to conflict, and not to be caught in feelings of hatred. We teach by giving Dharma talks, by writing articles, by any means we can to help people see that the path of hatred is a path of foolishness and ignorance.

"If there are great wars, the bodhisattvas make the strength on both sides equal." If one side is weaker, the strong side will kill everyone on the weak side. When both sides are equal in strength and do not dare to use armed force against each other, the bodhisattvas step in, manifest their spiritual authority, and convince people to reconcile. Efforts to bring both sides together in peace talks is the action of bodhisattvas. The poem continues:

"A lotus born in the flames
is something extremely rare.
Living in the desire realm and practicing meditation
is also something rare."

The image of a lotus blooming in a sea of fire is an image from Buddhist literature, specifically the Vimalakīrtinirdeśa. In 1964 when I had finished writing *Vietnam: Lotus in a Sea of Fire*[*] to call on both sides in the war to stop fighting and accept each other, I chose the title of the book from this image in the Vimalakīrtinirdeśa.

"Sometimes they appear as prostitutes
in order to seduce lustful men.
In the beginning they use desire as a lure
and then draw them into the wisdom of the Buddha."

---

[*] Parallax Press 2022.

The bodhisattvas can play the role of a prostitute. If a man is lustful the bodhisattvas use their beauty to attract him. Bit by bit they open up his understanding so that he begins to practice a spiritual path and is able to extract the poisoned arrow of sensual desire that is buried deep in him. In the Ratnakūṭa Sutra there is a similar line of thought. The Vimalakīrtinirdeśa continues:

> *"The bodhisattvas come to those who are fearful*
> *in order to reassure them.*
> *First they offer the gift of non-fear,*
> *then they teach them how to give rise to the aspiration*
> *to practice."*

These are people who are afraid of so many things and they need someone to come and offer them peace of mind, and comfort them and do what is necessary to offer them the practice of fearlessness; and that is the gift of non-fear (*abhaya dāna*). This is a gift that Avalokiteśvara Bodhisattva offers everyone. It is the most precious of all gifts.

The three gifts in Buddhism are: material gifts, the gift of the Dharma, and the gift of non-fear. Here the teaching of the Universal Door Chapter of the Lotus Sutra: "The bodhisattva appears in many different bodies according to the circumstances in order to help the world," is already found in the Vimalakīrtinirdeśa, which is an earlier sutra.

This long poem recited by Vimalakīrti is a teaching on the sphere of activity of a bodhisattva and all the members of the large family of the Tathāgata.

CHAPTER 9: ENTERING THE DOOR OF NONDUALITY

The Sanskrit word for nonduality is *advaya*. Not only is nonduality opposed to duality, it is also opposed to monism. Monism is the opposite of pluralism. Nonduality means that things are not one and they are not two. The teachings of nonduality have already been presented in an informal way in the first chapters of the sutra. An example is the decaying matter and the flower which, although they are two things, could never exist apart from each other. Without decaying matter we could never have flowers. Without flowers we would not have decaying matter. The afflictions and the awakened mind are the same.

At that time Vimalakirti said to the bodhisattvas, "Sirs, how does the bodhisattva enter the gate of nonduality? Let each one explain as they understand it."

"The bodhisattva Dharmavikurvaṇa said: "Sirs, birth and death are two. But since all dharmas are not born to begin with, they must be without death. By mastering and learning to accept this truth of birthlessness, one may enter the gate of nonduality."

The bodhisattva Virtue Guardian said, "'I' and 'mine' are two. Because there is an 'I,' there is also a 'mine.' But if there is no 'I,' there will be no 'mine.' In this way one enters the gate of nonduality."

Another bodhisattva said, "Perception and nonperception are two. But if dharmas are not perceived, then there is nothing to take hold of. And because there is nothing to take hold of, there will be no grasping, no rejecting, no action, no volition. In this way one enters the gate of nonduality."

The bodhisattva Śrikūṭa said, "Defilement and purity are two. But if one sees into the true nature of defilement, it is without the marks of purity but leads into the extinction of all marks. In this way one enters the gate of nonduality."

The bodhisattva Bhadrajyotis said, "The agitated mind and mindfulness are two. But if the mind is not agitated, then there will be no mindfulness. And if there is no mental attention, there will be no discrimination. The one who has thoroughly mastered this may in this way enter the gate of nonduality."

The bodhisattva Subāhu said, "The bodhisattva mind and the voice-hearer mind are two. But if one regards the mind as empty in form, like a magic display, then there is no bodhisattva mind and no voice-hearer mind. In this way one may enter the gate of nonduality."

The bodhisattva Puṣya said, "Wholesome and unwholesome are two. But if one understands the nature of wholesome and the nature of unwholesome and the nature of sign and signlessness, in this way one may enter the gate of nonduality."

The bodhisattva Siṃha said, "Demerit and merit are two. But if one penetrates the true nature of demerit, it is no different from merit. When one can dispose of signs with the diamond wisdom that cuts through afflictions, and see that they are neither bound nor liberated, they may in this way enter the gate of nonduality.

The bodhisattva Siṃhamati said, "Presence of āsravas* and absence of the āsravas are two. But if one can grasp the fact that all dharmas are equal, then one will not give rise to the concept of āsravas or no āsravas. One will not be attached to form nor dwell in formlessness either. In this way one may enter the gate of nonduality."

The bodhisattva Śuddhādhimukti said, "The conditioned and the unconditioned are two. But if one does away with all formations, then the mind is like empty sky, freed of all obstacles through pure wisdom. In this way one enters the gate of nonduality."

The bodhisattva Nārāyaṇa said, "The mundane and the supramundane are two. But since the nature of the mundane is empty, the mundane is in fact the supramundane. There is no coming and no going, no lack and no excess. In this way one enters the gate of nonduality."

The bodhisattva Dāntamati said, "The realm of birth and death (saṃsāra) and that of nirvāṇa are two. But if one sees the true nature of birth and death, one sees that there is no birth

---

* These are taints caused by desire, ideas of being and nonbeing, wrong views and ignorance

or death, no bound, no liberated. One who understands in this way may enter the gate of nonduality."

The bodhisattva Pratyakṣadarśana said, "The destructible and the indestructible are two. But whether dharmas are destructible or indestructible, they are all without the marks of destructibility. And if they are without the marks of destructibility, they are empty. And if they are empty, they are without the marks either of destructibility or indestructibility. If one enters this realm of understanding, one may enter the gate of nonduality."

The bodhisattva Parigūḍha said, " 'I' and 'not-I' are two. But since one cannot grasp 'I' how can one grasp 'not-I'? One who has seen into the true nature of 'I' will no longer give rise to these two concepts, and in this way enter the gate of nonduality."

The bodhisattva Vidyuddeva said, "Enlightenment and ignorance are two. But the true nature of ignorance is none other than enlightenment. And enlightenment cannot be grasped but is apart from all calculations. One dwells in the Middle Way, in the sameness without duality, and in this way enters the gate of nonduality."

The bodhisattva Priyadarśana said, "Form and emptiness are two. But form is none other than emptiness. Emptiness is not the extinction of form. Form is itself empty by nature. In the same way feeling, perception, volition, and consciousness, and the emptiness of them, constitute dualities. Dwelling in the midst of these concepts and understanding them thoroughly, one may enter the gate of nonduality."

We think the mind of the bodhisattva and that of the śrāvaka are two different things. In fact they are not. This is one of the contradictions in the Vimalakīrtinirdeśa. In many instances it teaches that we need to give up the śrāvaka mind in order to attain the bodhisattva mind. It clearly makes a distinction between śrāvaka and bodhisattva. Here when talking about nonduality, the sutra says that although the śrāvaka mind and the bodhisattva mind are two, they are not really two. Reading this we feel that the sutra is inconsistent.

The sutra says wholesome and unwholesome are two, merit and demerit are two but in truth they are not two. The state of having āsravas and no longer having āsravas, the mundane and the supramundane seem to be two, saṃsāra and nirvāṇa seem to be two but in origin they are of the same nature. The finite and the infinite are two, self and nonself are two, wisdom and ignorance are two, form and emptiness are two, but in fact they are not two. Although nonduality is the ultimate nature of all these pairs of opposites, if we are caught in the idea that they are the same, it can be very dangerous.

The bodhisattvas take turns to proclaim the nonduality of all phenomena until the end of the chapter.

When the bodhisattvas had finished speaking, they asked Manjushri, "How then does the bodhisattva enter the gate of nonduality?"

Manjushri replied, "To my way of thinking, to say nothing about dharmas, not to speak about them, not to cognize them, not to ask questions or give replies about them, is to enter the gate of nonduality."

Mañjuśrī does not need to talk about A and B and then conclude that A and B are not two separate realities. He says that the nature of all phenomena cannot be described in words and concepts and that is truly nonduality.

After saying this the bodhisattva turned to look at Vimalakīrti and asked: *"Everyone has spoken including myself. Now it is your turn to tell us what is nonduality. Vimalakīrti kept silent. Some seconds later Mañjuśrī Bodhisattva smiled and praised Vimalakīrti: "Excellent, your silence is the best expression of nonduality."*

CHAPTER 10: BUDDHA SUGANDHAKŪṬA

In this sutra Śāriputra is portrayed as someone who is very practical. When he stepped into Vimalakīrti's hut and saw it empty of all furniture, he wondered where the bodhisattvas would sit. In this chapter after some time has passed in discussion and people are beginning to feel hungry, he thought to himself: "What is the sangha going to eat?" That morning there had been no alms' round, only discussion of the teachings; now when people were hungry what was to be done?

Vimalakīrti was able to read his mind and said to Śāriputra: *"While listening to the Dharma how come your mind is distracted by thinking of food? But if you are hungry I shall offer you a very special meal that you have never eaten before."*

At that Vimalakīrti entered meditative concentration. He used his miraculous power to enable the sangha to see a land called the Land of Fragrance. In this land everything is made of fragrance. The Buddha of that land and all his disciples are made of fragrance. The Dharma that is taught there is also made of fragrance. The food is made of fragrance. The houses are made of fragrance. Walking meditation is practiced on the ground of fragrance. The fragrance of the meals wafts out into the ten directions. The Buddha of that land is known as Sugandhakūṭa, which means the Accumulation of Fragrance.

Thanks to the miraculous power of the layman Vimalakīrti the sangha was able to see Buddha Sugandhakūṭa and his community enjoying the midday meal.

Vimalakīrti asked the bodhisattvas: "Is there a bodhisattva who could volunteer to go to the Land of Fragrance to ask for some food and bring it back here for the sangha to eat?"

Mañjuśrī Bodhisattva used his spiritual power to make all the bodhisattvas silent. Then Vimalakīrti said: "Bodhisattvas, are you not ashamed? Do none of you have the ability to go to that land and ask for food?"

Mañjuśrī Bodhisattva replied: "Please do not look down on those who are new to the practice."

This is a sentiment that the Buddha had expressed to King Prasenajit: "Do not despise a little fire." Actually the bodhisattvas were not new to the practice. We could interpret this as meaning: Do not look down on those who have no more to learn, those who are *aśaikṣa*, and have completed their training.

Vimalakīrti stayed where he was and conjured up a bodhi-sattva who had all the auspicious marks, majestic, brilliant and imposing, more beautiful than all the bodhisattvas in the assembly. Vimalakīrti proposed that this conjured up bodhisattva should go to the land of fragrance, pay respect to Buddha Sugandhakūṭa, and say that Vimalakīrti bowed at the Buddha's feet, asked after his well-being, wished him good health, with few afflictions, and asked for a little food to be brought back to the sahā world to support the work of the awakened ones.

The conjured up bodhisattva obeyed his instructions and flew off to the land of fragrance. He bowed down before Buddha Sugandhakūṭa and transmitted the words of Vimalakīrti. When the sangha in the Land of Fragrance saw the conjured-up bodhisattva they uttered words of praise and asked Buddha Sugandhakūṭa:

"Lord Buddha whence comes this bodhisattva who has so many miraculous powers?

Buddha Sugandhakūṭa explained: "There is a world called Sahā that is found at a distance of as many Buddha lands as there are grains of sands of the Ganges multiplied by forty-two. In that land is a Buddha, whose name is Śākyamuni, teaching and practicing the way of enlightenment. In that world there is a layman by the name of Vimalakīrti and he sent this bodhisat-tva here to ask for food."

Sugandhakūṭa Buddha had an alms' bowl filled with the food of fragrance and handed it to the bodhisattva. At that point there were nine million bodhisattvas in the Land of Fragrance who wanted to visit the sahā world and see how Buddha Śākyamuni was teaching and transforming living beings. With one voice they asked Buddha Sugandhakūṭa: "We your disciples ask to go to the sahā world to make offerings to Buddha Śākyamuni and be in the presence of Vimalakīrti along with all the bodhisattvas over there."

They also had a similar curiosity to that of living beings in the sahā world. You come to Plum Village to practice the Winter Retreat but you also want to go up to Paris for a couple of days to see what the capital city has to offer.

Sugandhakūṭa Buddha replied: "You may go, but you must be careful to preserve your body of fragrance. Do not allow living beings in that world to become infatuated with you. It would be better to leave behind your body of fragrance so that those who are seeking the bodhisattva path over there will not feel inferior. And you must not look on the sahā world with disdain or contempt or rouse thoughts that obstruct progress.

He meant: "Do not compare our plentiful and beautiful land with their land."

This section of the sutra is talking about the discriminatory tendency that living beings have. This tendency is something all human beings have in common. The congregation of one temple is always comparing itself with, commending, or disparaging the other temples in the area.

The conjured-up bodhisattva accepted the alms' bowl of fragrant food, joined his palms, and bowed to Buddha Sugandhakūṭa in parting. Then with nine million bodhisattvas of that land he flew back to the sahā world. Vimalakīrti had a premonition that nine million guests were about to arrive so he used his spiritual power to bring into his meditation hut nine million more lion thrones. Up until now there were only thirty-two thousand people in the house and now nine million guests are arriving. Fortunately they had already eaten!

When the conjured-up Bodhisattva offered the alms' bowl of food from the Land of Fragrance to Vimalakīrti, the wonderful fragrance wafted out into all directions of the universe. Everyone in the town of Vaiśalī received a whiff of the fragrance and in their minds they felt more relaxed and light than they had ever felt before.

This kind of fragrance was not like the sandalwood incense that we sense through our nose. This fragrance was the incense of the heart: the incense of mindfulness trainings, concentration, insight, liberation, and the recognition of liberation. These are the five kinds of incense of the heart that people seek. The aspiration to realize this fivefold incense of the heart is the condition that brings us into the land of Buddha Sugandhakūṭa.

When the śrāvakas saw the alms' bowl they were concerned that the food it held would not suffice for thirty-two thousand people.

They thought to themselves "There is only a little rice—how can it feed all the people in this great assembly?"

But the phantom bodhisattva said, "Venerable Śāriputra, venerable śrāvaka disciples. do not use the limited merit and wisdom of the śravaka vehicle in appraising the immeasurable merit and wisdom of the Tathāgata. Though the four seas run dry, this rice will never come to an end. Why? Because this food is the leftovers from a meal eaten by those who have acquired inexhaustible merits through their practice of the precepts, concentration, insight, liberation, and the knowledge of liberation. Therefore it can never be exhausted."

The alms' bowl contained rice that had the taste of the nectar of the Tathāgata. It had been perfumed by great compassion. So you should not use the limited mind of the lower vehicle while eating the food of the Mahāyāna. The limited mind cannot eat this food. Before eating you should establish yourselves in the mind of the Mahāyāna. You have to make your stomach the stomach of the Mahāyāna if you want to be able to digest this food.

At that point everyone sat down and for the first time ate the wonderful food of the Land of Fragrance. While eating this food, their bodies became light and at ease, their appearance became beautiful and pure as the bodies of the guest bodhisattvas from the Land of Fragrance. From each pore of their skin a wonderful fragrance arose. It was as fragrant as the trees in the Land of Fragrance.

The layman Vimalakīrti asked the bodhisattvas from the Land of Fragrance: "Venerable sirs, in your homeland what kind of Dharma does Buddha Sugandhakūṭa teach? The bodhisattvas replied: "The Tathāgata in our land does not use words to teach. He just uses various fragrances to induce heavenly and human beings to undertake the observance of the precepts. Each bodhi-sattva sits under a fragrant tree, and when they smell the mar-velous fragrance, they immediately attain the samādhi known as the Storehouse of All Bodhisattva Virtues. Those who are able to attain this samādhi all become endowed with the quali-ties of a bodhisattva."

To put it more clearly, the kind of scent that is in the Land of Fragrance is the scent of the fivefold incense of the heart and it is therefore able to describe the Bud-dhadharma. The sangha only needs to smell the fra-grance of the practice of the spiritual path and the sangha understands the Buddhadharma. On the other hand the scent in the sahā world is a strong, enticing, and deluding fetter and has strange names to describe it like "Samsara," "Je Reviens," "Scorpion," "Poison." When you smell these kinds of perfume you only become more infatuated and more confused.

After they had replied, The bodhisattvas of the Land of Fra-grance asked: "And in the sahā world, how does Śākyamuni Buddha teach the Dharma?"

Vimalakīrti replied, "The living beings of this land are stubborn and rebellious and hard to transform. Therefore the Buddha uses the necessary language in order to tame and contol them....

These people who are difficult to convert have minds like monkeys. Therefore the Buddha must resort to various methods in order to control and regulate their minds. Only then can they be tamed and made obedient.... The bodhisattvas of this land are indeed steadfast in their great compassion for all living beings. The enrichment and benefit they bring to living beings in one lifetime here is greater than that bestowed in other worlds over the space of a hundred thousand kalpas. Why? Because in this sahā world there are ten wholesome practices that do not exist in any of those Pure Lands."

This means our Buddha has to use words. It takes a long time to give a teaching. Many terms have to be used. Many skillful means have to be used in order to teach and transform living beings in this sahā world. Although our land has the cloudiness of many wrongdoings and all kinds of suffering, we do not have a complex about this. That is because our land has many great advantages. These advantages are ten wholesome practices. These do not exist in the various Pure Lands.

Firstly we practice generosity to put an end to poverty:

In our land there are many poor people so we can use generosity to help liberate poor people from suffering. In the other Pure Lands, rice is always available, curry is always available, so no one needs generosity and practitioners there do not have a chance to practice generosity.

Secondly we practice the precepts to put an end to breaking the precepts.

In our land people are inclined to drink alcohol; they become inebriated, commit adultery, and kill others, transgressing all the rules of conduct. Therefore we are able to practice the *śīlapāramitā*, teaching people to transform by practicing the Five Mindfulness Trainings, the Ten Mindfulness trainings, and the bhikṣu and bhikṣuni Pratimoksha. In your land you do not need to practice the precepts. So you do not have that means to liberate people from their suffering.

Thirdly we practice patience to put an end to anger

Our land has many hot-tempered people. You only have to touch a sensitive point and they fly into a rage. This gives us an opportunity to practice the *pāramitā* of patience in order to liberate them from their suffering.

Fourthly we practice diligence to put an end to idleness

In our land people are lazy, therefore we can use the practice of the pāramitā of diligence to transform them and liberate them from their suffering.

Fifthly we practice meditative concentration to put an end to a distracted mind.

We can use the pāramitā of meditative concentration to help liberate people from the dispersed mind.

Sixthly we practice insight to put an end to ignorance.

Our land has so many people who are caught in ignorance but think that they are highly intelligent and have realized the highest peaks of human under-standing. That is why we can use the *Prajñāpāramitā* to help liberate them from suffering.

*Seventhly we teach those who have fallen into the eight unfavorable conditions how to overcome these conditions.**

Eighthly we teach the Mahāyāna to those who follow lesser paths.

Ninthly we practice cultivating wholesome roots for those who have not put down wholesome roots.

Tenthly we practice without ceasing the Four Means of Conversion (generosity, loving speech, beneficial conduct, and accompanying others) to bring beings to maturity in the practice.

In our sahā world we have much suffering and many problems so we have many bodhisattvas practicing these four means.

The bodhisattvas in the Land of Fragrance asked:

"What Dharma doors must these bodhisattvas in the sahā world practice in order to attain safely a pure Buddha land?"

---

* The eight unfavorable conditions are 1. falling into the hell realms. 2. being born as a hungry ghost. 3. being born as an animal. 4. being born as a long-lived god who does not suffer and so is not motivated to practice. 5. being born in the realm of no perceptions. 6. being blind, deaf, or unable to speak. 7. living in uncivilized tribes. 8. being born at a time when there is no Buddha.

The layman Vimalakīrti replied: "These bodhisattvas have to practice the following eight Dharma doors in order safely to reach a pure Buddha land.

1. They should benefit living beings without any wish to be requited.

2. They should take upon themselves all the suffering of living beings; and the merit they acquire thereby, they should offer up for those beings.

3. They should practice inclusiveness with regard to all living beings, humbling themselves and not erecting barriers between themselves and living beings.

4. They look on bodhisattvas as if they were looking on the Buddha.

5. When listening to sutras of deep meaning they have not yet heard, they have no doubts. They do not dispute with or oppose the śrāvaka vehicle.

6. They have no jealousy or envy when others receive offerings. They do not boast about their own advantages.

7. They master their thinking. They reflect on their own short-comings and they do not censure the shortcomings of others.

8. They remain vigilant at all times and accumulate all the virtues."

The fifth Dharma door is one that Vimalakīrti needs to remind himself of.

When Vimalakīrti and Mañjuśrī Bodhisattva had given this Dharma teaching, a hundred thousand heavenly and human

*beings all set their minds on attaining the highest, right, and
equal enlightenment, and ten thousand bodhisattvas realized
the truth of no-birth (and no-death).*

In this chapter we come across the basic idea of "The
lotus can only grow out of mud." If there are not suffering and hardship, the mind of love and the insight of a
Buddha can never arise.

CHAPTER 11: THE COMPORTMENT OF THE BODHISATTVA

While Vimalakīrti was teaching the Dharma to the
bodhisattvas from the Land of Fragrance and the sangha,
Buddha Śākyamuni was giving a Dharma talk in the
Mango Grove of the courtesan Āmrapāli to a number of
disciples and an assembly of others.

*Suddenly the Mango Grove grew full of light, widened out, and
everyone in the Buddha's audience had an aura of golden light.
Ānanda asked the Buddha about the reason for this unusual
occurrence and the Buddha replied: "Vimalakīrti, Bodhisattva
Mañjuśrī and their assembly are about to come and visit us,
and this is a presage of their coming."*

Buddha had only just finished speaking and the
sangha led by Vimalakīrti and Mañjuśrī Bodhisattva
arrived. All bowed down at the feet of the Buddha. They
asked after the Buddha's health, made offerings to the
Buddha, and withdrew to one side. The Buddha also

asked after the well-being of the bodhisattvas and other visitors and then told them to be seated.

The Buddha looked at Śāriputra and asked: "Have you seen the spiritual power of self-mastery in these bodhisattvas?"

Śāriputra replied: "Lord Buddha, I have."

The Buddha asked: "What is your impression?"

Śāriputra replied: "My impression is that these bodhisattvas are inconceivable. Their activities, spiritual powers, and qualities are inconceivable."

Then Ānanda asked the Buddha: "Lord Buddha, I am aware of a strange and wonderful fragrance that I have never smelled before. What is that fragrance?"

The Buddha replied to Ānanda, "This is the fragrance that comes from the pores of these bodhisattvas."

Then Śāriputra said to his younger brother in the Dharma: "This fragrance comes from the pores of our bodies too."

Ānanda asked: "What brought the fragrance about?"

Śhāriputra replied: "It comes from the rice left over from the Buddha's meal that the householder Vimalakirti had brought from the Land of Many Frangrances. The pores of everyone who ate it at his house emit this kind of fragrance."

Ānanda asked Vimalakīrti: "Layman, how long will this fragrance emanating from your pores last?"

Vimalakīrti replied: "When the food has all been digested, the fragrance will cease."

"How long does this food take to digest?"

"For some it is digested in seven days." Then he instructed Ānanda further: "Those śrāvakas who have not yet given rise to the highest determination have to wait for that determination to be realized for the food to be digested. Those who have not given rise to the Mahāyāna aspiration have to wait until they have given rise to that aspiration. Those who have set their minds on the Mahāyāna aspiration still have to realize the no-birth no-death nature of dharmas for this food to be digested. Then they have to go on to attain the fruit of the bodhisattva who will in the next lifetime become Buddha so that the food can be digested.

"Once they have eaten such food they have to practice until it has removed the toxicity of all the afflictions and then will it be digested."

Then Ānanda said to the Buddha: "This fragrant food of Sugandhakūṭa Buddha is inconceivable. It is able to do the great work of the Buddha."

The Buddha said: "What you say is correct, Ānanda. There are Buddha lands where people use the radiant light of the Buddha to do the work of the Buddha. There are lands where bodhisattvas do the work of the Buddha. There are lands where Bodhi trees do the work of the Buddha. There are lands where people use clothes or furniture to do the work of the Buddha. There are lands where people use food to do the work of the Buddha. There are lands where people use gardens, forests, palaces, and houses to do the work of the Buddha. There are lands where people use space to do the work of the Buddha. There are lands where people use similes such as dreams, magical illusions,

images in a mirror, the reflection of the moon in water, and
mirages to do Buddha the work of the Buddha."

In fact anything can be used to do the work of the Buddha. For example we pick an autumn leaf up from the ground and use it as the subject of a Dharma talk on "the one is the all and the all is the one."

"There are lands where they use sounds, the spoken word, and
syllables to do the work of the Buddha. There are lands where
they use silence, not saying or explaining anything, the non-
doing and non-conditioning, to do the work of the Buddha.
There are lands where they use non-action and not causing any-
thing to be done (which does not mean laziness) in order to do
the work of the Buddha. All the daily activities of the Buddhas,
their coming in, going out, every action they do, is the work of
the Buddha.

This means you can use walking, standing, lying down, sitting, smiling, and breathing to do the work of the Buddha. Fine manners, daily actions, and work can all be used to do the work of the Buddha.

The translation of Master Xuanzang reads: *"Walking, standing, lying down, and sitting, our comportment and daily activities are all elements to be used for the work of the Buddha."*

When we wish someone like an elder monk, an abbess, or a layperson: "May you fulfill the work of the Buddha," we generally think that the work of the Buddha is to build temples, cast bells, publish sacred texts, print scriptures, organize the Ulumbana festival, Wesak, or offering ceremonies for the Hungry Spirits. Here we have a very interesting teaching that means: whenever we walk, stand, lie down, or sit, the way we look at someone, smile, and breathe are the work of the Buddha. When we are mindful, peaceful, and joyful, everything expressed by our body and mind can be the means to liberate people from suffering. This is the basic work of the Buddha.

The Buddha continued: "Ānanda, the four kinds of Māra * and the eighty-four thousand afflictions, which wear living beings out, can be used to do the work of Buddha." This is like using refuse matter to make compost and plant flowers.

After the Buddha had spoken, nine million bodhisattvas from the Land of Fragrance joined their palms and said: "World-Honored Lord, when we had just arrived in your Buddha land, we saw it as impure and ugly, but now we regret our thoughts and have been able to remove them from our mind. We have seen that the skillful means used by Buddhas are inconceivable. In order to transform and liberate beings, Buddhas manifest different Buddha lands that are appropriate to the needs of different living beings."

Similarly we see that people who live in a situation of plenty, with all kinds of material luxuries in the West are

---

* Māra of the Afflictions, Māra of the Five Skandhas of Grasping, Māra of Death, and Māravatthu (the king of a heavenly realm).

not able to understand the suffering and happiness that people in developing countries have. When they hear about famine in the developing world they are afraid to go and visit those countries. In fact if they do go to those places they will discover some wonderful things. Although there is hardship there, nevertheless the sense of sisterhood and brotherhood is much deeper and it is something very beautiful. Because there is suffering, people vow to help those who suffer and their spirit grows more beautiful as they devote themselves to this work. In the developing countries there are daily joys that in the developed countries no longer exist. In the over-developed world people no longer have time to look at each other, to take a cup of tea together, or sit side by side every day without needing to say very much.

Nevertheless when people first come to developing countries they have a superiority complex. They think: "What an ugly country!" But after they have been there three or four months, for instance in India or in Vietnam, they find so many happy things that they would never find in any developed country.

This is just how the bodhisattvas from the Land of Fragrance felt. In that land they lived in great contentment so they could not see that afflictions are the very essence of awakening. This is why the ancestral teachers often say, "Our principle of practice is that the Pure Land is here." We want to stay here in the sahā world because we are able to find happiness right here.

The bodhisattvas from the Land of Fragrance said: "Lord Buddha, before we go back to the Land of Fragrance, please gives us a teaching that we can take back with us to practice there and remember you by."

The Buddha said: "There is a Dharma door called the "destructible and indestructible as a means to liberation." You can learn it and bring it home to practice."

Liberation has two aspects: destructible and indestructible. The Sanskrit words are kṣaya (destructible) and akṣaya (indestructible), (Chinese 盡 and 無盡). *Kṣaya* means something that can be destroyed, that can come to an end; *akṣaya* is the opposite.

The Buddha said: "What does destructible mean? It means those things that are conditioned. What does indestructible mean? It means those things that are unconditioned. The bodhisattvas do not destroy [or have done with] the conditioned, nor do they dwell in the unconditioned."

Conditioned dharmas are the phenomena subject to birth and death, creation and destruction. Suffering can arise with regard to such phenomena. The unconditioned belong to nirvāṇa, the realm of the unborn and undying, the end of suffering.

"What is meant by not removing the conditioned? It means not setting aside great loving kindness, not losing great compassion; not forgetting the determination to realize the mind of understanding all; never growing weary of teaching and transforming living beings.

The first practice of liberation discussed in this chapter of the sutra is "liberation by means of the destructible" also called "conditioned liberation." The practice of liberation by means of the destructible is that although life has suffering, shortcomings, and impurities, our mind does not give up in distaste. We are determined to stay in the world to practice great loving kindness, great compassion, and great understanding.

The second practice of liberation discussed is the "liberation in terms of the indestructible."

"What is meant by saying that the bodhisattva does not dwell in the unconditioned? It means that they study and practice the teachings on emptiness, but do not take emptiness to be enlightenment. They study and practice the teachings on signlessness and aimlessness, but do not take signlessness and aimlessness to be enlightenment…. They view things as impermanent, but do not neglect to cultivate the roots of goodness. They view the world as marked by suffering, but do not hate to be born and die in it. They see that there is such a thing as tranquil nirvāṇa, but do not dwell in nirvāṇa.

This means "not abiding in the unconditioned." Although we have realized the true face of all phenomena as unborn, undying, not perfect, not imperfect, signless, aimless, we do not abide in that realization in order to avoid suffering. We have realized the true nature of phenomena but we do not use that realization as an escape. "We have realized the peaceful nourishing of the unconditioned (where nothing needs to be

done 然後不為安養 平入娑婆) and we re-enter the
sahā world" is a phrase in the early morning liturgy
of Chinese and Vietnamese monasteries. The phrase
means that we have no desire to escape into a personal
quietude. We are determined to come back to the sahā
world. We do not abide in the unconditioned and abandon the conditioned.

The attitude of a bodhisattva is one of acceptance of
this sahā world with all its suffering as their home. They
fulfill the work of liberation of themself and other beings
right here.

CHAPTER 12: BUDDHA AKṢOBHYA

There are many Pure Lands; the most well-known among
present-day Buddhists is Sukhāvatī, the Pure Land in
the Western direction that is presided over by Buddha
Amitābha, the Buddha of Limitless Light. Another Pure
Land often referred to in the Buddhist scriptures is the
land of Akṣobhya. It is called Abhirati, which means
"delight" in Sanskrit, 妙喜, "Wonderful Joy" in Chinese,
and is found in the Eastern quarter of the cosmos. It is
also a well-known paradise but the conditions for doing
the practice in this land are a little more difficult to meet.
Since the nature of beings in the sahā world is a little bit
lazy they usually register to go to the Western Sukhavati.
Not many register for the land of Buddha Akṣobya in the
Eastern quarter. Therefore the number of practitioners

in this Eastern paradise is less than that of those in the Western paradise of Amitābha.

This chapter on Akṣobhya Buddha begins with a section that talks about the practice of looking at the Buddha.

The Buddha looked at Vimalakīrti and asked: *"Now you have come to visit me and have met me, how do you see me?"* This question means: "What is the layman's notion of the Buddha?"

Vimalakīrti said: "World-honored Lord, I look on the Buddha in the same way as I look on my own true form." These lines are very famous in the world of Zen. In the Records of the Eminent Master Tuệ Trung,* these eight words: "觀身實相 觀佛亦然" "looking at your own true face, you naturally look at Buddha," are found in a koan that the Master transmitted to his disciples.

Vimalakīrti continues: *"I do not look on the Buddha as arising in the past, abiding in the present, or departing in the future. I do not see the Buddha as body, feelings, perceptions, mental formations, or consciousness. I do not look on him as this or that, as conditioned or unconditioned or as something that can be explained."*

Vimalakīrti says that the true reality of the Buddha is not different from the reality of himself. Buddha does not

---

* Master Tuệ Trung was a Vietnamese lay Zen master; he died in 1291.

arrive or depart and does not abide. Buddha is not self and is not other. Buddha is not conditioned or unconditioned. Buddha is not past, present, or future. We cannot use words or notions to describe the Buddha. If you say: "I look on the person of the Buddha like that," that is the correct way of looking. Looking otherwise at Buddha is incorrect vision. The way of looking at Buddha described by Vimalakīrti is the Mahāyāna way. In our practice we have gāthās praising the Buddha. One of them reads as follows:

> *The Buddha jewel shines infinitely,*
> *enlightened for countless lifetimes.*
> *The beauty and stability of Buddha sitting*
> *is seen in the mountains and rivers.*
> *How splendid is the Vulture Peak!*
> *How beautiful the light that shines forth from*
> *Buddha's brow,*
> *illumining the six dark paths.*
> *To the Nāgapuṣpa Assembly we will go*
> *to continue the true teachings and practices.*
> *We take refuge in the Buddha ever-present.*

In this gāthā we recollect the Buddha body according to the Mahāyāna.

The body of the Buddha is unborn and undying, it has no after and no before. If we look with the eyes of relativity we shall never be able to see the true nature of the Buddha body. It is like a gāthā in the Vajracchedikā

Sutra, which we can translate from the Sanskrit as follows:

> *Those who wish to find me in a form*
> *or seek me in a voice*
> *are wrongly attached to an abstraction.*
> *They will not see the Tathāgata.*
>
> *They should see me through the Dharma,*
> *for our guides in the world are the Dharma body.*
> *The nature of dharmas is unknowable*
> *and cannot be discerned.*
> *They are looking in the wrong way*
> *and they will not see the true form of the Tathāgata.*

Next in this chapter we find out about the origins of Vimalakīrti. He originally came to the sahā world from the Abhirati paradise.

Śāriputra asked: "Layman, in your previous lifetime where were you, before you were born in this world?"

Vimalakīrti said: "In the Dharma that you have practiced is there such a thing as birth and death?"

"There is no birth and death."

"If there is no birth and no death why do you ask where I died before I was born here?

"Death is the sign of something that is empty and illusory coming to an end. Ending of illusory phenomena and birth is

the sign of the continuation of something that is empty and illusory. Although the bodhisattva dies, his roots of goodness are not lost, although the bodhisattva is born he does not continue unwholesome actions."

The Buddha told Śāriputra: "Śāriputra, Vimalakīrti has come to manifest in the sahā world from the Paradise of Delight, the abode of Buddha Akṣobhya (Unshakeable)."

Śāriputra said: "It is amazing, World-Honored One! How could someone abandon such a Pure Land as Abhirati for a Buddha land so defiled by vice?"

Vimalakīrti said: "What do you think, venerable monk? Is the brightness of the sun accompanied by darkness?

""No, when the light of the sun shines, all darkness ceases at once to exist."

Vimalakīrti asked: "Why does the sun visit the continent of Jambudvīpa?"

The Venerable Śāriputra replied: "Because the sun wants to bring its light in order for this world not to be in darkness."

" Bodhisattvas are the same, they are born in the impure Buddha lands with a view to helping living beings transform their suffering. They do not abide with the afflictions but remove the darkness of the afflictions of beings."

In this chapter of the Vimalakīrtinirdeśa we see Śāriputra portrayed as a fool who asks feather-brained questions. Clearly those who were writing the text of this sutra intentionally used the character of Śāriputra as a means to expound the ideas of the Mahāyāna. Even though we know this we still feel very sorry for the historical Śāriputra.

The whole assembly was very eager to see the Abhirati paradise and Akṣobhya Buddha with his community of bodhisattvas and śrāvakas. Knowing what the assembly had in mind the Buddha said to Vimalakīrti: "Layman, make it possible for the assembly here to see the Abhirati paradise of Buddha Unshakeable. They long to see what it is like."

Vimalakīrti entered samādhi and performing a miracle, lifted the Land of Delight out of its place with his right hand and set it down on the ground.

Then Śakyamuni Buddha addressed his great assembly, saying, "Friends, do you see the Abhirati paradise, the tathāgata Buddha Unshakeable, and the splendors of his land, the purity of the practices carried out by his bodhisattvas, the purity of his śrāvakas?"

All replied, "Yes, we see them."

CHAPTER 13: ON OFFERING THE DHARMA

In this chapter Śakra, the king of the Gods, is present in the sangha. He comes forward and praises the Vimalakīrtinirdeśa and vows he will support and protect those who put it into practice.

Then Buddha said to the King of the Gods: "O Lord of the gods, in former times, inconceivable ages ago, there was a Buddha

by the name of Bhaiṣajyarāja, Medicine King (藥王). At the
same time there was a Wheel-turning King by the name of
Ratnacchattra who possessed all the seven treasures and ruled
over the four continents of the world. He had one thousand
sons. At that time king Ratnacchattra came with his followers
to make offerings to the Buddha Medicine King, providing him
with all he needed for his well-being. He did this for five whole
kalpas, and when the five kalpas were over, he said to his sons,
'You too should make offerings to the Buddha with the same
deep respect as I have shown.' The thousand sons, obeying their
father's command, proceeded to make offerings to the Buddha
Medicine King for another five kalpas, providing him with
everything needed. One of the sons named Chandracchattra
thought to himself: 'I and my children are practicing generosity
in this lifetime and have done so in many previous lifetimes
without knowing what is the most valuable way to practice
generosity.' Then thanks to the spiritual power of the Buddha,
there came from outer space the voice of a god saying: 'Making
offerings of the Right Dharma is the most valuable offering of
all.' Prince Chandracchattra then went in search of the Buddha
Medicine King to ask how one could make offerings of the
Dharma.

"The Tathāgata replied: 'Son of a good family, the sutras of deep
meaning spoken by the Buddha are difficult to believe in and to
accept by people of the world. They are wonderful but difficult
to see. They are pure and unsullied. You will not understand
them by using discriminatory thinking.

'If someone hears these sutras, has faith in them, understands,
accepts, memorizes, and preserves them, reads, recites, and uses
the power of skillful means and analysis to teach them, that

is making the offering of the Dharma. If someone gives clear instructions for living beings to practice them, then they are preserving and protecting the Right Dharma; that is offering the Dharma.'"

Among all the ways of offering the Dharma the most precious is the offering of action. This means putting into practice the teachings that the Buddha has transmitted. For example,

'Someone understands interdependent origination and lives according to that understanding. Someone abandons wrong views and embraces the understanding of no-birth. Someone goes beyond the idea of self and what belongs to self, relies on the spirit of the sutras rather than the word, relies on intuitive insight rather than habitual patterns of thought, relies on the sutras of the deep teachings, rather than the teachings that are not deep, relies on the teachings not on the person who gives them, ... that is called the higher way of offering the Dharma.'

"The prince vowed to ordain as a monk in order to practice when he had heard this teaching, and not long after he become enlightened."

This is a Jātaka or previous birth story of something that had happened in ancient times. Buddha Śākyamuni recalled it to prove that protecting the Right Dharma, offering the Right Dharma and sharing the Right Dharma are the most valuable of all the actions of giving. Buddha lets us know that King Ratnacchattra of that time has now become the Buddha Ratnārcis and the prince Chandracchattra of that time is a former life of Buddha Śākyamuni. This chapter has shown us clearly that the gift of the Dharma is a very precious gift, the most valuable of all gifts.

If we are able to receive and hand on the essential message of the Vimalakīrtinirdeśa without being caught in its discriminatory ideas, the merit resulting from this action is immeasurable.

CHAPTER 14: ENTRUSTING

The meaning of the title of this chapter is to entrust the responsibility of preserving the teachings of the Vimal-akīrtinirdeśa and transmitting them to future generations. Śākyamuni Buddha knows that bodhisattva Maitreya will take his place in continuing to teach and transform beings in the sahā world so the Buddha counsels him to take care of the learning, preserving, and transmitting of the teachings of the Vimalakīrtinirdeśa.

"Maitreya, I now entrust to you this highest, right, and equal awakening that has been gathered over countless millions of long eons. In the age after the Buddha has passed into parinir-vāṇa, use your supernatural spiritual power to preserve sutras such as this and disseminate them throughout the continent of Jambudvīpa not allowing them to disappear. Why? Because in the ages to come there will be good men and good women, as well as gods, nāgas, and other beings, who will give rise to the aspiration for the highest, right, and equal awakening and

delight in the Dharma. If they are unable to hear sutras such
as this, they will lose the opportunity to gain their excellent
benefits."

In this chapter we are shown the difficulties that
people who taught the Dharma in the time of the com-
pilation of the Vimalakīrtinirdeśa encountered. The
details show us the difficulties that presented themselves
to those teaching the Mahāyāna in the first and second
centuries CE.

Buddha told the bodhisattva Maitreya: *"Maitreya,*
you should understand that there are two types of bodhisat-
tvas. What are these two types? The first type is attracted to
words and beautiful literary forms. The second is not afraid
of deeper teachings of the sutras and is able to enter into the
true meaning."

Two different tendencies can generally be attributed
to bodhisattvas. In the first case a bodhisattva is attracted
to beautiful and good expression in words (bodhisattvas
are poets and writers). In the second case the bodhisattva is not afraid of new ideas. They may like well-
phrased and pleasing verbal expression, but they bring
out from the beautiful phraseology the deep ideas in
order to learn from them, put them into practice, and
realize the practice of them.

"The bodhisattvas who just like the well-phrased and pleasing
verbal expression are bodhisattvas new to the practice. Those
who know how to make good use of deep and wonderful

teachings and without fear penetrate the deeper meaning and,
having heard these teachings, put them into practice, are those
who have been practicing for a long time.

"Maitreya, there are two attitudes of bodhisattvas new to the
practice which prevent them from penetrating the deep teachings. The first is that there are sutras that have a deep meaning
that the bodhisattva has not heard before. When they hear
these teachings for the first time they develop an attitude of
doubt and fear. So they do not rejoice in these sutras. They say:
'I have never heard these teachings before. Where do they come
from?'"

This is a weakness to which a new bodhisattva is subject. Although you have never heard or read such ideas,
this sutra could contain many precious jewels, so do not
develop an attitude of doubt. Open yourself to receive it.

"The second attitude is that when they meet those who preserve,
uphold, understand, and expound profound sutras of this type,
they are unwilling to come close to them, to offer them alms or
treat them with respect, but at times may even criticize them
before others. Where you find these two attitudes, you may
be sure those who hold them are new bodhisattvas. They do
injury to themselves and cannot train their minds to accept the
Dharma."

The second attitude to avoid is that when you encounter someone who is transmitting, reciting, or teaching a
sutra with new ideas, you discriminate against it, criticize it, and refuse to draw near to receive the teachings.

This is another harmful attitude that the new bodhisattva should not adopt.

This section shows us that in first and second centuries CE, the teachings of the Vimalakīrtinirdeśa had still not been accepted widely by the people. The sutra calls on students of the sutras to have an open mind. Do not be in a hurry to condemn sutras with a deep and revolutionary meaning. Be open to accept them. Do not discriminate against people who transmit such sutras. Rather, you should support them.

Maitreya bodhisattva said: "World-Honored One, your words are extraordinary, your words are wonderful. I shall avoid the faults you have spoken about and strive to preserve the Dharma that leads to the highest, right, and equal awakening that the Tathāgata has accumulated over numberless eons. If in the ages to come there are good men and good women who seek the Mahāyāna, I will see to it that deep sutras on the ultimate meaning such as this come into their hands.

IV

CONCLUSION:

THE ESSENCE OF THE

VIMALAKĪRTINIRDEŚA

THE IDEAS

Now is the time to summarize the teachings and special characteristics of the sutra. We know that the Vimalakīrtinirdeśa first appeared in the second half of the second century CE, 150–200 years after the birth of Christ. Although the original Sanskrit version has been lost, the Vimalakīrtinirdeśa in Sanskrit has been quoted a great deal in sutras and commentaries that appeared later on so that today we can still read many sections of the sutra in the original Sanskrit.

The Vimalakīrtinirdeśa shares with other sutras of the early Mahāyāna many ideas. Here we list the ideas found in the Prajñāpāramitā collection, that are also found in the Vimalakīrtinirdeśa.

1. *All dharmas are without a self-nature. They do not have a separate self.*

In chapter three Vimalakīrti says: "*If you want to give a correct explanation of suffering, you have to realize the truth that the five skandhas do not have a separate self. There is no true self to be found in any of them.*"

In the Heart Sutra (in the new translation by the Venerable Thich Nhat Hanh): "*That is why in emptiness, body, feelings, perceptions, mental formations, and consciousness are not separate self-entities.*"

2. *All dharmas are unborn and undying, not produced (anutpanna) and not destroyed (aniruddha).*

A bodhisattva explains in chapter nine of the Vimalakīrtinirdeśa: "*But if one sees the true nature of birth and death, one sees that there is no birth or death.*"

In the Heart Sutra: "*all phenomena bear the mark of emptiness; their true nature is the nature of no-birth, no-death....*"

3. *All dharmas are originally silent of all concepts and quiescent. All are already by nature in nirvāṇa.*

"Quiescent" here means they do not belong to pairs of opposing concepts like: perfect/imperfect, born/dying. The meaning of quiescent is similar to the meaning of nirvāṇa.

In chapter three Vimalakīrti says: "*If you want to talk about nirvāṇa and cessation, you should know the truth that all phenomena are all lying in their nirvāṇa nature already.*"

4. *All dharmas are signless (animitta) and inexpressible (anabhilapya).*

In chapter five Vimalakīrti says: "*My sickness has no form. It is signless.*"

In the Vajracchedikāprajñāpāramitā Sutra: *The Buddha said to Subhuti, "In a place where there are signs, in that place there is deception. If you can see the signless nature of signs, you can see the Tathagata.*"

5. *All dharmas are equal (sama) and nondual (advaya).*

The teaching of nonduality is stressed many times in the Vimalakīrtinirdeśa. In fact a whole chapter is devoted to it.

In the verses on the Middle Way reflecting the Prajñāpāramitā, Nagārjuna has a famous verse that states that there is no difference between nirvāṇa and saṃsāra. (Chapter 25, verse 20.)

In the gāthā praising the Buddha that the layman Ratnakāra speaks in chapter one, he says: "*The Buddha has penetrated the equalness of all dharmas.*"

In the Vimalakīrtinirdeśa are frequent references to skillful means. All dharmas can be used to lead to the inconceivable liberation (acintya vimokṣa). They are the ways of transforming and liberating living beings that we are not able to measure with our minds. Bodhisattvas can liberate living beings in ways that our ordinary rational ways of thinking cannot understand.

The sutra wants to tell us that although someone is a layperson it does not stop them from making a significant contribution to the transformation and liberation of living beings. A king, a minister of government, a Prime Minister, a woman, a child, a prostitute, a politician can transform and liberate living beings without ordinary people knowing. A bodhisattva can go into wine bars and casinos to transform and liberate beings and those of narrow vision will not recognize them and what they are doing. They can use time and space, making a long age last only seven days. They can make a second into an eternity in order to liberate and transform living beings, and living beings do not know it.

A bodhisattva can even manifest as Māra to transform and liberate people who think the bodhisattva is truly Māra.

In short, bodhisattvas can use ways that people could not imagine to liberate living beings, and that is what is meant by inconceivable liberation.

HANDING ON THE TEACHINGS

We have seen how the Vimalakīrtinirdeśa hands on the teachings of the Prajñāpāramitā Sutras. It also has elements shared with the Avataṃsaka Sutra and makes them more concrete.

Here "making concrete" means that the Vimalakīrtinirdeśa presents the teachings of the Prajñāpāramitā and Avataṃsaka Sutras as ways of action, ways of life, and concrete practices—the practices of a bodhisattva who wants to rescue all beings from their suffering.

The Prajñāpāramitā and Avataṃsaka Sutras present the truth of interdependent origination in their own ways. "All events and all phenomena are present because of interdependent origination. So they have no real separate self and they are empty." This is the doctrine of Prajñāpāramitā. In the Avataṃsaka Sutra all events and all phenomena are also present because of interdependent origination. In the Vimalakīrtinirdeśa, however, interdependence is expressed in terms like: "*I am sick because living beings are sick*," the nonduality of the lotus and the mud, of the sahā world and the Buddha land.

You could say that when we study the Prajñāpāramitā, we see emptiness as the ground of being. The teaching of emptiness is to help us not be caught in the idea of being. The teaching of emptiness is specifically to help us correct our wrong perception of being.

When we enter the Avataṃsaka world we see that True Emptiness has become Wonderful Being. The world of Avataṃsaka is a world of light and wonder. Whatever takes place in the Avataṃsaka world is wonderful. The people are beautiful, the flowers are beautiful, the Bodhi tree is beautiful. When we have realized True Emptiness we can dwell in Wonderful Being.

When studying the Vimalakīrtinirdeśa, we see that although it takes ideas from both the Prajñāpāramitā and Avataṃsaka Sutras, it is closer to the Avataṃsaka because it is more practical and uses elaborate and beautiful imagery to take us into many worlds. The Avataṃsaka Sutra had an enormous influence on the Vimalakīrtinirdeśa.

The aim of the Vimalakīrtinirdeśa is to argue against the doctrine of the śrāvaka vehicle with the heaviest kind of artillery that the householder Vimalakīrti can manufacture. He does not treat anyone with consideration.

The artillery that the Vimalakīrtinirdeśa sends into the citadel of the lesser vehicle was the heaviest artillery that the Mahāyāna of that time could muster.

Although it takes the Prajñāpāramitā as its backdrop, its attitude is never one of negating. On the contrary the Vimalakīrti goes along with the Avataṃsaka in proclaiming the truth of Wonderful Being. In the Vimalakīrtinirdeśa the view of the Pure Land and the view of the world is presented very clearly. Whether a land is beautiful or full of suffering, our environment and our environmental retribution are all determined by our personality. Our world is as our mind is. Therefore we do not need to run away, we only need to change our state of mind and adjust our mental attitude. When our mind is purified, any world can be the Pure Land.

In the Vimalakīrtinirdeśa the basis is our life in the present moment. The sutra teaches us to dwell where we are. Our two feet should be firmly on the earth of this world. Never try to escape, even to a Pure Land, because the Pure Land can only be produced by our mind. The Vimalakīrti gives significance to our life as it is now and does not aim at running away from suffering to another world of bliss. Everything depends on how we live today. Whether our life today is the Pure Land, the sahā world, peace and joy, suffering, liberation, or the impurity of the afflictions, all depends on our attitude and our personality and our way of living in the present moment.

The principle of inconceivable liberation and skillful means is the same. This teaches us that we should not distance ourselves from society. We should live in the midst of our society. We have to plant the lotuses in the mud of the pond. Out of this mud the most beautiful lotuses will bloom. It is only in this world of afflictions that we can attain liberation and nirvāṇa. The self-centeredness and self desire which we see as ugly and unclean can, if we know how to use them, become the kind of compost from which the flowers of Buddhahood and the mind of love can grow.

THE AIM OF THE SUTRA

The aim of the Vimalakīrti is to attack the śrāvaka vehicle and it has no hesitation in making the Venerable Śāriputra its target. The Venerable Śāriputra represents what was considered to be the substance of the lesser vehicle. We could say that the Vimalakīrtinirdeśa is the result of a movement to resist the idealization of the monastic life. Buddhism is not reserved for monks and nuns. It is not a path for monks and nuns who are weary of this world and looking for the peace and joy of an individual nirvāṇa. Buddhism is the path for all human beings and other species to enjoy. If we are not skillful we can turn Buddhism into an ideology for a minority who are monks and nuns and it will lose its nature of being open to all.

The intention of the Buddha is that all realms of life, not only the human species, but the animal, vegetal, and mineral species as well can participate in a life of peace, joy, and purity that arises from our mind. The aim of the Buddha is not to give the opportunity for a small group of practitioners to enter peace, joy, and purity for themselves alone.

There were a number of people who wanted to turn Buddhism into an ideology, a path for just a small number of monks and nuns, and therefore Buddhism could not be engaged in the world. We could say that the Vimalakīrtinirdeśa reflects a movement of laypeople who opposed a monastic ideology that made Buddhism a tool available to monks and nuns alone. What made this more serious was that some of these monks and nuns were just interested in their own advantage.

Of course there were monks and nuns who thought in a similar way to Vimalakīrti, and in the movement for a more engaged Buddhism there was also the participation of monks. Nevertheless we have to say that the majority of people involved in this movement were laypeople who wanted to bring Buddhism out of its ivory tower of monastic idealism. This idealism propounded that laypeople only needed to make offerings in order to have merit. They could not participate in practicing what the Buddha taught.

READING AND UNDERSTANDING THE VIMALAKĪRTINIRDEŚA

When we study the sutras, especially the famous ones like the Lotus Sutra, Srīmāladevi-siṃhanāda, or Vimal-akīrtinirdeśa, we do so with the preconceived idea that many scholars and high monks have commented on them. Therefore we think that if we do not base our understanding on these commentaries and the masters who have gone before us, we shall never be able to understand the sutras. This is a way of thinking that we need to re-examine. Of course we should read the commentaries of the masters of old. Nevertheless each one of us has our independent means of understanding and we should have trust in our own capacity to understand. That is our own Buddha nature—the awakened nature that is innate in all of us. The independent capacity of understanding is the most precious thing human beings have.

When reading a sutra, the first thing we have to do is use our own independent vision in our approach to understanding it. If we think that without reading the commentary first we shall never understand the sutra, we have underestimated our independent capacity to understand or, in other words, our own Buddha nature. In *The Admonitions and Encouragements of Master Guishan** (part of the novice disciplinary code) there are the following words: "Others have been heroes, I can do likewise." We should not underestimate ourselves so that we regress and inhibit our capacity.

What I suggest is that we should not be in a hurry to attach ourselves to the commentaries of old. When we come to study the sutra, we should do so with all our heart and confidence in our own mental capacity. If we can encounter the Buddha directly it is best to do so; we should not come to Buddha through Śāriputra and Maudgalyāyana. The sutra is the teaching of the Buddha. Our mind is also the Buddha. When these two Buddhas meet each other there is a sympathy between them and the dialogue is very deep. This does not mean that we ignore the way of looking at the commentary of others, including that of our ancestral teachers and our present teacher. We can read or listen to them to know how they understand the sutra. Nevertheless, we do not

---

* Thich Nhat Hanh, *The Admonitions and Encouragements of Master Guishan: Text and* Commentary, Parallax Press, 2022.

need to understand the sutra in exactly the same way as our teacher does. If it was like that there could never be any progress. We should always be going back into past discoveries. Why? Because how can we understand our teacher's way of understanding 100 percent? At the most we shall understand 99 percent, and our own disciples at the most will understand 98 percent and over successive generations the understanding will continue to decrease. We have to have our own understanding, and that understanding will be our root teacher. We shall transmit all we have of our own understanding to our students, and they will not be satisfied and will then go on to make their own discoveries. This is the method I have used during fifty years of studying Buddhist sutras.

When we study the Vimalakīrtinirdeśa we should come to it as the original text that has not yet been commented on. In the past our spiritual ancestors did not have the opportunities or conditions as we have to be in touch with many different traditions of Buddhism. A student of Buddhism born in China could only be in touch with the Chinese tradition of Buddhism. One born in Tibet would only know about the Tibetan tradition and know very little or nothing about the Thai or Vietnamese Buddhist tradition. Therefore people were molded in their own tradition and could only understand the Buddha and the sutras according to their own tradition. In our own time, the doors of all traditions are open and we have many opportunities to visit other traditions. Each tradition has its own point of view and way of looking. It has its own historical and philological data to shine light on the path of the practitioner. If many different rays of light can shine together on the subject of our research, we can discover things that the ancestral teachers of the past were not able to discover. The ancestral teachers in the past had only one source of light.

At present in the West we have to be very happy that all the Buddhist traditions from 2,500 years are beginning to be present. It is not difficult for us to study and learn about these traditions. Through what we learn from different traditions we can have a wider view of what already lies in our own tradition. Those who study Buddhism in our own time should profit from these advantages.

Our predecessors who studied the sutras in the past gave much weight to the ideas and thoughts contained in the sutras. They were very little concerned with historical evidence. In our own time, thanks to historiological and philological research, we can discover many facts that were not available to our predecessors. During the last two hundred years, new discoveries of ancient Buddhist texts have been made in Central Asia and Nepal. There are scientific methods for dating these manuscripts. We should know how to make good use of these discoveries in comparing different versions of the sutra. In the Dunhuang caves of western China, many Buddhist texts have recently been discovered. The Buddhist congregation in Taiwan have reprinted these texts and we can compare them with the versions that are presently found in the Buddhist canon. This kind of scholarship is very necessary.

Apart from historiological studies, philological studies are also very important. We can make many new and interesting discoveries through philology. If we want to know about the origins of a race we can use both historiological and philological studies to help us. The same is true for Buddhist texts. Philological studies can help us establish the place and date of origin of the text. We know which version is early and which is later.

In the Ugraparipṛccha, the content concerns the monastic and the lay bodhisattva. When this sutra appeared, the bodhisattva precepts had not yet been formulated. The Mahāyāna Brahmajāla Sutra, which is the text that formulates these precepts, appeared after the Ugraparipṛccha in which the lay bodhisattva practices only the five mindfulness trainings. This comparative dating of sutras was something that Buddhist masters of old knew nothing about.

When I lived in Paris, I taught Buddhism through historiological and philological studies in the École Pratique des Hautes Études. I belonged to the Faculty of History and Philology. During this time I discovered many interesting facts. For example I discovered that the Eminent Master Tuệ Trung (thirteenth century

Vietnam) was the blood brother of the hero Trần Hưng Đao and not his son as people had previously thought. Scholars in Hanoi have now accepted that this is so. This discovery was only possible by the historiological and philological comparison of various historical texts.

A Buddhist scholar of our time must know how to use historical and philological studies. They have to use analytical methods. They have to discover more about what they are interested in. There has to be curiosity and a desire to discover something new for their studies to go far. On the other hand, if you only want to know about the ideas of the ancestral teachers concerning the various sutras, you will simply be a slave your whole life, very faithful to your master but unable to make any new discoveries to light up the path for generations to come. You can transmit what you have received but you cannot contribute to any new advance or discovery. The strength of Buddhism is its ability to open up new paths of discovery. Buddha was not satisfied with the spiritual path that had been handed down from previous generations. It was his deep aspiration to find a new way, and he rejected the throne of his father in order to make new discoveries and hand them on to future generations. As we read the sutras, we should follow the example of the Buddha in making new discoveries.

RELATED TITLES BY THICH NHAT HANH

The Admonitions and Encouraging Words of Master Guishan

The Art of Living

At Home in the World

Awakening of the Heart

The Blooming of a Lotus

Cultivating the Mind of Love

Enjoying the Ultimate

Fragrant Palm Leaves

Freedom Wherever We Go

Happiness

The Heart of the Buddha's Teaching

Inside the Now

Interbeing

Joyfully Together

Living Buddha, Living Christ

Old Path White Clouds

Peaceful Action, Open Heart

Present Moment Wonderful Moment

Stepping into Freedom

The Other Shore

Understanding Our Mind

Zen and the Art of Saving the Planet

Zen Battles

Monastics and visitors practice the art of mindful living in the tradition of Thich Nhat Hanh at our mindfulness practice centers around the world. To reach any of these communities, or for information about how individuals, couples, and families can join in a retreat, please contact:

PLUM VILLAGE
33580 Dieulivol, France
plumvillage.org

LA MAISON DE L'INSPIR
77510 Villeneuve-sur-Bellot, France
maisondelinspir.org

HEALING SPRING
MONASTERY
77510 Verdelot, France
healingspringmonastery.org

MAGNOLIA GROVE
MONASTERY
Batesville, MS 38606, USA
magnoliagrovemonastery.org

BLUE CLIFF MONASTERY
Pine Bush, NY 12566, USA
bluecliffmonastery.org

DEER PARK MONASTERY
Escondido, CA 92026, USA
deerparkmonastery.org

EUROPEAN INSTITUTE OF
APPLIED BUDDHISM
D-51545 Waldbröl, Germany
eiab.eu

THAILAND PLUM VILLAGE
Nakhon Ratchasima
30130 Thailand
thaiplumvillage.org

ASIAN INSTITUTE OF
APPLIED BUDDHISM
Lantau Island, Hong Kong
pvfhk.org

STREAM ENTERING
MONASTERY
Porcupine Ridge, Victoria 3461
nhapluu.org

MOUNTAIN SPRING
MONASTERY
Bilpin, NSW 2758, Australia
mountainspringmonastery.org

For information visit: *plumvillage.org*
To find an online sangha visit: *plumline.org*
For more resources, try the Plum Village app: *plumvillage.app*
Social media: *@thichnhathanh @plumvillagefrance*

PALM LEAVES PRESS aims to develop a complete catalog of the scholarly works of Thich Nhat Hanh to contribute to the study and practice of Engaged Buddhism and Applied Buddhism, to share what spiritual practice can offer to counteract social injustice and climate change, to develop a global ethic, and to facilitate the awakening of the collective consciousness. Infused with the rich tradition of Vietnamese Buddhism, Palm Leaves Press's mission is to preserve Thich Nhat Hanh's legacy so his teachings can continue to nourish practitioners now and for many generations in the future.

THE MINDFULNESS BELL, a journal of the art of mindful living in the tradition of Thich Nhat Hanh, is published three times a year by our community. To subscribe or to see the worldwide directory of Sanghas (local mindfulness groups), visit mindfulnessbell.org.

AROUND
MANCHESTER
Guide

PETER HADDINGTON

Willow
PUBLISHING

First published in 1990
by Willow Publishing
36 Moss Lane, Timperley
Altrincham, Cheshire, WA15 6SZ

© Peter Haddington 1990

ISBN 0 946361 31 2

Printed by The Commercial Centre Ltd.
Clowes Street, Oldham

Cover photograph: City of Manchester
Town Crier Douglas Britton

*Whilst every care has been taken to
ensure the accuracy of the information
contained in this book, neither the
publishers nor the author can accept
any responsibility for any errors or
ommissions.*

CONTENTS

INTRODUCTION *5*
MANCHESTER *6*
SALFORD *30*
WIGAN *38*
BOLTON *44*
BURY *56*
ROCHDALE *62*
OLDHAM *70*
TAMESIDE *76*
DERBYSHIRE *82*
STOCKPORT *88*
TRAFFORD *98*
CHESHIRE *104*
INDEX *128*
TOURIST INFORMATION
CENTRES *129*
ACKNOWLEDGEMENTS *129*

Publishers Note:

While the places mentioned have been generally grouped within existing Borough boundaries, certain attractions have been moved into chapters for the convenience of the visitor. eg. Helmshore Textile Museum is, administratively, in Lancashire but has been included in the 'Bury' chapter.

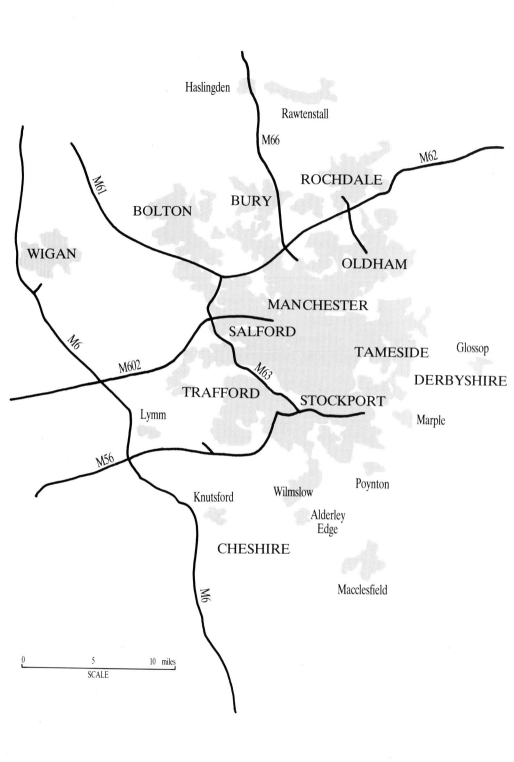

Haslingden

Rawtenstall

M66

M62

M61

ROCHDALE

BURY

BOLTON

OLDHAM

WIGAN

MANCHESTER

M6

SALFORD

TAMESIDE

Glossop

M602

M63

DERBYSHIRE

TRAFFORD

STOCKPORT

Lymm

Marple

M56

Poynton

Knutsford

Wilmslow

Alderley
Edge

CHESHIRE

M6

Macclesfield

0   5   10 miles
SCALE

INTRODUCTION

This book is designed to show people the full range of interesting afternoons-out to be enjoyed in Greater Manchester and the countryside immediately around it.

Within Manchester and the nine big metropolitan boroughs that surround it, from Rochdale in the north to Stockport in the south, there is a lot to be seen. Each town has its own heritage and tourist attractions to go with it. So the region is richer in places to see than many more rural areas of Britain.

Despite that, many people have little idea of what is on their doorstep, even if they may have lived here all their lives. They tend to go on exhausting drives to see something new, unaware of what is on the other side of Manchester. The owner of Adlington Hall, near Macclesfield, told me that some visitors to his home said they had driven through Adlington for years before they finally stopped to see the hall, being in the habit of driving 50 miles to see a stately home.

The book covers an area which extends from the moors above Bolton down to Gawsworth, just south of Macclesfield, and from Wigan in the west to the western slopes of the Pennines.

I have restricted entries to places which are likely to occupy visitors for half-an-hour, up to a full day. Therefore I have not listed most of the pretty villages around Manchester, since they do not afford an afternoon out in themselves, but are rather places to stop for a few minutes only.

The book is therefore not intended as an exhaustive account of the treasures of the area. It is a description of those treasures which are worth making a special journey to see. I have listed many museums and art galleries because they are open all year, in most cases, and are good places to go on a wet or freezing day!

Every effort has been made to ensure that the information given is accurate and up-to-date. As opening times, admission prices, and exhibits are likely to change at short notice, telephone numbers have been included so readers can check information, particularly opening times, before they set out. I hope this book will prove a handy aid for years so that you will never be at a loss for somewhere to go.

Chinese Arch, George Street

MANCHESTER

The city has a range of splendid free-of-charge attractions, including Heaton Hall and Wythenshawe Hall. Here, however, are a few suggestions for city centre viewing.

At George Street, in the Chinatown area, a stone's throw from Piccadilly, stands the fantastic Chinese Arch. It is a riot of colour and as high as a house and fronts a small Chinese garden with pagoda.

At the back of Marks and Spencers, off Market Street, is an ancient black and white timbered gem known as The Old Shambles. The Old Wellington Inn, and the adjoining Sinclair's Oyster Bar, were jacked up several feet in an amazing operation when the site was redeveloped. The Inn, thought to be of 1500's vintage, has had the date 1328 stuck on it to confuse us.

Another old gem, known as The Hidden Gem, is St. Mary's RC Church at Mulberry Street, off Deansgate. The G-Mex exhibition centre, created out of the former Central railway station near St. Peter's Square, is a stunning sight inside if you can manage to have a peep. It stages a wide range of exhibitions plus sports and music events. Have a look, too, inside the former Royal Exchange building at St. Ann's Square and see the extraordinary theatre in the round they constructed in the middle of the floor.

If you are in the Oxford Street area there may be something on show at the Corner House arts centre, which has a cafe. And, of course, Manchester's Arndale shopping precinct is a truly vast place. It dwarfs the region's other shopping centres.

Old Shambles

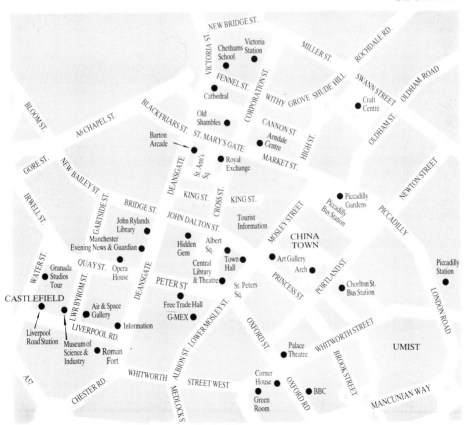

Manchester City Art Gallery, Mosley Street

A tremendous display of 'Old Masters' is here—many so large that they would fill your lounge wall from floor to ceiling! Outside the national gallery collections, the collections at Manchester and Liverpool are regarded as Britain's best in public ownership.

At Mosley Street the City Art Gallery has room to display only part of its stocks. The Gallery is noted for its pre-Raphaelites, Turners, Stubbs, and Dutch collection. And not forgetting The Crucifixion, attributed to Duccio di Buoninsegna, worth £1·8 million).

City Art Gallery Extension, Princess Street

More pictures, including modern art, can be found in what was once a gentlemen's club, The Athenaeum.

Gallery opening times: Mon.–Sat., 10 am–6 pm. Admission Free. Tel: 236 5244

National Museum of Labour History

It is housed in the Mechanics Institute, the first meeting place of the TUC in 1868. There is a colourful display of banners, badges, posters and everyday objects. See

the worlds largest collection of banners being conserved along with a changing programme of temporary exhibitions on both contemporary and historic themes.

103 Princess Street. Open Wed.–Sat.,10–5 pm, Sun. 2–5 pm.
Bank holiday Mons. 10 – 5 pm. Tel: 228 7212.

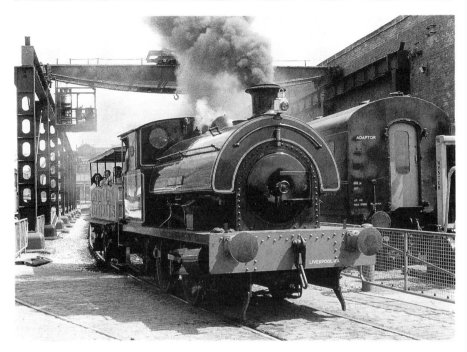

Castlefield Urban Heritage Park

The Greater Manchester Museum of Science and Industry occupies what was the Liverpool Road railway station of 1830 and its carriage shed and warehouses. In addition the Castlefield canal basin,where the Bridgewater and Rochdale canals meet, has been cleaned up and is an impressive sight, straddled by railway viaducts. The Grocers' warehouse beside the canal has been reconstructed to first floor level and you can walk through and look down on an excellent reconstruction of the historic machinery that was used to lift coal from canal to street level. Coal was brought here from the Duke of Bridgewater's mines at Worsley.

▊ UNDERGROUND MANCHESTER

Here you can walk through a section of main sewer of the type laid under Manchester streets. This exhibition explores the city beneath our feet and describes the horrors of poor sanitation and living conditions in the 19th century.

▊ THE MAKING OF MANCHESTER

Like the sewer show, this exhibition is housed in Liverpool Road station's old carriage shed, now reconstructed. This display presents a fascinating social history of Manchester and shows how the city grew.

▊ XPERIMENT!

Visitors are able to carry out experiments involving light and power, including a photographic feature that freezes your shadow on the wall. There are some 30 to 40 working models in this gallery.

Castlefield Urban Heritage Park (continued)

■ POWER HALL

Working engines are a fascinating sight and they are stars of this impressive show in an equally impressive hall which gives everyone plenty of space.

People look hypnotised as they watch the Firgrove Mill engine from Rochdale, with its steam boiler and huge thrusting shaft. Then there is the enormous Haydock beam engine from a colliery, possibly 150 years old, for which a replica brick engine house has been built in the hall. Also working busily is an undershot water wheel from a mill at Otley.

The exhibition shows some of the inventions that helped to make Greater Manchester the world's first industrial region. It includes a huge South African Railways' articulated loco, built by Beyer Peacock of Gorton between the wars, the largest class of engine to be made in Europe. There are veteran cars and a Rolls-Royce jet engine, plus a cute Isle of Man Railways' engine. And you can view textile and paper-making machinery in a separate gallery plus an exhibition of machine tools.

■ ELECTRICITY EXHIBITION

The big surprise here is the full scale power station interior specially built into the old railway warehouse. From the steel catwalks you look down on a generator moved here from Bolton's Back o'th' Bank power station after its closure.

The other galleries tell of the history of electricity generation, from the first public electricity supply service at Godalming, Surrey, in 1881. There is a steam turbine built by Charles Parsons—his invention in 1884 was to revolutionise electricity generation. There are also kitchens and living-rooms containing typical furniture and electrical appliances of 1935 and 1955.

■ AIR AND SPACE GALLERY

Here is a wonderful show which is mainly a collection of military aircraft from the Air Force Museum at Hendon. The exhibits are housed in the Lower Campfield Market, which was used as the City Exhibition Hall for many years.

The newest attraction is the major civil aviation display, the flight deck of a Trident airliner open to the public to inspect, with a video charting the history of Trident.

Military aircraft include a Supermarine Spitfire MK VB fighter bomber used in squadron service in 1942 and 1943. This was the most widely used Spitfire. Locally made planes include a replica Avro triplane of 1908, which produced the first British

sustained flight. One smaller exhibit I found of particular interest was a one-seater Japanese Navy suicide aircraft of 1945. They were launched at targets, with their doomed pilots, from a bomber at 11,500 feet.

Don't miss the space exhibits on the gallery above—they include a 20ft long model of a Space Shuttle and Tom Stafford's 1966 Earth Orbit space suit. There is also a section on the famous trans-Atlantic flight by Alcock and Brown which won them a £10,000 prize in 1919.

Greater Manchester Museum of Science and Industry Tel: 832 2244

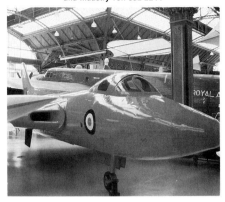

■ ROMAN FORT

The Romans built a fort at Castlefield around AD79 and later rebuilt the wood and turf structure in stone. The North Gate of the fort has been reconstructed in stone and includes a guardroom over the gate, furnished in Roman style. In summer you might meet guides dressed in Roman military costume (a Flixton couple who dress in Roman garb at home and enjoy special Roman feasts in their semi-detached have helped to man the ramparts).

A second section of Roman wall, with a terrace, has been constructed near the North Gate, and foundations of the village that stood in front of the fort are on show. A new Roman exhibition can be seen in Castlefield Visitors' Centre.

Granada Studios Tour

Since television is the most popular entertainment ever devised, Europe's first TV studios guided tour could hardly fail to be a success.

Allow at least three hours if you want to see everything on the $3\frac{1}{2}$ acre site and have a drink or a meal. The guided tour itself lasts about 90 minutes. It starts with a visit to the mega production control panel, and a mock-up studio featuring the original Minnie Caldwell 'snug' in the Rover's Return.

In the next room I found myself pictured on a TV screen as the surprised party was ushered on to a large, storm tossed raft in an eccentric audience participation slot. We were then shown a mock-up of the stars' make-up room, and a typical star's dressing room, followed by the costume department (with its own ghost). The visitors seemed impressed by a planetarium style

presentation of Los Angeles by night. A Downing Street set was followed by the Baker Street interior used to make the Sherlock Holmes films.

The children were intrigued by the enormous Goliath like furniture from the set used to make *The Return of the Antelope*. The indoor part of the tour is completed with a jungle walk representing the TV series *The Disappearing World*.

Once outdoors you board one of the cute double-decker trams (fitted with bus wheels, ditto engine and no rails) which crawls past the Baker Street set, with the Great Detective's home in the middle. Then the tram stopped at the Berlin "Checkpoint Charlie" border post. A highlight of the tour was the sinister 'German' guard who boarded and demanded to see our tickets, stared sternly at us and made sarcastic remarks. We survived the interrogation to walk over the cobbles on the famous Coronation Street set, built with bricks from a demolished Salford street. (You can often see them filming outdoor scenes on Monday mornings.)

The Coronation Street museum at the Graffiti Club contains a big photographic exhibition, plus mementos of the stars and the original Hilda Ogden living-room set with its famous wall ducks. The tour ends at the full-size House of Commons set, used for the filming of Jeffery Archer's novel "First Among Equals".

In addition to the guided tour extras include a cinema show about the history of

film making, and a replica of the Rover's Return in which you can drink and pretend you are Mike Baldwin. In a little room not far away you can pose and see yourself on screen in a Rover's Return scene with members of the cast, taking part in an exchange of lines with them.

There is an admission charge and entrance is in Water Street, at the bottom of Quay Street. There is a big car park opposite the entrance, plus other car parks not far away. For year round opening times ring 061-833 0880. From April to the end of September the site is open seven days a week. From October to March, Wednesdays to Sundays.

The Booking Hall

Liverpool Road Station

Stand in the spacious booking hall and imagine the excitement on September 15, 1830, when the Prime Minister, the Duke of Wellington, came to open the world's first passenger railway station here.

The Duke arrived from Liverpool on a train pulled by George Stephenson's famous locomotive, Rocket. Unfortunately a mob that was apparently protesting about the Peterloo Massacre, in Manchester 11 years previously, looked so menacing that the Duke did not get off the train. He went back to Liverpool and missed a banquet in Manchester!

The booking hall that has been preserved was for first-class passengers only. The second-class peasants had their own booking hall and walked up separate stairs to the trains. First-class carriages were fully boxed-in from the weather— everyone else had open carriages and had to suffer the rain, soot and engine sparks.

The triumphant opening was marred by the death of William Huskinsson,

President of the Board of Trade, who was run over at Liverpool by Rocket. This loco, which won the Rainhill Trials in 1829, worked on the Manchester to Liverpool line until 1836.

At the station, lifesize figures dressed in period costume are on view, plus a small exhibition of Liverpool–Manchester souvenirs. And you can sit down and view an interesting colour slide show about the construction of the line and the great men who planned what was, for that time, a staggering engineering achievement.

Liverpool Road station soon lost its passenger traffic when Hunts Bank (now Victoria station) opened in 1844. Liverpool Road was kept open as a goods traffic centre until after the second world war, and so survived intact.

Passenger traffic has returned to Liverpool Road now that tourists are given short steam train rides past the old station, on a standard gauge track. The open wooden cattle truck-style carriages are like the 1830's rolling stock.

Manchester Town Hall

Opened in 1877, this monolithic Gothic building, crowned with a clock tower 286 feet high, cost a million pounds, a lot of money in Victorian days. The big Town Hall extension was built in 1938. A highlight of the tour is the Great Hall, the walls of which are covered by 12 mural paintings by Ford Maddox Brown. They depict famous men and incidents in Manchester's proud history.

You also see the Lord Mayor's Parlour. Visitors see the banqueting room with its minstrels' gallery, the council chamber, conference hall, and other rooms. There is much fine original furniture, and even the corridors offer beauties in stone.

From Monday to Friday there are usually free guided tours of what is one of the largest and most impressive town halls in Britain. Anyone can turn up without prior notice, although occasionally tours are cancelled if the Town Hall is in special use. Ring the information office (234 3074) if you wish to check.

Central Library

Next to the Albert Square civic centre stands Manchester's fantastic circular Central Library. It is worth inspecting inside even if you do not open a book.

Rochdale Canal Walk

See Manchester city centre from a new angle—by walking along the towpath of the disused Rochdale Canal. One point to join the canal is at Whitworth Street West, between Deansgate railway station and Albion Street.

A gap in the wall near Albion Street gives access to steps down to the towpath. Turn right to walk between office blocks and old warehouses to Princess Street, where the towpath finishes temporarily. Follow the canal along Canal Street to the bridge at Minshull Street. From here there is more towpath which ends at Dale Street because of a wall built over it.

Grocers Warf, Castlefield

A 'hidden' exit brings you onto Dale Street for a short street diversion. Turn right along Dale Street past the old Rochdale Canal Company headquarters to China Lane. Turn right into China Lane, then along a cobbled path, turning left into Brewer Street and quickly right into Tariff Street. This leads to a bridge over the canal and access to a further towpath which takes you to Great Ancoats Street. Here you walk alongside the canal on Redhill Street to the next bridge. The towpath entrance is between some 'corkscrew' walling. From here it is plain sailing through Ancoats and Newton Heath.

This urban canal walk is more interesting than some canal walks through featureless fields. From Whitworth Street West, our starting point, you can also turn left and soon come to the Castlefield Canal Basin, recently restored.

John Rylands University Library

Most people who walk down Manchester's Deansgate never think of entering this extraordinary building, described as the best piece of modern Gothic in Europe. The majority of passers-by probably don't realise that it is open to the public.

The library is said to contain the best collection of ancient, rare books in Britain outside Oxford and Cambridge. They are not available to examine unless you are a member of the library or have a letter of recommendation from an academic institution. But interesting rare books are usually on display in the exhibition hall.

The building is worth visiting for a look at its

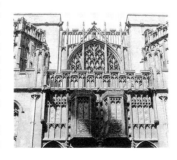

beautiful interior. The exterior is in dark red sandstone, but the interior is in Penrith sandstone or shawk, which varies in colour here from grey to red to pink.

The building was erected as the John Rylands Library between 1890 and 1899 by Mrs. Enriqueta Rylands as a memorial to her dead husband John Rylands, a noted Victorian textile manufacturer and philanthropist. The library, designed to house religious books, was built on the lines of Mansfield College. Oxford. It has the atmosphere of a cathedral and I can't remember seeing a more impressive memorial to a spouse!

In the main reading room John Rylands and

his wife still gaze at each other—they are modelled in white marble, standing at each end of the huge room. The couple lived at Longford Hall, Stretford.

The library contains manuscripts which range from the third millennium before Christ to modern times—written on every material used by man. There are papyrus collections and a fragment of St. John, the oldest New Testament extract in existence in any language (it is second century). There are illuminated manuscripts of stunning beauty.

The staff allow people doing research to examine rare books on application.
Opening times: Mon.–Fri., 10 am–5.30 pm. Sat., 10 am–1 pm. Closed Sunday. Tel: 834 5343.

The Guardian and Manchester Evening News Tours.

See the miracle of daily newspaper production by joining one of the parties that are shown behind the scenes of the Manchester Evening News or the Guardian. The free conducted tours of the Evening News starts at 1.30 pm from Monday to Friday – contact the M.E.N. Marketing Dept. 832 7200 ext. 2313. The Guardian production tour commences each week night at 7.45 pm and finishes at approximately 11.00 pm – further details re booking and numbers contact the Guardian Circulation Dept. 832 7200 ext. 2418. Visitors see the composing room as printers set stories on VDUs for the computerised typesetters. The other process departments are visited, and the tour ends with a look at the presses as they churn out the finished product.

Manchester Craft Centre

Professional craftsmen ply their fascinating trades in this 1982 conversion of a former Victorian fish market, once part of Smithfield. The glass building houses 20 shops producing jewellery, ceramics, leather work, enamelling, weaving, engraved glass and much more.

There are demonstration days and craft workshops. The cafe is open daily. The craft centre is open Tuesdays to Saturdays (but seven days a week prior to Christmas). Located between Shudehill and Tib Street in the city centre. Tel: 832 3416.

Barton Arcade, off St. Ann's Square and Deansgate

Manchester Cathedral

While most churches are shut for much of the time these days, to stop vandalism, cathedrals are still available for inspection, thank goodness. Manchester Cathedral is open all day, every day until 6.30 pm except Saturdays, when it closes around 5pm.

The Cathedral's greatest glory are the beautifully carved choir stalls, executed by Tudor craftsmen. There are 30 canopied stalls, and wood carvers were brought here from France and accommodated in Long Millgate while they weaved their magic to create the south side stalls. The north side stalls were carved by a man called Richard Bexwicke. On the miserere seats are amusing pictures. *e.g.* A man flees from his wife after dropping a jug of ale; rabbits roast a huntsman; pigs dance to bagpipes.

The Cathedral is also famous for having the widest nave in the country. The width of the building is two-thirds of its length, if you discount the front porch and a tiny chapel which sticks out at the other end.

A Saxon church originally stood here, and part of the existing structure dates from the 15th century, although many parts have been rebuilt since. In 1421 Henry V granted a charter making the church a College of Clergy, with a warden and eight fellows. The Early English nave and aisles were then rebuilt in the perpendicular Gothic style to give pier arches of great beauty and a more impressive structure.

The collegiate church became a cathedral in 1847 and it was considerably enlarged and embellished by the Victorians. One delightful touch is that the main roof beams end in 14 angels, each playing a different musical instrument.

It is, of course, worth attending services here to hear the glorious music from organist and choir. Services to attend for this

Manchester Cathedr

Chetham's School of Music

People who visit this place are often amazed to find mediaeval buildings of 1421 around a huge courtyard on a site opposite Manchester's Victoria railway station.

You can take advantage of a tour of part of this edifice in red sandstone if you attend one of the short lunchtime concerts of classical music that are held at 1.40 pm each Wednesday during term times throughout the year. The concerts are free and are frequently used as rehearsals by outstanding young musicians before important contests and other public appearances.

Concerts are given in the splendid 15th century stone hall, and guides talk about the school and lead visitors down cold, draughty corridors where monks used to pray in their freezing cells. Also visited are the audit room, with its magnificent table and Chippendale chairs, followed by a look at Chetham's Library, which was the first free library in north-west Europe. Here, towering 12 feet high, shelves made in the 17th century hold priceless books in a 70,000 volumes collection. The public can use this library but visitors must get permission.

The tour covers only one wing of the mediaeval buildings, as the main wing is in constant use by pupils. This contains the music library and studies, and a commonroom used by the 80 day pupils. The 200 or

so boarders live and sleep in nearby modern buildings, including pre-fab classrooms!

The 15th century buildings were erected as a college for priests. Then in 1653 the famous landowner and clothier, Humphrey Chetham, turned the place into a school and home for boys from poor families. When he died he endowed the school and also the library (where you can still see ancient books that were chained up to prevent theft).

Three hundred years later, in 1952, Chetham's Hospital School became a grammar school. It was only in 1969 that Chetham's was turned into a specialist school for the musically gifted.

In addition to Wednesdays, public concerts are often held on other days, but without a guided tour. For details ring 061-834 9644/7961.

Manchester Cathedral (continued)

purpose are the 10.30 am Sung Eucharist and the 3.30 pm Choral Evensong (Sundays) plus 5.30 pm services in midweek.

The Cathedral stages frequent professional concerts (phone 833 2220 for details) and its brass-rubbing centre is open every day except Sunday.

Manchester Museum

The museum has been collecting things since 1821—it's so big you can't take everything in on one visit. Even so the displays are only a part of the treasures in store. If you have children of primary school age they will enjoy the aquarium and vivarium, with its pythons, lizards, tree frogs, giant toads and so on.

The rest of the zoo's animals are all stuffed—and what an enormous collection, including a full grown Bengal tiger, lion, polar bear and bizarre animals like the giant anteater, armadillo and wombat. There's also a full gallery of British and foreign birds.

The Egyptology collection, which features 21 mummies, is the best in Britain next to those in London and Oxford. The University's Egyptian Mummy Research Project has examined in depth the human and animal mummies and developed new techniques.

Museum open Mon.–Sat., 10 am–5 pm. Closed Sunday. Admission free. Tel: 275 2634.

Manchester University and Museum

Gallery of English Costume, Platt Hall

Whitworth Art Gallery

Owned by Manchester University, this is one of Britain's leading provincial galleries and it has very large collections in store. There is an important collection of British and foreign watercolours and drawings, and the Gallery is second only to the Victoria and Albert Museum in its range of textile exhibits from many parts of the world. Other rooms feature modern art, temporary exhibitions, and an eccentric collection of historic wallpapers.

The familiar red brick gallery was gifted to the University in 1958 by the private Trust which owned it and could not afford to continue to do so. It was built with money from the will of the famous Stockport born

(Right) Wythenshawe Hall

machine tool manufacturer Sir Joseph Whitworth (1830–1887). He was the first man to introduce uniformity into screw threads.

Gallery open Mon.–Sat., 10 am–5 pm (Thurs. 10 am–9 pm). Closed Sundays. Meals available at popular Gallery bistro. The Gallery is on Oxford Road, almost opposite to Manchester Royal Infirmary. Tel: 273 4865

Gallery of English Costume, Platt Hall

Clothes dating from the 17th century to modern times are displayed at Platt Hall, which stands at the north end of Platt Fields at Rusholme.

The City Council's dress collection is the largest of its type outside the Victoria and Albert Museum, but sadly there is exhibition space for only a quarter of the clothes, so exhibits are changed from year to year.

I was intrigued by a display of stays and corsets, dating from the 1830's, to the liberty bodice of the 1930's. What a shame that women had to have their bodies squeezed into such monstrosities in the name of fashion. No wonder ribs were sometimes broken in the process! When I visited Platt Hall I saw a glittering collection of Victorian ball gowns and 1920's evening dresses. And there was a doublet of 1625 and a shirt from the same century.

Platt Hall, a red brick Palladian house built in the mid-1700's was bought with its estate by Manchester Corporation in 1908. Platt Fields was opened as a public park in 1910. The hall was later used as an art gallery until the Gallery of English Costume was opened in 1947.

Location: Junction of Wilmslow Road and Platt Lane. Opening times: Mon.–Sat., 10 am–6 pm (closed Tuesdays). Sundays, 2 pm–6 pm. Gallery closes at 4 pm November to February. Admission free. Tel: 224 5217.

Wythenshawe Hall and Park

There's plenty to see in the vast 250 acres Wythenshawe Park near the southern tip of Manchester. Wythenshawe Hall was built by the Tatton family and occupied by them from 1540 until 1926, when Robert Henry Greville Tatton sold the hall and park to Lord Simon of Wythenshawe. Simon immediately presented his magnificent purchase to the city of Manchester.

There are several rooms on view with two of real note—the dining-room and drawing-room. The dining-room is the building's most complete survival of the Tudor hall built by Robert Tatton. It contains wall paintings which celebrated a marriage that united the Tatton and Booth (Dunham Massey) families between 1540 and 1570. The dining-room was used as such from at least the 17th century.

The house contains some fine pictures, being administered as a branch of the city art galleries. There's also a gallery which houses visiting exhibitions. As part of a recent renovation the black and white face of the front was removed (it was put on in the 1940's). The timbers have been exposed and the front has been restored to give a 19th century effect.

In front of the hall, on a towering plinth, stands a statue of Oliver Cromwell, whose troops captured the hall in 1644. Behind the hall are beautiful Victorian gardens, hidden away behind walling. They are open throughout the year.

Hall opening times: Mon.–Sat., 10 am–6 pm (Closed Tuesdays). Sunday 2 pm–6 pm.
Free admission is open from the beginning of April to the first week of October.
Tel: 998 2331

Wythenshawe Park Horticultural Centre

Manchester City Council has a vast area under glass at Wythenshawe Park, open to the public almost every day throughout the year. There is a fantastic display of cacti and succulents. The tropical house contains exotic things like bananas, palms, paw-paw, pineapples. But no plants are for sale.

The park's other facilities include a big pitch and putt course, pets' corner, and large children's playground.

Park main entrance on Wythenshawe Road, Northenden (B5167). Tel: 945 1768.

Fletcher Moss Museum and Art Gallery and Parsonage Gardens

The old parsonage which houses the art gallery stands in peaceful gardens opposite Didsbury Parish Church. Palm trees which grow in front of the museum testify to the sheltered nature of the high walled garden.

There is a rose garden, glorious herbacious border, orchid house, and unusual and rare trees, shrubs and plants. The old parsonage contains an interesting collection of paintings of Manchester scenes and events, plus visiting exhibitions.

In 1884 the house, was bought by Fletcher Moss, who became a Manchester alderman. Moss, who had an obsessive love of the house and gardens, left the property and adjoining land to Manchester Corporation, on his death in 1919, for the benefit of the people of Didsbury.

Museum location: Next to the Old Cock hotel on the A5145 on the Stockport side of Didsbury village. Museum and Art Gallery open from April 1 to Early October. Mon.–Sat., 10 am–6 pm (closed Tuesdays). Sundays 2 am–6 pm. Admission free. Garden open throughout year. Tel: 445 1109.

Fletcher Moss Botanical Gardens

It is situated out of sight a few yards down the road from the Parsonage Gardens. Near the Didsbury pub you will see a sign for Fletcher Moss Park. Walk past some tennis courts here and you find yourself gazing upon the large and lovely rock garden, occupying a steep slope below you.

Paths wind between attractive specimen trees and shrubs and at the bottom there is a lily covered pond containing goldfish. It is a place of considerable charm, with sheltered corners in which to sit, and children have an exciting time exploring the intriguing little paths. There are council owned grass tennis courts for hire here.

Manchester Jewish Museum

There are no horror photographs of Nazi tyranny on view in this former synagogue. This is a charming, happy exhibition about the history of the Jews in Manchester.

Old school groups, choirs, theatrical productions and pictures of old Manchester adorn the displays. Here, for instance, are shots of Manchester's Bessie Cohen, one of the original Tiller Girls when that group was founded in the city in the 1890's. Among pictures of grinding poverty in north Manchester is a queue of men at the Jewish soup kitchen in 1930.

The museum, on Cheetham Hill Road, opened in 1984, is housed in a synagogue built by Spanish and Portuguese Jews in 1874. The striking exterior of the building is in the Moorish style, and the interior also has Moorish features. The exhibition is laid out on the balcony, while the ground floor of the building has been left as it was when used for services. You can see the Torah Scroll (Scroll of the Law) consisting of the five books of Moses on parchment, and a massive chair in which children were held down while being circumcised.

Additional temporary exhibitions are staged regularly in a rear room, and throughout the year special events are put on. Heritage Trail walks are organised from the building (for details ring 834 9879). Museum open from 10.30 am from Sunday to Thursday (closed on Friday and Saturday). Small admission charge.

Greater Manchester Museum of Transport

One of the largest collections of public service vehicles in Britain is housed in a former bus garage at the rear of GM Buses' Queens Road depot. At least 60 vehicles are on view and others are stored elsewhere.

The exhibits range from a horse bus of the 1890's to rear-engined buses of the 1970's. The museum also features a wealth of smaller exhibits, from old ticket machines to destination indicator blinds.

Ranks of beautifully restored buses sport the liveries of the 14 municipal bus undertakings which merged to form Greater Manchester Transport. There are the maroons of Oldham, Wigan and Bolton, the blues of Rochdale and Ashton, the green of Stalybridge, the red and white of Stockport and so on. There are single and double-deckers from the old North Western Road Car Company, and a bus run by Mayne's, a private operator that survived the big merger.

Boyle Street is very much a 'workshop' museum, with vehicles being restored here so they can be driven on the roads. The 1890's horse bus, an arresting sight in its red and cream livery, was built at Pendleton and is thought to be the largest of its type in existence.

Try to visit on the opening day on the first Saturday in April, a festival day with visiting exhibitors from model transport societies. The other highlight of the year is on the first Sunday in September, when a cavalcade of vintage buses, cars, commercial vehicles and motor-cycles leave Boyle Street for a historic vehicles rally at Heaton Park. Admission to the museum is free on this day. The rally is organised by the Greater Manchester Transport Society, whose members run the museum.

Admission Charge. Museum opening times: Saturdays, Sundays, Wednesdays, also Bank Holidays, 10 am–5 pm. Tel: 205 2122. Cafe open Sundays only. Boyle Street is off Queens Road, near to its junction with Cheetham Hill Road, a mile north of Manchester's Victoria station.

Heaton Park and Heaton Hall

Heaton Park, with its 650 rolling, bracing acres north of Manchester, is claimed to be the largest local authority owned park in Europe.

Its undulations give it scenic charm as well as space and there is plenty do do, with Heaton Hall, a farm full of animals in the former estate's stables, a pets' corner nearby, and much more.

▋ HEATON HALL

Of the rooms on view the cupola, originally a dressing-room for the Dowager Lady Egerton, is the most arresting. The octagonal room has eight

mirrors between painted column-like sections of wall and Roman triumphal arches, all trimmed with gold leaf. The dome of a ceiling is a splendid sight with its delicately painted panels and a gold leaf centre. This room is a rare survivor of the popular 'Pompeian' style of the 1770's (there are apparently only three such rooms left in Britain). A chandelier completes the stunning effect. Another repainted ceiling of great beauty is to be found in the saloon.

Heaton Hall's library, with its dark green walls and high, green and white ceiling, is another striking room. Here is a picture of one of the horse race meetings which were held at Heaton Park from 1825 to 1837. There are many other rooms on show, notably the dining room and a music room which has an 18th century organ filling up one wall.

All the many pictures here, and the pieces of furniture, have been imported from the city council's art galleries' collection. The hall's original contents were auctioned in 1902 when the hall and park were sold to Manchester Corporation. Until then the property had been in the hands of the Egerton family since 1684, when Sir John Egerton married heiress Elizabeth Holland. The Holland family had owned the estate since the Middle Ages. Sir Thomas Egerton, builder of the present house, was created first Earl of Wilton in 1801. Heaton Park was laid out from 1770 by William Emes, a pupil of the famous Capability Brown.

The hall is open from the beginning of April to early October. Admission free. Weekdays 10 am–6 pm. Sundays 2 pm–6 pm. Closed Tuesdays. Free guided tours Saturdays. Cafe near hall. Tel: 773 1085.

▮ HEATON PARK

The farm is a big favourite with children, featuring cattle, sheep, pigs, poultry, and a shire horse. It is open throughout the year from 10.30 am (closed Mondays). Horse riding facilities are here. Rare breeds of cattle roam the park.

Other park attractions are boating on a 10-acre lake installed in 1914; a full size 18-hole golf course open to all visitors (professional and equipment hire); pitch and putt course; orienteering course and tennis.

In summer, on Sundays, a vintage single-decker Manchester Corporation tram gives rides between the Middleton Road entrance and boating lake. Also rides are available round the park on a vintage double-decker bus.

The park is at Prestwich, main entrance on A576 Manchester to Heywood road.

Boggart Hole Clough, Blackley

This wooded ravine runs through part of north Manchester's urban wastes, yet is unspoilt. Visit it if you can in late May or early June, for the masses of rhododendrons then in flower in the bottom of the glen are worth seeing.

I walked along the Clough from the Rochdale road on the bottom path, returning part of the way on a higher level. There is boating on a large lake featuring a tree-covered island.

Conducted Tours of Manchester Soccer Grounds

Manchester City: Free conducted tours of the Maine Road ground, take place usually at 10 am or 2 pm, on weekdays when the guide is available. The tours, during the soccer season, generally last an hour and include the boardroom and dressing rooms. Phone 226 1191 if you want to be included in a party.

Manchester United: Conducted tours of Old Trafford can be arranged on weekdays or Sundays but not, of course, on Saturday match days. There is an admission charge, but this includes admission to the Manchester United Museum, which features gear worn by famous players, trophies, and films of great United victories. The museum is open to everyone but it is advisable to phone 872 1661 first if a tour is desired.

Manchester Airport

The airport, situated south of the vast Wythenshawe council housing estates, is included as a reminder that an interesting afternoon out can be had watching the non-stop cavalcade of aircraft. Viewing promenades are high above the tarmac. Or you can sit inside the main hall and enjoy a meal or drinks as you peer out of the windows.

Worsley

SALFORD

In the past the city of Salford had never been thought of as a place for the tourist. However, redevelopment, landscaping, tree planting and reclamation of derelict sites have helped to change its image.

Worsley, is a gem of a place and the ongoing Salford Quays development at the former docks make it a fine place for water sports and waterside promenading.

Salford has a centre of sorts beside the River Irwell at Windsor Crescent, although

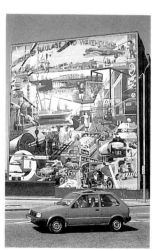

Trafford Road

the Town Hall is at Swinton. Salford University rubs shoulders with the art gallery and museum. Across the road is Viewpoint, a new photographic exhibition centre. Not far from The Crescent stands Salford's RC Cathedral, in Chapel Street.

I recommend a walk from Windsor Crescent along the Irwell, following the newly designated Irwell Way. You can walk through the Irwell Valley all the way to the moors of Rossendale if you have the legs for it.

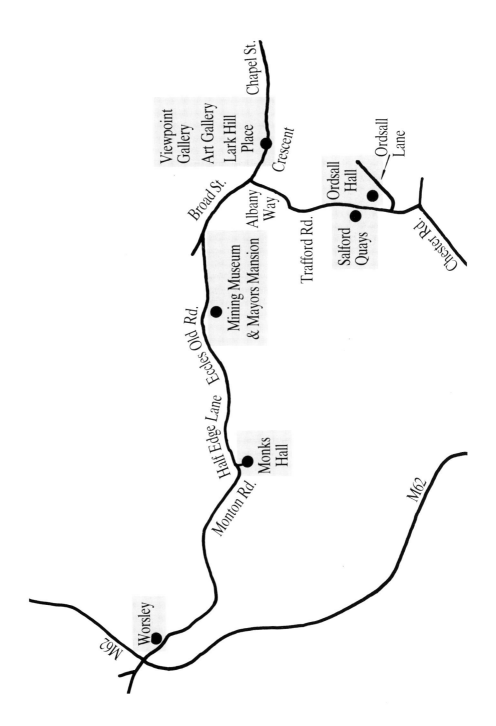

Monks Hall Museum, Eccles

This small museum occupies a house which has a 19th century frontage covering a timber-framed 16th century structure. Exhibits include a steam hammer and other machinery by James Nasmyth, plus a toy museum. Exhibitions of painting, sculpture and local history are held regularly at Monks Hall. There is a walled garden.

The museum is at Wellington Road, off Half Edge Lane, beside the M602. It can be quickly reached from Eccles town centre via Peel Street, which takes you over the M602. Museum open: Monday to Friday and on Sunday afternoon from 2 pm. Tel: 789 4372.

Salford Quays

Walk round the former Salford Docks at Trafford Road and see the unique Salford Quays development. In 1981 Salford City Council bought much of the docks area from the Manchester Ship Canal Company. They are now turning this potentially super marina into a waterside leisure, housing, and commercial centre. Hundreds of trees will be planted and walkways provided, and water sports will be introduced.

Features already completed included a cinema with eight studios, a 166-bedroom four star hotel, a pub-restaurant, and waterside houses.

Worsley and Worsley Woods

At Worsley you come upon one of the most photographed views in northern England. The famous black and white Packet House is mirrored in the vivid orange water of the Bridgewater Canal, which starts at this showpiece village of beautiful old houses.

The canal water is orange because of iron ore which seeps out of the underground canals to the long since closed coal mines north of Worsley.

The man responsible for the building of the canal to carry coal to Manchester was Francis Egerton, third Duke of Bridgewater and owner of the mines. In Worsley village centre you can see the rock face from which the underground canal section emerged. There were 46 miles of canals between the various pits, with four underground levels with connecting shafts. Coal boats were pushed by hand pressure on rails on the tunnel walls. Some tunnels were 550 feet below the surface.

James Brindley, who could neither read nor write, was the engineer of the canal which started our modern transport system.

The aqueduct he constructed over the River Irwell was a wonder of the age (it was superseded by the present swing bridge at Barton when the Ship Canal opened). The canal from Worsley into Manchester was completed in 1764, and the route through Cheshire to Runcorn was completed in 1776. But work on the underground canals at Worsley was done gradually to service new pits, and went on into the 19th century.

The Worsley estates passed out of the hands of the Egerton family in 1923, when the fourth Earl of Ellesmere sold out to a syndicate of local businessmen who formed Bridgewater Estates Ltd., which still runs the 'empire'. Members of the Egerton family once lived at Worsley Old Hall, now a mediaeval banquets restaurant. Parts of the hall date back 900 years. Turn up the Walkden road to get to the lane which leads to the hall.

At the canal in Worsley there are always many narrow boats to look at, and there are boat trips from the Packet House in summer. The black and white Worsley Court House

Worsley and Worsley Woods (continued)

was at one time the local magistrates' court. Nearby is a house called The Old Nick. It was once the police station and two of the rooms inside are the old cells, complete with cell doors and peepholes.

▮ WORSLEY WOODS

From the centre of Worsley village a lane leads upwards past attractive cottages to the hidden Worsley Woods, which afford a worthwhile and popular walk. The path leads you past a lake and eventually goes under the M62 motorway.

If you feel equal to a longer walk carry on alongside a stream which takes you to the pleasant village of Roe Green.

Ordsall Hall

On Ordsall Lane, stands the mediaeval manor house called Ordsall Hall, part of which is 600 years old.

Salford Corporation bought the property, then semi-derelict, in 1959 and spent a lot of money restoring it. The hall was not opened to the public until 1972. There is free admission to the half-timbered section, the oldest part being the Star Chamber bedroom, so called because the ceiling is covered with stars. The Great Hall is a beautiful riot of black and white timbering. Another room is fitted out as a farmhouse kitchen with ancient cooking implements. Two rooms upstairs, used as a small museum, complete the short tour.

A brick wing was added to the hall in 1639, but this is not open to the public. Ordsall Hall, home of the Radcliffe family for centuries, once had a moat. It stands in Taylorson Street, off the south end of Ordsall Lane.

Opening times: Mon.–Fri., 10 am–12.30 pm and 1.30 pm–5 pm. Closed Saturday. Sunday 2 am–5 pm. Open all year. Tel: 872 0251.

Lark Hill Place

Old shop fronts from a radius of two miles from the gallery have been assembled in a street scene with cobbled roadway, gas lamps, horse-drawn carriages and penny farthing bicycles. It is fascinating to peep into the shop windows and see goods that were sold in Victorian or Edwardian times.

There is a blacksmith's unit (with clanging sounds), pawnbroker, toy shop, pub, clogger, antiquated chemist and a door bearing a plaque which says: "Mrs.

Driver, bleeder with leeches". The house of a rich family contrasts with the cottage of a poor man.

I imagine that most Manchester and Salford children are taken to see this wonderful street. Lark Hill Place was the name of the mansion that now houses the art gallery. It was the home of a landowner, Lt.-Col. James Ackers, who bequeathed the property to Salford Corporation.

Open Monday – Friday 10 am–5 pm. Saturday closed. Sunday 2–5 pm.
Tel: 736 2649.

A Lowry painting

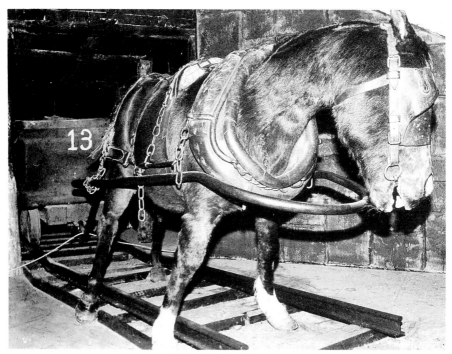

Salford Mining Museum

L. S. Lowry Gallery, Salford Art Gallery

With photographs of Lowry and interesting biographical captions to his work, this imaginative display traces the artist's life. Comprising more than 200 paintings and pencil drawings, Salford's is the largest Lowry collection.

The caption to one oil, a traditional portrait of a man, explains that the man's wife refused to have it in her house, even though he had painted it to please them. "Very, very few people liked my work at all", said the eccentric bachelor. He realised, however, that artists had ignored Britain's industrial scene, so he made a name for himself by filing the gap.

Salford's gallery is located on the main Manchester to Bolton road (A6). Cafe at gallery. Mon.–Fri. 10 am–5 pm. Sunday 2 pm–5 pm. Closed Saturday. Tel: 736 2649.

Salford Mining Museum

This museum is highly recommended as an interesting free admission place to take the children on a wet day. They will like walking through the subterranean gloom of the drift mine constructed in the cellars of the imposing mansion in Buile Hill Park, Eccles New Road, Salford.

From the pit head offices and miners' lamp room you walk down steep steps to the tunnel, shored up with pit props. There are two coal faces. One represents a typical face of the 1950's, with coal cutting machinery. The second is a face of the 1850's. Down here you can see drills, coal tubs, and other gear. Upstairs, in the entrance hall, is a stuffed pit pony, wearing its harness and pulling a big coal tub along rails.

The museum includes an excellent gallery of relics on an upper floor. There is an enormous wooden horse-pulled gin—the main type of pit cage winding device until the early 19th century. Examine an impressive range of mining artefacts from the past, plus huge photographs depicting the hard life of miners in the bad old days when there were no pit head baths, no bathrooms at home, and not much money. A weary pitman is seen scrubbing the coal dust off his body in his tiny tin bath in front of the fire.

The museum also features an art gallery of pictures on pits and pitmen by distinguished artists. Here, in a frame, is a memorial serviette produced in large numbers to raise funds for the families of 344 men and boys who died in the Pretoria pit explosion at Westhoughton in 1910. The names of the victims are printed in tiny type.

■ **MAYOR'S MANSION**
The mansion in which the mining museum is housed was built 1825–27 for textile merchant Sir Thomas Potter, first Mayor of Manchester 1838–40. He helped to launch the Manchester Guardian in 1821 and helped promote the Liverpool–Manchester railway of 1830. Buile Hill was bought by Salford Corporation in 1902 and opened as a park and natural history museum in 1906.

The mining museum is open every day of the week except Saturday. For further details phone 736 1832.

WIGAN

The Wigan area, famous for its coal and Rugby League, is not the scene of industrial desolation that it once was. During the last decade 2,000 acres of derelict land (the equivalent of 1,250 soccer pitches) have been cleared in Wigan and its surrounding towns. Slag heaps have been removed or grassed over and the Wigan Pier canal development has put the town on the tourist map.

If you see Wigan for the first time you will find some Tudor-style buildings to give a touch of class to what is actually an ancient town—its charter dates back to 1246.

Industry began here with the town's first coal pit in 1450. By the late 1800's there were more than 1,000 pit shafts

Haigh Hall Country Park

within five miles of the town centre. Have a look at the 13th century Wigan Parish Church (All Saints in Market Street). Here is the altar tomb of Sir William Bradshaw and his wife Mabel, who lived at Haigh Hall 600 years ago. In 1314 the Knight was away at war in Scotland, and Mabel heard that he had been slain. He came home 10 years later to find she had remarried.

Sir William slew his usurper, and the bigamous Mabel was ordered to walk barefoot from Haigh Hall, on the outskirts of town, to Wigan Cross once a week for the rest of her life. The story (how much of it is true, I wonder) was made into a novel by Sir Walter Scott and is marked by Mab's Cross in Wigan Lane.

Wigan Pier

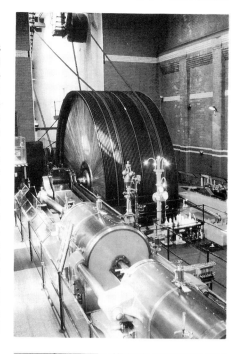

The famous Pier consists of rail sidings warehouses, loading bays, and barges, all there to shift coal and cotton. For more than 100 years this was the hub of industrial Wigan. The story of the place is told in the Heritage Centre on the waterfront. It also features a historical exhibition called 'The Way We Were', a show enlivened by actors. You step back to 1900 and learn how the people of Wigan and Leigh spent their lives. Visitors experience life at the coalface and feel the horrors of the Maypole Colliery disaster. Also on display are the workshops of various trades, from clogging to textiles.

Further along the canal is the Trencherfield Mill, containing the world's largest working mill steam engine, with its giant flywheel. This is under steam daily, and working examples of mill machines tell the story of cotton spinning. There are separate admission charges for the mill and heritage centre.

Other attractions here are a waterbus service and The Mill at the Pier, a new concert hall which stages big name concerts and Sunday jazz sessions.

Wigan Pier is situated on the A49 at Wallgate, just south of the town centre. It is open daily throughout the year from 10 am to 5 pm. Tel: 0942 44888 (recorded information) or 0942 323666.

Pennington Flash Country Park, Leigh

The Flash, a mile long lake covering 170 acres, is the centrepiece of this 1,000 acres country park. It is regarded as the best place to go bird-watching in Greater Manchester—at least 200 species have been recorded here.

On the lake's north bank, not far from the visitor centre and car park, lie several reed-fringed lagoons and ponds that teem with wildfowl and rarely-seen birds. On my visit I watched a great crested grebe diving for fish—this bird is common here. There is a butterfly garden with special plants to attract them.

Opened in 1981, the country park offers interesting walks, including a four miles complete circuit of the Flash. The lake was formed by subsidence of this large area of land due to extensive mine workings from Bickershaw Colliery, to the north of the lake.

The subsidence between 1892 and 1905 interfered with the drainage of the local brook and brought a massive build-up of water. A railway line ran across what is now the centre of the lake—but it closed in 1942 due to flooding problems!

So now the area is a marvellous nature reserve, including a special wetland area. Birds are attracted all year round—but especially in winter. You can watch them from several hides. A local Sailing Club is allowed to use a section of the lake, but other water-sports are barred because of the wildlife. A municipal golf course near the car park is open to everyone. The park's display centre is open April to September only.

Location: Drive along East Lancs Road from Manchester to its junction at Lowton with A572 Newton to Leigh road. Turn right along A572 for two miles to country park entrance. Tel: 0942 605253.

Turnpike Gallery, Leigh

The gallery has specially mounted exhibitions, plus a collection of prints you can take home on loan.

The gallery forms part of Leigh's town centre library complex. Open Mon.–Sat. Tel: 0942 679407.

Haigh Country Park

If you have not taken your children to this 250 acres park, then do so! They will love the small zoo and pets' corner, which features many exotic animals, including zebra, lynx and baboons (small admission charge). The former estate of Haigh Hall (now used for functions) also boasts a model village, a narrow gauge steam railway, and an excellent children's playground; and all in lovely woodland surroundings. Adults can play golf, mini golf, or just crazy golf, and there are miles of paths and trails through acres of woodland called the Haigh Plantations, plus a cactus house and tropical plant house.

Tel: 0942 832895. 3 miles north of Wigan off 135239. Open daily. Admission charge to zoo, model village etc.

Three Sisters Country Park

The Three Sisters were huge colliery slag heaps over 150 ft high, known as the Wigan Alps. The mountains were removed in a gigantic clean-up operation but the fringe of the bottom of one was left intact to form a natural bowl. The arena is used for both kart and motor-cycle racing on most Sundays in summer. Kart racing continues about once a month in winter.

This unusual country park also includes what is reputed to be one of Britain's finest BMX tracks. So pack junior's cycle in the boot of your car if you come here! The park, one mile from the centre of Ashton, has been created from 200 acres of derelict colliery workings. There is a visitor centre. Adjoining this recreation centre is Bryn Marsh, which was formed by mining subsidence. It is a wildlife haven and centre for windsurfing.

Bryn Road. Tel: 0942 720453.

Astley Green Colliery Heritage Centre

I think that few readers will have visited the backwater village of Astley Green.

The Colliery opened for business in 1912 and closed in 1970 because it was no longer economic to run, although there was still coal to be mined. Members of the Red Rose Steam Society are restoring some of the old buildings so that they can create an industrial museum. There is a superb engine winding house, looking like an immense church with its arched windows. Inside it is the largest pit winding engine of its type ever built.

The pit headgear with its unusual tower of latticed metal stands next to the engine house. There are steam and diesel locomotives on site and a small exhibition in the visitor centre (the former pit lodge). The former pit garage is a workshop and tea room.

Admission is free and you can walk or drive through the attractive village, over the canal, and across Astley Moss. Meals are available in a pub-restaurant at the canalside.

The Heritage Centre is open every Sunday throughout the year from noon to 5 pm. For weekday visits by arrangement ring (061) 790 7804 after 5 pm. It lies on the south side of the East Lancs Road (A580) near Boothstown, up a cul-de-sac of a lane that goes on to cross Astley Moss and ends at the Manchester–Liverpool railway line.

BOLTON

Of all the towns around Manchester, Bolton must possess the finest shopping centre. All the big national stores are here, plus two local department stores in Whitaker's and Whitehead's, and they stand in a small, compact area. A new shopping complex has been built a little further away at Knowsley Street, next to the big Market Hall, and at Moor Lane there are excellent fish and vegetable markets.

Bolton's glory is its magnificent Town Hall, backed by a lovely matching

Olde Man & Scythe, Churchgate

buff-coloured stone crescent which reminds one of Bath. The Town Hall square and adjoining shopping streets make up an excellent traffic-free pedestrian precinct.

About 150,000 people lined the streets of Bolton when the Prince and Princess of Wales, later Edward VII and Queen Alexandra, opened the Town Hall in 1873. But there had been much criticism of the building's enormous cost, bearing

in mind the appalling housing conditions then in Bolton. Two huge stone lions guard the building's front entrance under the five-columned Greek temple style façade. The Albert Hall, a fabulous concert hall inside the Town Hall, was destroyed by fire in 1981, but it was rebuilt as double-decker halls and reopened in 1985.

Places to see in Bolton town centre include the craft centre shops inside the former St. Georges Church, which still has its choir stalls, stained glass, and gallery. Also Ye Olde Man and Scythe pub in Churchgate, dated 1251. Here James Stanley, seventh Early of Derby, was executed in 1651 as a result of his activities leading Royalist troops in the Civil Wars. Outside the pub is a cross bearing plaques telling the story of Bolton through the ages. The nearby Bolton Parish Church, cathedral-like in its size, is worth visiting if it is open.

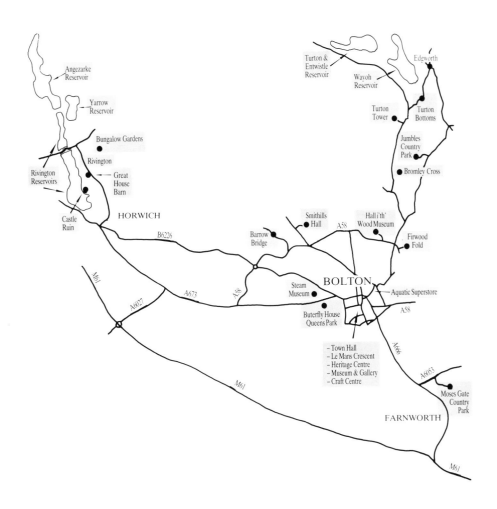

Bolton Town Hall

Bolton Museum of Local History, St. George's Street

Walk down Bridge Street from the town centre shops and turn right into St. George's Street, the location of this small but well laid out museum. It is housed in a sandstone building known as Little Bolton Town Hall even today. Bolton's first town hall, it was opened in 1826 and contained a police office and cells as well as municipal offices. It was used for sittings of magistrates and the dock can still be seen on the first floor.

In 1839 rioting Chartists stormed the building, using a lamp-post as a battering ram, in a bid to free the leader of a mob. He had been arrested following a "sit-in" at Bolton Parish Church in protest at local grievances.

When Bolton's present town hall was opened in 1879, Little Bolton Town Hall became a library.

The Museum is open from 10 am–5 pm (closed Thursdays, Sundays and Bank Holidays). Admission free. Tel: 0204 22311 ext. 2192.

Central Museum, Art Gallery & Aquarium

The glorious stone crescent behind Bolton Town Hall is partly occupied by an unusual four-in-one complex—a museum, art gallery, library and aquarium.

The museum is notable for its collection from ancient Egypt, with mummies from Egypt and Peru. The museum also features a marvellous natural history section, also in mummified form, in that the British and foreign birds and animals are all stuffed! The aquarium in the basement is well worth visiting.

Le Mans Crescent

In the art gallery you may not see the permanent collection on view because there are a lot of special exhibitions.

Centre opening times: Mon.–Fri., 9.30 am–5.30 pm (closed Wednesdays). Saturday 10 am–5 pm. Tel: 0204 22311 ext 2191

The Water Place

This new super baths at Great Moor Street in the centre of Bolton is described as "an amazing aqua adventure for all the family". The largest leisure pools complex in Greater Manchester, The Water Place offers "lagoons" on four levels, two aquaslides 100 metres long, a tidal wave feature, and a "wild water" channel. Visitors climb into inflatable rubber rings to go on the Raging River ride, which includes a whirlpool. There is a slanted beach for children, and a Jacuzzi with two geysers. One concession to serious swimming is a training pool! Charges are higher than those of "straight" baths, but a family of four qualify for a cheap group ticket. During "off peak" periods, when the odd water feature may be closed, admission charges are lower.

Open Mon. – Fri., 9 am – 9 pm. Sat. and Sun. 9 am – 7.30 pm. Tel: 0204 364317 or 364616.

Free Flight Butterfly House, Queen's Park

Tropical butterflies flutter past you in free flight in the large conservatory in Queen's Park, Bolton. The large glasshouse has been turned into a jungle-like hothouse to suit beautifully marked specimens from many parts of the world.

But visitors first enter a smaller and cooler section reserved for British and other European butterflies. While the tropical house, with its pools and exotic plants, is inhabited by butterflies all year, European butterflies are not on view in winter. There are also less lovely creatures to see here, like stick insects and huge spiders.

Open from Easter to end of October in 1989. Open seven days a week, 10 am–5 pm. Tel: (0204) 363528. Queen's Park is near Bolton town centre.

Turton Tower, Turton

Turton Tower is just over three miles north of Bolton town centre, on the B639. It was built in sections between the 14th century and 1850. The stone-built block which gives the tower its name is a Pele tower, the oldest part of the house. Cruck-framed buildings were added in the 16th and 17th centuries and part of the resulting whole was a farmhouse.

The tower's contents include furniture of many periods, paintings and armour. In 1930 the last occupant, Lady Nina Knowles, presented the tower to Turton Urban Council after the death of her husband. It was then used as a council chamber until local government reorganisation in 1974.

The tower's most famous owner was Humphrey Chetham (1580–1653) the founder of Chetham's Hospital and School in Manchester. He was Lancashire treasurer for the Roundheads during the Civil War—and had to entertain troops.

Opening times: November and February, Sunday afternoons only. March, April, October, Sat.–Wed., 2 pm–5 pm. May to September, open seven days a week (Sat. and Sun., afternoons only, 1 pm–5 pm). (Closed December and January.) Admission charge. Further details, ring 0204 852203.

Bolton Steam Museum, Atlas Mills

The Northern Mill Engine Society exhibits half a dozen former textile mill engines in the engine room of a former cotton mill.

Also textile industry artefacts, including photographs.

Corner of Mornington Road and Chorley Old Road, open every Sunday throughout the year. Free admission except on occasional steaming days, when engines are working (small admission charge). For steaming dates phone (0204) 74557.

Tonge Moor Textile Museum

This collection of early textile machines is housed in a separate hall at Tonge Moor Library, a mile north of Bolton town centre on Tonge Moor Road (A676). The machines include the only surviving example of a Spinning Mule built and used by the inventor, Samual Crompton.

The library and museum is open Mon. & Thurs. 9.30–7.30 pm, Tues & Fri 9.30–5.30 pm. Sat. 9.30–12.30 pm.
Tel: 0204 21394

Turton Tower

Jumbles Country Park, Turton

This 250 acres country park comprises Jumbles Reservoir and the surrounding land. There is a walk of nearly two miles right round the reservoir—the path is on higher ground, away from the reservoir, along part of the western side.

I visited a large, impressive bird hide constructed for the public on the east bank. Sitting on a form inside, you can watch birds feeding on food laid out for them on rocks about 40 yards away. Bring your binoculars!

Opened in 1972, Jumbles Reservoir does not provide drinking water. It is used to provide compensation water to keep Bradshaw Brook at a steady flow. This enables the same amount of water to be released for drinking from the larger Wayoh Reservoir a mile to the north.

There is a walk northwards from the north end of Jumbles Reservoir. An interesting half mile walk brings you to the picturesque village of Turton Bottoms.

From Turton Bottoms it is half a mile to Wayoh Reservoir, which also provides a circular walk. From Wayoh a further half mile brings you to the most scenically grand stretch of water in these parts—Turton and Entwistle Reservoir.

A circular walk taking in all three reservoirs is about 10 miles.

The main entrance to Jumbles Country Park is on the left of Bradshaw Road (the A676 to Ramsbottom). It is a three mile drive north from Bolton town centre. The lane down to the reservoir centre is clearly signposted. Free angling is available at Jumbles. Tel: 0204 852473.

Barrow Bridge

A picturesque village on the edge of the moors north of Bolton, Barrow Bridge was once a textile manufacturing centre, and later a day trippers' favourite.

After the last war people still went in droves to the boating lake and cafe, regarding it as a good day out. But now the site of the lake—built as a reservoir for a mill—is occupied by a car park and lawn.

The Dean Brook rushes past old stone cottages and there is a flight of 63 stone steps to climb at the end of the village. These were built in the late 18th century for the convenience of quarry and coal mine workers up on the moors. You can enjoy a circular moorland walk from here because paths criss-cross the moors above the village.

Barrow Bridge, formerly known as Dean Mills, was a 'model village' built to give textile workers of the 19th century living conditions which were then regarded as almost utopian. Robert Lord erected a water-powered carding mill in the late 18th century. This was demolished in the 1830's by industrialist Robert Gardner and two larger mills were built. Gardner and the mills manager, Thomas Bazley, erected excellent houses for workers, and a marvellous school they called the Institute (1846). By 1850 the workers had themselves established a successful co-op shop here. In 1862 Bazley, then the sole owner, sold the mills and estate. The mills were demolished in 1913.

Edgworth

This stone-built village on the edge of the moors boasts 400-years-old cottages, special 'antique' gas lamps and cobbled streets. The village is ideally placed for a walk round the nearby Wayoh and Entwistle reservoirs, set in rugged country. Half a mile from Edgworth is the attractive riverside hamlet of Turton Bottoms. Edgworth is four miles north of Bolton town centre. Not far from Edgworth is the village of Affetside, a one street affair on top of a hill. Parts of Watling Street, the Roman road, are visible here. Homes on one side of Affetside's street are in Bolton, the other side in Bury. The Pack Horse Inn contains the skull of the 17th century executioner of Lord Derby over the bar.

Smithills Hall

You step back to the 14th century when you enter the oldest part of Smithills Hall. The great hall, with its huge oak beams and pillars, is part of one of the oldest manor houses in northern England, and has been restored to its original state as far as possible.

The great hall would have had a raised dais at one end on which the Lord-of-the-Manor and his family sat. Their servants ate and possibly slept in the body of the hall, which would be furnished with trestle tables and benches, and the floor covered with rushes, with a fire in the middle. At one end of the hall you enter the bower, or bedroom for the Lord's family.

Of the other living-rooms open to the public, the largest one is the withdrawing room, built as part of the east wing extension about 1540 by Andrew Barton. The wonderful oak wall panelling is the only surviving example of this type of work in Lancashire. There are dozens of panels containing portraits in profile, possibly of members of the Barton family and other people associated with Smithills Hall. One

joking panel illustrates the name Barton—it features a bar over a barrel, or tun, of ale.

At the end of the east wing is Smithills Chapel, which contains some stained glass coat-of-arms panels that are Tudor work. The chapel is used for services on most Sundays and for weddings.

The rest of Smithills Hall, built as later additions, houses handicapped children and is not open to the public, although it can be viewed from the terraced walk at the rear.

The affluent Ainsworth family, which owned a local bleachworks, were the last occupants of Smithills Hall (for more than 130 years) and in 1875 they added the new building. The hall was sold to Bolton

Smithills Hall (continued)

Corporation in 1937 but it was not opened to the public until 1963 because the war delayed restoration the converted stables were opened as a restaurant in 1967.

Smithills had one martyr—a clergyman called George Marsh who fervently preached Protestantism during the reign of Catholic Queen Mary. Marsh was examined by a magistrate on a heresy charge at Smithills. As he left Marsh stamped his foot angrily in the stone floored passage alongside the withdrawing room. His alleged footprint is preserved in the stone. Marsh was burned at the stake near Chester.

Admission charge. Location: Smithills Dean Road, off Crompton Way (two miles north of town centre). Open every day, except Thursdays, from April 1 to September 30. Weekdays 11 am–5 pm, Sundays 2 pm–5 pm. Open to parties in winter. For further details ring 0204 41265 .

Hall I' Th' Wood Museum

Samuel Crompton, inventor of the Spinning Mule, lived here. That is the chief claim to fame of this small manor house, in one of the northern suburbs of Bolton.

It has been preserved as an interesting museum thanks to Lord Leverhulme, the Bolton man who made a fortune from his soap works at Port Sunlight.

He bought the place and rescued it from decay in 1899. Soon afterwards he presented Hall i' th' Wood to Bolton Corporation, along with money for its

Hall i' th' Wood Museum (continued)

restoration. He continued to buy sixteenth and seventeenth century furniture for the house until his death in 1925!

The Hall, viewed from the front, looks like a cannibalised car. On the right is the black and white, original house built by Lawrence Brownlow in 1483. The half-timbered frame lies on a base of sandstone. On the left side is the stone wing built by Alexander Norris in 1648. He pulled down the west side of the original hall to do so.

There are 10 rooms to view, including the dairy, which houses a collection of ancient household implements. Upstairs is the Crompton Room, where Crompton built the prototype of his Mule while his family occupied part of the Hall, which was let off as tenements in the 18th century.

Here you can see facsimilies of Samuel's letters concerning his fight to obtain a Parliamentary grant for his invention.

Also, a spinning wheel used by Crompton for spinning flax yarn, his favourite chair, his grandfather clock, the trunk in which he kept his papers, and an organ he built. In the next room are more Crompton relics, including his violin (he was choirmaster at a local church).

The museum is located at Green Way, off Crompton Way. Open April 1 to end of September. Tues.–Sat., 11 am–5 pm. Sunday, 2 am–5 pm. Closed Mondays. Open to pre-booked parties in winter. Small admission charge. Tel: 0204 51159.

Firwood Fold

Inventor Samuel Crompton was born here in a quaint cottage which is still thatched. A plaque above the tiny front bedroom window records the historic date—December 3, 1753. Firwood Fold's 300-years-old cottages are tucked away out of sight less than 100 yards from bustling Crompton Way. When you see the cobbled enclave it is like stepping back in time.

One cottage, the oldest inhabited house in Bolton, dating from the 16th century, has a tree trunk section embedded in its gable end. This is a rare survival, a cruck-framed house which was built onto trees, bent upwards like the prow of a boat. I was told that this house was one of only two of its type in England.

The Fold's big stables block, sold off for housing development in 1986, backs a village green which boasts an 1857 horse trough. The yellow stonework of the cottages makes a fine sight when the sun shines.

To get to Firwood Fold from Bolton town centre drive 1½ miles along the A676 (Folds Road and then Tonge Moor Road). At the traffic lights at the Castle pub turn right along Crompton Way and first left into Firwood Lane. Park in Firwood Lane and walk down the path at the end of the lane to Firwood Fold just below.

Rivington and Lever Park, near Horwich

Enjoy a wonderful scenic drive along country lanes round four big reservoirs, followed by tea at the picturesque Great House Barn in Lever Park. Thousands flock here at the weekend, so go in midweek if you want solitude!

The Great House Barn, which may date from the Middle Ages, is supported by huge cruck beams, from which baskets of flowers hung when I was last there. Nearby is a gift shop and art gallery, and paths lead in all directions through woodland. Not far away is Rivington Hall (used for functions and not open to the public) and Rivington Hall Barn, now a restaurant. On the bank of Lower Rivington Reservoir stands a replica of Liverpool Castle, which once stood in the centre of that city.

At the north end of Lever Park is Rivington village with its 16th century parish church, a charming spot at the junction of the Lower and Upper Rivington reservoirs (the Anglezarke and Yarrow reservoirs complete a scene worthy of the Lake District). High on Rivington Moor stands the famous Rivington Pike tower, built in 1773 by the owner of Rivington Hall. The Pike is a traditional climb for picnic hordes at Easter, and can be reached from the Great House Barn.

■ BUNGALOW GARDENS

From the rear of Rivington Hall a footpath leads up the side of Rivington Moor to the amazing terraced gardens which were

constructed by William Hesketh Lever, otherwise Lord Leverhulme, the Bolton man who made a fortune from his Sunlight soap. He planted thousands of bushes and trees on what was an inhospitable heather-covered slope to shelter his garden from the harsh climate. The grounds include lakes, a Japanese garden, and a ravine crossed by a stone bridge.

Lord Leverhulme bought the manor of Rivington for £60,000 in 1900 and shortly afterwards built a large timber bungalow and started the gardens. In 1913 a suffragette set fire to the bungalow and destroyed it. Lord Leverhulme then built a palatial stone bungalow. This and three entrance lodges were demolished by later landowners, Liverpool Corporation Waterworks, in 1948. The gardens, long neglected and overgrown, have been restored to something of their old glory.

A Gardens' Trail Guide is obtainable at the Visitor Centre at Great House Barn. Tel: 0204 691549.

Moses Gate Country Park, Farnworth

This attractive area beside the River Croal has been created from a hideous industrial tip, almost moon-like in its desolation.

Even Rock Hall, now the Visitor Centre, was semi-derelict before its restoration. John Crompton, owner of a paper-making mill that once stood here, erected the Georgian house in 1806. It was later used by managers of the paper works. Near the hall are Crompton Lodges, three stretches of water created to serve the paper mill. Fishing, canoeing dinghy sailing and sailboarding are enjoyed here. Camping and caravanning are allowed on a nearby field.

The Croal is no longer the grossly polluted stream it was, and kingfishers inhabit the area for the first time for 100 years.

The country park extends to where the Croal joins the Irwell at Nob End, south of Rock Hall. But you can now walk down the steep-sided Croal–Irwell valley all the way from Bolton to Salford, an interesting mixture of unspoilt landscape and industry. In 1987, ramblers inaugurated the Irwell Way, leading from Salford to Ramsbottom.

Location: The entrance to Moses Gate Country Park is on the A6053 Moses Gate, Farnworth, to Little Lever road. Ring Visitor Centre on 0204 71561 for details of guided walks.

Last Drop Village, Bromley Cross

A collection of old farm buildings on the edge of the moors was transformed in the 1960's into a smart upmarket leisure centre. This includes a pub, a restaurant in a former cow shed, a bistro, craft shops, hotel and conference centre.

Location: Hospital Road, Bromley Cross, off B6472 (not far from B6472 junction with A666 Bolton to Blackburn road). Tel: 0204 591131.

Britain's Aquatic Superstore

This store, occupying a former factory in Folds Road, Bolton, is one of Europe's largest commercial aquariums. 50,000 fish and other forms of marine life swim in nearly 1,000 tanks. Some tanks in the form of baths are as big as ponds. Most fish are exotic tropical species. There are also foreign birds and small pets, plus plants.

A cafe is on the premises which is open every day of the week. A garden centre is up the road. Folds Road is the A676 from Bolton to Ramsbottom (aquarium half a mile from the town centre).

Peel Statue

Castle Street

'Two Tubs'

BURY

Bury has become a tourist attraction at last with the opening of the East Lancashire Railway, described in this section. But the town has long been famous for its wonderful open-air market that draws coachloads of shoppers from many parts of the Northwest. The thrice weekly market is held on Wednesdays, Fridays and Saturdays and is renowned for its Bury black pudding stall (although these days the puddings are made outside the borough!).

Outside the parish church stands a statue of Bury's most famous son, Sir Robert Peel, Prime Minister on two occasions and founder of the Metropolitan Police Force. Kay Gardens features a statue of John Kay, the Ramsbottom-born inventor of the fly shuttle, which helped to revolutionise the textile industry.

Bury Town Hall, set beside pleasant gardens, is a striking modern building that was officially opened by the Queen in 1954. Work on it began in 1938 but it was left partially completed for the duration of the war! The oldest building in Bury is believed to be the 'Two Tubs' pub in the Market Place. It was constructed round two oak trees and is early 18th century.

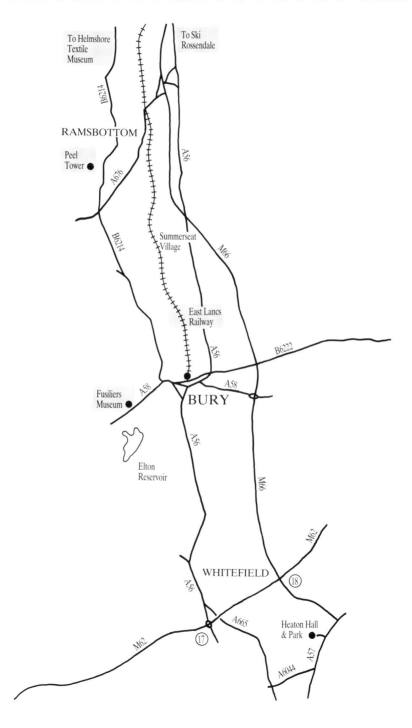

Helmshore Textile Museums

Woollen and cotton mills once operated here side by side—and that is how these twin working museums are presented today (the original machinery is on view in both mills). The museums, run by Lancashire County Council, were set up after cotton production finished here in 1978.

■ HIGHER MILL

Higher Mill was one of the first fulling mills to be built in the Rossendale Valley. The Turner family bought the mill site land in 1759. In this mill they received woollen cloth woven by cottagers. The fulling process involves causing the fibres in wool cloth to interlock and form a shrunken surface, giving a heavy, dense fabric suitable for blankets and overcoats. Originally this was done by cottagers stamping on the cloth.

Step inside the windowless machine room at Helmshore and you see an early stage of the industrial revolution. The

treading action is done by huge wedge-shaped hammer heads which crash down on the fabric in open topped boxes. A magnificent backshot water wheel revolves at one end of the room. This provided the power for the Heath Robinson fulling stocks. Next to the hammer head fulling stocks are the more advanced, but still quaint, rotary milling machines installed in 1900, using rollers rather than hammers.

Step outside and you see the lodge built by the Turners to feed the three water wheels that have been used here.

The Turners owned several textile mills hereabouts and were all powerful. One William Turner (1793–1852) built a local chapel and houses, and became a JP, but

he obviously stood no nonsense. Apparently he caused one man who had been spinning yarn too thick to be sent to prison for six months. Local worthies were so upset at the man's treatment that they organised a petition demanding the man's release. He was freed before he completed his sentence. The Whittaker family ran this mill for the last 100 years of its commercial operation.

■ WHITTAKER'S MILL

This mill was built by William Turner early in the last century, and was rebuilt after a severe fire in 1857. It finally became a condenser cotton plant run by L. Whittaker and Son.

Condenser mills take waste cotton from other mills and produce a soft yarn suitable for making sheeting, cheap towels and cleaning cloths. You can watch machines transforming the raw waste and the condenser cotton Mules in motion—each machine can product 714 stands of yarn.

The Helmshore cotton mill includes a room known as the Devil Hole. Here hard waste was fed into the breaking-up machines, known as devils. Devilling was dangerous and old devil minders usually had fewer than 10 figures. The machines also caught fire regularly.

Tel: 0706 226459
Open March to October. Admission charge.

Hand spinning and weaving at Helmshore.

Ski Rossendale

This is one of the largest dry ski centres in Britain, and is probably the most popular. You don't even need to book in advance, unless you want to engage the services of an instructor for special lessons. The hire cost of equipment is reasonable and it is cheaper if you ski midweek.

At the time of writing there was a main slope 180 metres long, plus a 60 metres intermediate slope and two nursery slopes. All skiing areas are floodlit and served by ski tows.

Ski Rossendale is open six days a week all year (closed Mondays). Licensed cafeteria and hotel. Children's playground museum. Tel: 0706 228844.

Regimental Museum of the Fusiliers

This museum is all that is left of the former Wellington Barracks, headquarters of the Lancashire Fusiliers. It is a mile from Bury town centre on the Bolton road (A58). The museum's relics cover the history of the Regiment and the British Army from 1688 to the 1980's, with an outstanding collection of period uniforms and medals.

Open daily from 9.30 am, except Thursday and Sunday. Tel: 764 2208.

East Lancashire Light Railway

At last Greater Manchester has its own steam railway. Nearly four miles of the Irwell Valley line, from Bury to Ramsbottom, were re-opened in July, 1987, by the volunteer workers of the East Lancashire Railway Company. And another four miles of line, between Ramsbottom and Rawtenstall, are being restored.

During the first two months of weekend services in 1987 a staggering 20,000 people travelled on the trains, to the delight and surprise of the operators.

The Bury to Rawtenstall line was the northern section of a route which connected the Manchester to Bolton railway at Clifton with Rawtenstall, via Radcliffe. This line opened in 1846 and in 1852 it was extended to Bacup. In 1972 passenger traffic was ended, but coal trains continued to run until the line closed in 1980. Fortunately the line was preserved, thanks to pressure from local authorities and the East Lancashire Railway Preservation Society, which now works alongside the private railway

company to run the line.

The journey to Ramsbottom includes some charming rural scenery. Most dramatic views are of Holcombe Hill, crowned with the enormous Peel Tower, and Summerseat village. The train passes over a viaduct at Summerseat, with a splendid view of the Irwell (crossed five times during the ride) and Brooksbottom Mill, which has been turned into flats. Straddling the river is the former mill canteen, opened as a restaurant in 1987. The sandblasted mill buildings of buff coloured stone look most attractive, and you can break your journey here to explore this interesting village.

At least six trains* run per day on Saturdays, Sundays and Bank Holidays, with a reduced service out of season. There are normally no midweek trains. Near the Bury station there is a small transport museum containing locos and other forms of transport. Bury station enquiries on 764 7790 (weekends only).
*A small number of trains are pulled by diesel locos.

Peel Tower, Ramsbottom

On a clear day . . . all is revealed from the top of Peel Tower. The 120 ft high Tower stands 1,100 feet above sea level on the crest of Holcombe Hill. Its original 148-step internal staircase became unsafe by the 1940's and the Tower was bricked up. The construction of a new staircase has enabled local volunteers to re-open it to the public. From the top of the millstone grit monument you can see to Jodrell Bank radio telescope in Cheshire, the Peak District, to Frodsham and Helsby Hill in the west, and to the mountains of North Wales.

The Tower was erected in 1852 as a tribute to the memory of Bury's most famous son, Sir Robert Peel, Prime Minister and founder of the first police force in Britain.

The nearest you can get by car, prior to a short walk up the hillside to the Tower, is up Lumb Carr Road, Ramsbottom (the road runs uphill from the Bolton Road/Bolton Road West junction). When the Tower is open the Union Flag is flown from the top. Open Saturdays, Sundays and Bank Holidays. Summer 11 am–6 pm. Winter 11 am–2.30 pm. Small admission charge. Tel: 705 5900.

Bury Art Gallery and Museum

The art gallery houses an attractive collection of Victorian paintings, including works by Turner, Constable, and Landseer. The Gallery in Moss Street, in the town centre, stages two exhibitions per month by contemporary artists. The museum is centred on local history.

Open: Mon.–Sat Tel: 705 5878.

Rochdale Town Hall

Broadfield Park

Rochdale Art Gallery

ROCHDALE

Rochdale has an elegant town centre, thanks partly to The Esplanade, which is built over the River Roch for 445 metres and is claimed to be the widest river bridge in the world. Standing on the wide promenade is the striking stone building housing the library and art gallery, and Rochdale's beautiful Town Hall, an outstanding example of Gothic architecture that was completed in 1871. Have a look inside if you can, for the interior is even better than the exterior (see guided tours in this chapter).

Rochdale is lucky to have Broadfield Park right in the town centre. The park rises steeply from The Esplanade up to the lovely St. Chad's Church, with its 13th century arcades and impressive woodwork. The church is reached by 122 steps and a magnificent view of the town and the surrounding hills is obtained.

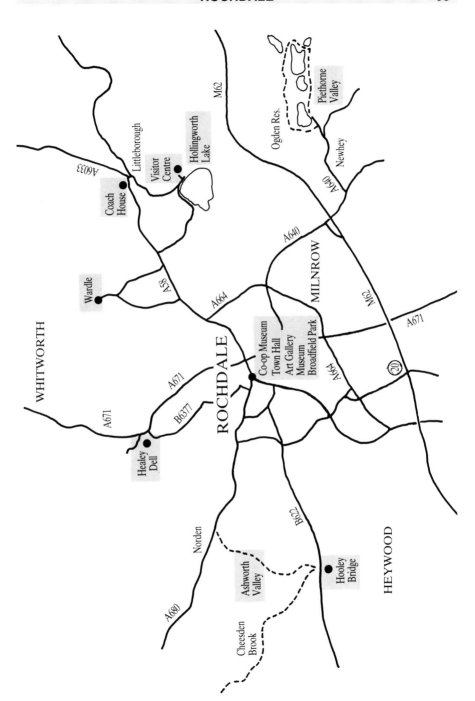

Rochdale Town Hall Guided Tours

Free guided tours of Rochdale Town Hall—surely one of the most beautiful civic centres in Britain—are available for both casual visitors and groups. The one-hour tours generally take place at 10 am and 2 pm, Monday to Thursday, and at 10 am only on Fridays.

Highlight of the tour is the assembly hall, a truly baronial sight with its marvellous hammer-beam roof resting on 16 angels. The hall boasts an outstanding 35 ft long fresco that shows King John at the signing of the Magna Carta. The 11 windows are a glorious sight with life-size portraits in stained glass of many of our monarchs, from William the Conqueror to Queen Victoria. Leading to this

mediaeval-style hall is a fine staircase adorned with carvings.

Visitors are also shown the old council chamber downstairs, the present council chamber upstairs (this was once a courtroom), and the Mayor's parlour and reception rooms.

The Gothic exterior of the building is impressive, with ranks of gargoyles looking down. The clock tower, a smaller edition of the Big Ben tower at Westminster, is a delight to the eye. This tower replaced an original spire that was destroyed by fire in 1887, six years after the Town Hall was completed.

It is best to confirm that Town Hall tours are available by ringing Rochdale 0706 47474.

Toad Lane Co-op Museum

This museum is famous all over the world, for the Co-operative Movement now has 155 million members. The tiny Co-op shop that workers established here in 1844 was the start of the modern Co-operative colossus. Pilgrims from every continent come here to view the relics of the Rochdale Equitable Pioneers' Society and their modern successors.

Visitors are sometimes touched to see the birthplace building. Some Japanese who have come here (the Co-op is big in Japan) have been seen to kiss the walls. A Greek visitor became so emotional that he burst into tears.

The 28 Rochdale Pioneers set up the shop because working folk, living in the 'hungry forties', often had to pay a high price for their food from local traders. To earn more, shopkeepers adulterated many foodstuffs. Sand was mixed with oatmeal, plaster-of-Paris with flour. Sometimes they gave short weight.

The new Co-op bought pure and wholesome food and sold it at a reasonable price. Part of the profits were divided among members in the form of a dividend.

The Pioneers set up their shop with just 25lb of butter, 56lb of sugar, 6cwt of flour, a sack of oatmeal, and 24 tallow candles. Unfortunately they were unable to sell the candles. The local gas company refused to supply gas to their premises, so they had to burn the candles themselves to light the shop (it was evening trading only at first, twice a week).

As you enter the door of the museum you step into the atmosphere of that simple shop. There is a bare wood top across beer barrels that served as a counter, and a pair of giant scales circa 1844. The rest of the ground floor is a history of the Co-op movement, including prize exhibits like the first minute book of the Pioneers' business

meetings. Thirteen founder members stare out of a huge photographic mural on the wall, including one James Standring, an ancestor of Rochdale MP Cyril Smith.

There are more exhibits in the lofty hall upstairs.

The museum is open throughout the year from Tuesdays to Saturdays (10 am–12 noon and 2 pm–4 pm) and Sundays (2 pm–4 pm). Tel: 0706 524920. Toad Lane is reached on foot from the Town Hall square by walking up Yorkshire Street, turning left at Lennards shop. There is a Victorian-style pub-restaurant next to the museum.

Rochdale Museum

This museum is housed in a listed Georgian building (1725) which stands next to the beautiful St. Chad's Parish Church, for which it used to be the vicarage. The museum is in the parkland area which climbs steeply behind the Town Hall, so there are good views from it.

The building houses mainly local interest subjects, from textiles to pictures and mementos of singer Gracie Fields.

There is a room devoted to the revered Rochdale man John Bright, a 19th century campaigner for justice and freedom. A Quaker, he was a member of a family of cotton manufacturers. Another room is devoted to John Collier, Lancashire's first dialect poet.

Opening hours: Mon.–Fri. 12–5 pm. Saturday 10 am–5 pm. Closed in December. Tel: 0706 47474.

Rochdale Art Gallery

The Art Gallery shares a stone building with the Central Library on The Esplanade, not far from the Town Hall. It has a collection of more than 1,000 pictures and drawings, but these are on view only about twice a year, for a few weeks each time. Visiting exhibitions, some local, occupy the rest of the year.

Open: Mon–Sat. (Wed. 10 am–1 pm half closing). Tel: 0706 47474

Healey Dell Nature Trail

The ravine near Whitworth that is Healey Dell is the centre of a nature reserve. The River Spodden rushes over rocks and under a 100 feet high viaduct that once carried the Rochdale to Bacup branch railway line (closed 1967).

I found the three-mile nature trail to be a most interesting walk. At one stage you walk across the top of the viaduct, enjoying a bird's-eye view of the Dell. This railway line, built to Facit in 1870 and extended to Bacup in 1881, was never viable and had been constructed mainly by the Lancashire and Yorkshire Railway to keep another railway company out of the district. Such was the railway building mania of the Victorians, who invaded so many lovely places with uneconomic lines.

Much of the trail, being at the bottom of a ravine, is a good place to go to get away from biting east winds in winter. The trail starts near the Dell entrance road at the junction of the A671 from Rochdale to Whitworth, and the B6377 (Shawclough Road). You might be able to get a trail guide from the newsagent's shop near the Dell entrance; or drive into the Dell to the old mills, where the warden's office is situated (there is a car park here).

The Dell is only 2½ miles north of the centre of Rochdale. The warden can be contacted on 0706 350459.

Wardle Village

Two lanes lead from the Rochdale to Littleborough road into Wardle. And that's where they end, for this stone built village is up a cul-de-sac in the hills, amid splendid surroundings.

You will be impressed by Wardle's large village square, with its two big stone-faced chapels standing rather grandly side by side. Wardle is like a small town built in the middle of nowhere. A short uphill walk from the village brings you to Watergrove reservoir—when this was built a village of that name was submerged. The moors here are rich in footpaths.

Coach House Heritage Centre, Littleborough

The Heritage Centre in the middle of Littleborough makes a worthwhile stop for those who are visiting the narrow valley that runs between Littleborough, Todmorden, and Hebden Bridge.

The centre is houses in stables built to serve the stage-coach route across the Pennines. It tells the story of the conquest of the Pennines by canal, stage-coach, and railway. With information from the centre you can better appreciate the walk along the towpath of the Rochdale Canal through attractive hill scenery.

The Littleborough Heritage Centre is open daily throughout the year (Sun.–Fri. 2 pm–5 pm, Saturday 10 am–5 pm). Exhibitions of painting and crafts are held here. Tel: 0706 78481.

Ashworth Valley and Cheesden Brook

Two fabulous walks, starting from the same point, will surprise you by their scenic excellence, considering the area is midway between two big towns like Rochdale and Bury.

Cheesden Brook: This precipitous valley once contained several cotton and print mills, interesting traces of which remain. The walk starts along a precipice with a bird's-eye view of the brook below. It is a great moorland day out.

Ashworth Valley: A two-mile walk to Norden beside the river into a pretty, tree-fringed narrow valley.

Take the B6222 Bury–Rochdale road, and stop at Hooley Bridge. From here the Ashworth Valley runs north to Norden, and Cheesden Brook runs north-west and eventually reaches the Rochdale to Edenfield road (A680).

Piethorne Valley, near Milnrow

This 'hidden' valley, three miles east of Rochdale, contains five reservoirs surrounded by high hills which lead up to the top of the Pennines. The circular round the Ogden, Kitcliffe and Piethorne reservoirs is just over three miles and ideal for a family outing.

Put your car on the car park at the first reservoir (Ogden) where there are toilets. The path leads across the Ogden dam and goes along the hillsides on the north side of the reservoirs. There are sweeping views at every turn along this section. The path is well marked by arrowed posts. A lane returns you along the south side of the reservoirs to the car park.

Location: If you use the M62 leave it at exit 21 (Milnrow). Drive along the A663 for half a mile into Newhey village. Turn left up the A640 (Denshaw road) and after a mile turn left into Ogden Lane which leads into the Piethorne Valley.

Hollingworth Lake

Hollingworth Lake and Country Park

For more than 100 years Hollingworth Lake has been a celebrated pleasure spot for trippers. In the old days it was known as The Weavers' Seaport because this was the nearest to the seaside that many of them could afford to get to regularly. With its boats and amusements and funfair, the lake must have had a strong seaside flavour in its heady days in the 1890's.

The lake was created by flooding the fields from moorland streams. Three embankments were constructed to hold the water, and the vast lodge, completed in 1804, was used to supply compensation water to the newly opened Rochdale Canal. The lake still supplies water to the long closed canal, the water being used by factories alongside the canal.

Now a country park has been created

on the south side of the lake, complete with a wildfowl reserve. At the north end of the lake is an impressive purpose-built visitor centre, complete with a cafe, exhibition hall, and plush lecture theatre in which you can see a film about the area. More than 1,000 people often visit it on a Sunday.

Lake Bank, or the lake front, offers rowing or motor boat hire and there are motor launch trips round the lake from April to September. Amusement arcades, cafes, and pubs complete a lively scene. On foot it is two miles and 300-odd yards round the lake.

Hollingworth Lake owes much of its beauty to the hills which partly surround it. Rakewood Viaduct, which carries the M62 over a ravine-like valley here, is a dramatic sight with a maximum height of 140 feet.

The lake is on the Milnrow to Littleborough road (B6225). Visitor Centre tel: 0706 73421.

Saddleworth Church

OLDHAM

Go to Oldham if you wish to see a place of truly Lowryesque mood. I'm told that within the Metropolitan Borough, which includes Chadderton, Royton, Shaw and Failsworth, there are more large textile mills still standing than in any other town.

Oldham itself is built largely on the side of a hill, with the town centre at the top. Its famous Tommyfield Market is one of the largest of its type in Britain, with nearly 400 traders. The first market hall was built here in 1856. Tommyfield opens on Mondays, Fridays and Saturdays, with a second-hand market on Wednesdays.

But it is the marvellous hill country that surrounds Oldham that is the big attraction for tourists. No metropolitan borough in the Greater Manchester area has a more spectacular setting. An excellent car tour of the district would include

Tommyfield Market

the charming stone villages of Uppermill, Dobcross, Delph, Greenfield and Denshaw, all worth stopping to see.

Oldham's heritage tours by coach include a trip called 'Villages and Viewpoints of Oldham' (details from Oldham Tourist Information Centre on 061-678 4654). A walk from Dobcross to Delph is recommended; the former Delph Donkey railway line has been turned into a footpath. Delph boasts interesting craft shops. But Uppermill, largest of the villages and a one-time mill workers' community, is the 'in place' for trippers, who arrive in large numbers on summer Sundays.

Another popular car trip now is past Greenfield and Dove Stone Reservoir, up over the moors to Holmfirth, famed for its 'Summer Wine' TV series. That is a spectacular drive.

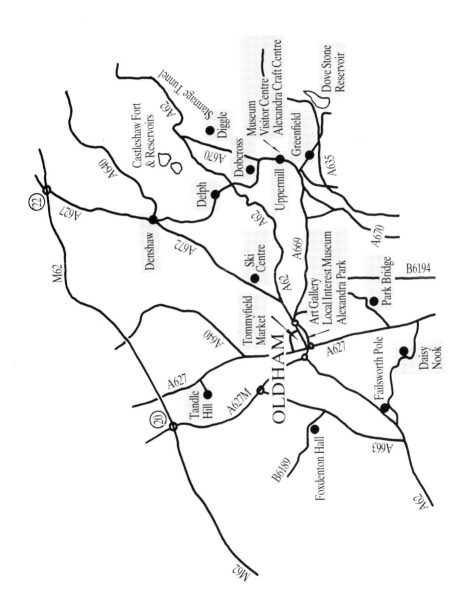

Uppermill

Saddleworth Museum and Art Gallery

This museum, in the centre of Uppermill, deals with the landscape and history of Saddleworth, the moorland district containing Uppermill and other villages. When I called there were vintage cars, motor-cycles and bicycles on view, plus textile machinery. Making cloth has been Saddleworth's most important industry (sadly only one of several textile mills is still working in the Uppermill area). Saddleworth museum is open seven days a week (admission charge). Tel: 0457 874093 or 870336

The Huddersfield Narrow Canal passes the museum and in summer barge trips are run most days up to the Brownhill Visitor Centre. The boat passes under the Saddleworth railway viaduct. Railings were installed on the top of this after one passenger fell to his death in 1866, when he stepped out of the halted train in the belief that it had stopped at Saddleworth station.

Brownhill Visitor Centre depicting the Saddleworth area is half a mile north of Uppermill near the junction of the A670 and the A6052 to Delph. It stands besides the Huddersfield canal at a scenic spot worth exploring on foot. Not far from here is the Clough Bottom Nurseries, a garden centre with animals and a farm implements museum.

Tel: 04577 2298

Oldham Ski Centre

The dry slope is at Counthill School, Moorside, Oldham, and is open to the public for daytime sessions on Saturdays and Sundays from September to April, with Monday and Tuesday evening sessions all year round. The fully floodlit centre offers a free ski tow, hire of skis, boots and sticks and qualified instructors.

Ring 678 4054 for details.

Daisy Nook Country Park

The valley of the River Medlock here is a surprisingly pleasant green oasis wedged between Oldham and Ashton-under-Lyne.

The country park is centred on an old canal system which once served local cotton mills and collieries. Crime Lake, which features a variety of wildfowl, is at the end of an isolated canal section, and was formed as a result of the canal construction in 1794. The canal severed the natural course of a brook, so a culvert was built. When a landslip blocked the culvert the water built up and flooded the area, swamping two cottages which still lie at the bottom of a lake.

There are cafes open throughout the year near Crime Lake, and at Daisy Nook Visitor Centre. From Crime Lake you can enjoy a circular walk along the Medlock Valley. Follow the canal to the Oldham to Ashton road (A627) and walk back on a path high above the River Medlock, where the National Trust owns land. You can cross the Medlock on an aqueduct.

Further up the valley towards Oldham, in a remote spot, stands Park Bridge, the old ironworks village created by the Lees family in the 1850s. Stables here have been converted into a visitor centre.

Medlock Valley Warden Service 330 9613.

Oldham Art Gallery and Local Interest Museum

Selections from the gallery's permanent collection of British paintings, and pottery and glass, are on show as well as exhibitions from out of town. So ring 678 4653 to find out what's on.

Just round the corner from the art gallery, Local Interest Museum presents long running special exhibitions dealing mainly with Oldham's social and industrial past. The current exhibition is the fascinating 'Going Up Town' with a full-sized recreation of pubs and shops.

Gallery, Union Street & Museum, Greaves Street, opening hours: Mon., Wed., Thurs., Fri. 10 am–5 pm. Tues. 10 am–1 pm. Sat. 10 am–4 pm. Closed Sunday. Museum Tel: 678 4657.

Tandle Hill Country Park, Royton

The small Park features a deep, aformitive glen. If you scramble to the top of the glen at the north end of the park you will get a fine view from the crest of Tandle Hill itself—it is crowned with an old war memorial from which the copper plates bearing the names of the fallen have long since been removed. From here one can see to Rochdale and Bury, and to Winter Hill at Bolton on a clear day. At the south end of the park there is a view of Oldham and its mill chimneys.

An inscribed stone informs us that the park was a gift to the public, just after the first world war, by a Mr. Norris Bradbury of Royton 'as a thanks offering for peace'.

To get to the park, drive north from Oldham through Royton along the main road. At the northern fringe of Royton turn left into Tandle Hill Road.

Alexandra Craft Centre, Uppermill

Uppermill, once a mill workers' community, is now a popular spot for trippers. The craft centre, set in the offices of a former woollen mill, offers about 40 shops, ranging from painting, pottery and toys to clothes and furniture. Part of the craft centre is across the mill yard in a former warehouse—the shops here surrounded a cafe in the centre of the floor.

The craft centre is open throughout the year, Wednesdays to Sundays. Uppermill straddles the A670 Huddersfield road, four miles from Oldham, and is surrounded by glorious moorland scenery. Tel: 0457 875984.

Castleshaw Reservoir

Dobcross, Saddleworth

Dovestones Reservoir Walk, Greenfield

The area east of Oldham comprises some of the grandest scenery in the North-west— (it has been dubbed 'the little Switzerland'). But the walk is easy and suitable for a family.

From Greenfield village the A635 climbs in spectacular fashion above the three reservoirs here and snakes over Saddleworth Moor to Holmfirth. Start at the Clarence Hotel at Greenfield and walk through a large white gate along the access road to Fletchers paper mill. Cross over a wooden bridge and proceed to the embankment of Dovestones Reservoir.

Turn south along the embankment to the ranger post and toilets and pass the south end of the reservoir. Here, if you have the energy, you can scramble up Chew Brook as it tumbles down from Featherbed Moss. But beware; in snowy weather the steep brook area seems prone to avalanches. In 1979 a climber died in one and in December, 1981, men from Bury and Eccles were rescued after being buried by an avalanche.

If you have no time for a scramble up the brook, just carry on up the east side of the reservoir. When you reach its north end you can turn back to Greenfield along the

west bank. Or you can press on along the bank of Yeoman Hey Reservoir to Greenfield Reservoir. The walk then takes you along the west bank of Yeoman Hey Reservoir back to Greenfield, completing an excellent circular with some wonderful moorland views. Maximum length of walk is six miles.

Ashton Market

TAMESIDE

Tameside consists largely of a packed group of adjacent towns which stand on both sides of the River Tame, with Mossley isolated further up the valley. Ashton is the administrative centre and offers a big open market outside its town hall.

If you are in Hyde visit Newton Hall, a 14th century manor house that has been restored. It has cruck beams and a glass panel stretches from ground level to roof, showing how a mediaeval timber-framed hall was constructed. Newton Hall, half a mile north of the town centre on the A627, is open to the public all year round, but it is very small and perhaps not worth a long special journey to see.

Ashton's town centre boasts the lovely Stamford Park, the gardens of which lead through woodland to a big boating lake, pets' corner, and a magnificently restored conservatory which features exotic specimens like bananas and rubber plants. Cheetham's Park, Stalybridge, has a bird sanctuary.

Mossley is a town of stone houses built on both sides of the hilly Tame Valley here, so a walk round affords grand views. To the west of the town stands Hartshead Pike, a former beacon site from which you can see for miles. The tower here, third on the site since 1426, is almost 1,000 feet above sea level and was built in 1863 to mark the marriage of the Prince of Wales and Princess Alexandra.

Also out of town is the hill village of Mottram-in-Longdendale, where the artist L. S. Lowry had his last home. There are fine views from the 15th century parish church, an ancient court house, drinking fountain and stocks.

Ashton-under-Lyne was the scene of a wartime tragedy that rocked England in 1917. The local munitions factory, which made high explosive for shells, blew up. Forty-seven people died, 350 were injured, and a host of factories and homes were wrecked.

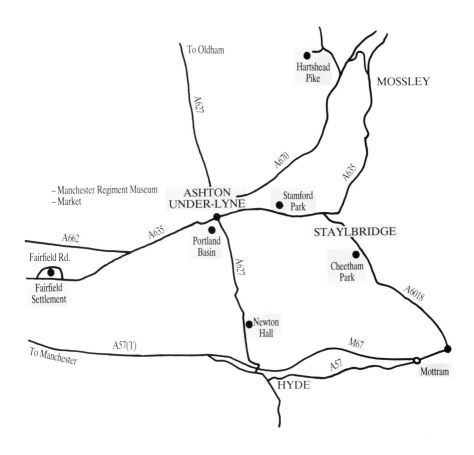

To Oldham

A627

Hartshead
Pike

MOSSLEY

A670

A635

– Manchester Regiment Museum
– Market

**ASHTON
UNDER-LYNE**

Stamford
Park

A662

A635

STAYLBRIDGE

Portland
Basin

Fairfield Rd.

Cheetham
Park

A627

A6018

Fairfield
Settlement

Newton
Hall

A57(T)

M67

To Manchester

A57

Mottram

HYDE

Portland Basin Canal Museum, Ashton-under-Lyne

This small museum occupies an old canal warehouse built in 1834, at the junction of the Ashton and Peak Forest canals. The canal basin is impressive with the River Tame far below, spanned by a bridge carrying the Peak Forest canal as it reached the basin junction. There is a splendid 1835 stone footbridge. These canals opened in the 1790's but were derelict by the 1906's. Now it is passengers cruising instead of coal, limestone, timber and cloth. Try short walks along the three canal arms from here.

Museum open Tues.–Sat., 10 am–5 pm. Closed Mondays. Location: At the bottom of Portland Street South (on southern side of A635 near centre of town). Tel: 308 3374.

Fairfield Moravian Settlement, Droylsden

The lovely cobbled streets of Georgian houses have been preserved to show the qualities of an 18th century Moravian community development. The Settlement is the largest of its kind in Britain and all the buildings have been listed as being of special architectural or historical interest. The streets are wide enough to

Fairfield Settlement (continued)

accommodate trees in the centre.

The Moravian Church, the first Protestant church in northern Europe, was founded in Moravia, Czechoslovakia, in 1457 by people disenchanted with the Roman Catholic Church.

The English Settlement at Fairfield was founded in 1785. The church of that date is still a busy place with its own clergyman who lives in an attractive house next door. The Moravians once had a theological college and boys' and girls' boarding schools here. The former theological college has been restored at great cost and turned into the Settlement's Christian social centre.

The Settlement, just off the busy Fairfield Road, is a place of peace and quiet. Only residents may park cars there so leave yours in Fairfield Road. Guided tours are available on Tuesday and Thursday afternoons and evenings in summer if you book in advance by ringing Wilf Lomax on 370 3461.

In the Moravian graveyard there are no headstones. Small plaques, laid on the ground in regimented rows, mark the graves. Single men are buried on one side of the dividing path and single women on the other. But there is no segregation for married couples, who are allowed to share the same grave.

Location: From Manchester drive along the A635, the main road to Ashton. Two miles from the city centre you reach traffic lights at the Half Way House pub. Turn left here into Fairfield Road and drive one mile to the Settlement, a neat, ordered place which looks as if it might be a make believe film set! Tel: 370 3461.

Museum of the Manchesters, Ashton-under-Lyne

The Queen Mother, a former Colonel-in-Chief of the Manchester Regiment, opened this museum in Ashton Town Hall in 1987.

This is one of the new breed of museums, with captions in big, easily read lettering to explain the wartime photographs and historic objects.

I stepped into a large darkened cubicle the size of an average bathroom and found myself in a reconstructed trench, like the ones at Havrincourt Wood on the Western front in April, 1917. The guns boom and the machine guns chatter and the sky over the top of the sandbags is lit by the flashes of exploding shells. The smell of the trenches is recaptured and soldiers crouch in the gloom, looking through slits at No Man's Land.

There is more realism in the Malaya section in the form of jungle hell noises (birds, frogs and insects I suppose). The museum covers the major conflicts in which the Manchesters were involved—the Boer War, the two great wars, Palestine and Malaya. The usual soldiers' personal equipment and uniforms can be seen, plus displays about wartime at home.

But the museum also covers social history, from the growth of Chartism, which caused Ashton's Ladysmith Barracks to be built to hold troops locally so they could suppress any working class agitation!

The Manchester Regiment, based at these barracks, was formed in 1881. It ceased to exist in 1958 when it amalgamated with the King's Regiment (Liverpool).

A big daily open-air market can be found in the square outside (there's an indoor market as well).

Museum open Mon.–Sat., 10 am–4 pm. Admission free. Tel: 344 3078.

Hartshead Pike

Astley Cheetham Art Gallery, Stalybridge

This gallery occupies the top floor of the library in Trinity Street, in the centre of Stalybridge. New exhibitions virtually every month.

Open weekdays 1 pm–7.30 pm (Closed Thursdays, Sundays). Sat. 9 am–5 pm. Tel: 338 3831.

Mottram

Stamford Park, Ashton

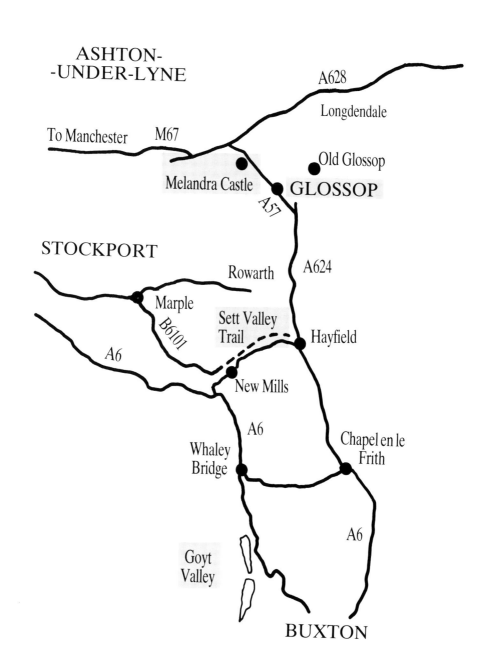

Buxton

The town remains a firm favourite for visitors with its many sights, attractions and bracing air which befits its location as the highest market town in England. There are walks and picnic sites by the River Wye off Spring Gardens, and Corbar Woods reached via Manchester Road, about half a mile from the Crescent. The Pavilion Gardens with 23 acres of walks, sports and pleasure facilities is a favourite place for families. Nearby are several buildings to admire – the Colonnaded Crescent built in 1870 on the site of a Roman bath, the Devonshire Royal Hospital with its huge dome to enable patients to exercise in all weathers, and the beautiful 1903 Opera House with its superbly restored marble stairs and ornamental ceilings.

The Crescent

■ BUXTON MICRARIUM

See a variety of real specimens under the easily operated microscopes. There are hundreds of microscopic objects projected onto large screens, which enables you to see the intricate and intriguing details of plants, water fleas, snowflake crystals and the curious Rotifer – an animal which seems to posses revolving wheels.

Opposite the Crescent. Open March to early November 10 am – 5 pm. Admission charge. Tel: 0298 78662.

■ BUXTON MUSEUM & GALLERY

The wonders of the Peak District are depicted here in a series of settings including a walk through a coal forest, a crawl into a tomb, a cure in a Roman Shrine and a look at 19th century shops in Buxton.

Terrace Road, open Tuesday to Friday 9.30 – 5.30 pm, Saturday 9.30 – 5.00 pm. Tel: 0298 24658.

■ BUXTON STEAM CENTRE

Steam train rides on all Sundays between July and September and many other special events. There are lots of locomotives and examples of rolling stock to see and a souvenir shop. The centre is part of Peak Rail – an organisation dedicated to reopening the scenic Buxton to Matlock line.

Adjacent to Buxton Railway Station. Open daily 10 – 5 pm. Admission charge. Tel: 0298 79898.

■ POOLES CAVERN

Described as "the most beautiful show cave in Britain' it is famous for its extraordinary 'poached egg' stalagmites and stalactites. On display are pieces from the Roman dig and there is a video of the Buxton Country Park through the seasons. There are a hundred acres of woodland including a nature trail and, for the curious and energetic – a walk up to Solomon's Temple – a folly on the summit.

Green Lane, open daily Easter to November. (Closed Wednesdays – April, May and October). Admission charge. Tel: 0928 26978.

Chestnut Centre, Chapel-En-Le-Frith

Otters, owls and birds of prey can be seen in this conservation park set in 40 acres of grounds amidst beautiful and natural surroundings. The centre is based at Ford hall, once the home of William Bagshaw known as the "Apostle of the Peak", and visitors have access to lovely walks through its grounds.

A625 Castleton Road. Tel: 0298 814099.

Kinder Reservoir

Melandra Castle

Those who visit the Dinting Steam Centre are only two miles away from Melandra Castle, the site of a Roman infantry fort designed to accommodate 500 soldiers.

It is worth visiting this windswept site, on a plateau high above the River Etherow, for the panoramic view of the surrounding hills alone.

Walking between opposite corners of the fort, I found that the distance was 175 paces. In the middle of the site you can see,

peeping above the ground, the walls of what was the principia, or headquarters, building. The walls of the fort were originally built of turf surmounted by wood, but later the wood was replaced by stone. Melandra Castle was established in the late first century A.D. as the Romans moved north. It was not occupied for long, being abandoned in 139–140 A.D. when its troops joined in the second Roman invasion of Scotland.

Melandra Castle lies just to the west of the A57 Glossop to Hollingworth road.
You can drive to the site via the Gamesley housing estate, which lies off the A626 road to Charlesworth.
I chose to climb to the fort on foot from a lane which runs beside the River Etherow from the A57.

Sett Valley Trail

The former branch line railway from New Mills to the terminus at Hayfield, that traditional paradise for hikers, is now a broad footpath along the pretty Sett Valley. There are wonderful views of the moorland on either side during the $2\frac{1}{2}$ miles trek. Hayfield is a peaceful village these days, thanks to the by-pass which has taken care of the Glossop to Buxton traffic which once roared up the steep streets. From Hayfield

I walked back to my car at New Mills along the pleasant lane on the north side of the valley, enjoying panoramic views from on high. You can, of course, return by bus instead if you have had enough!

On the east side of Hayfield there is a pretty walk along the narrow upper part of the Sett Valley up to Kinder Reservoir, in the shadow of Kinder Scout.

Upper Goyt Valley

The Goyt Valley between Whaley Bridge and Buxton is a deservedly popular place for both family trippers and ramblers.

If you drive to the car park near the dam of Errwood Reservoir, above the older Fernilee Reservoir, you are in magnificent hill country. I recommend the short walk up the narrow cleft in the hills on the west bank of Errwood Reservoir. This woodland walk brings you to the ruins of Errwood Hall, a remote mansion that must have been a desirable residence for those wanting to get away from the bustle of life. It was built by the Grimshaw family in 1830 but was abandoned after Fernilee Reservoir was built on the estate in 1938.

Keen walkers will enjoy the trek from Errwood Reservoir to Taxal, near Whaley Bridge, a distance of three miles. The path beside the east bank of Fernilee Reservoir is the track of the former Cromford and

The now demolished Errwood Hall

High Peak Railway. Then the path follows the Goyt through sylvan wooded scenery to the tiny hamlet of Taxal. I did a more ambitious walk from Whaley Bridge to Buxton via the Goyt Valley, returning to Whaley Bridge by train.

The lane south of Errwood Reservoir runs over Goyt's Moss to the famous Cat and Fiddle Inn on the Macclesfield–Buxton road.

Rowarth

Enjoy some grand moorland scenery with a visit to this isolated village high up in the hills above Marple Bridge. Rowarth, two-and-a-half miles east of Marple, up a cul-de-sac lane, is another world.

Not far from the village is a renowned drinking and eating spot in the Little Mill Inn. A stream rushes past the pub, set in a charming, sheltered spot away from the wind. Tables are on the grass outside the pub.

Glossop

Glossop, occupying the north-west tip of Derbyshire but only a short drive from Manchester, is a stone built town of Victorian mills, set below a crescent of towering moors. Consequently there are some wonderful walks from the town's outskirts.

To learn about the history of the place across the centuries visit Glossop Heritage Centre at the top of Norfolk Square, opposite the Town Hall. This centre (admission charge) features an audio-visual presentation, a permanent exhibition, plus changing exhibitions and an art gallery and crafts area. The centre is open seven days a week in spring and summer.

Manor Park, at the eastern side of the town centre, is a beautiful place that sports a boating lake and miniature train rides. If you visit this excellent park have a look at adjoining Old Glossop, an enclave of 17th and 18th century cottages. There are cobbled pavements and an old village square and market place as Old Glossop was the town's original centre.

Glossop has an indoor market (Thurs., Fri., Sat.) and outdoors (Fri., Sat.).

Old Glossop

Taxal Church

Whaley Bridge

Little Underbank

Market Place

Town Hall

STOCKPORT

Because Stockport spans the Mersey valley it is a town of steep streets and good views from the sandstone cliffs on which the place is built. The famous Stockport railway viaduct, a third of a mile long, is made of 11 million bricks and has 27 arches, although some of these are tiny ones on the hillsides.

The spacious Merseyway shopping precinct, built in the 1960's, stands on stilts over the Mersey. From the central square a hill leads to the 700-years-old Market Place, where the last wife to be sold in England was allegedly purchased (the market here is open on Tuesday, Friday and Saturday). There are attractive old buildings and specialist shops in Great Underbank.

The striking white faced Town Hall in Wellington Road South, was built in 1907, and visitors can wander round and examine the civic silver. The clock tower, like a wedding cake, was not given chimes so that patients in the Infirmary across the road would not be disturbed.

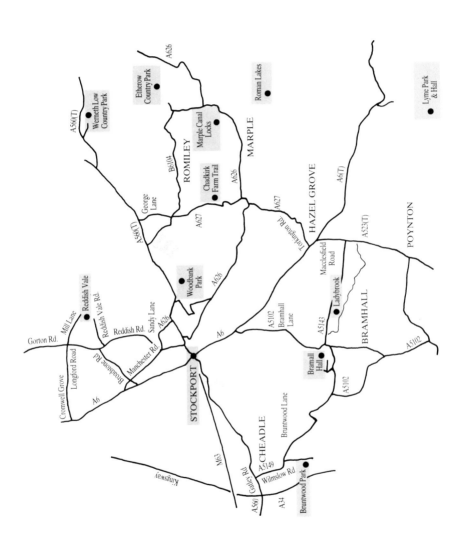

Stockport Museum, Vernon Park

The museum covers the social and industrial history of the town. An outstanding exhibit is an 8 ft by 3 ft 6 in window in Blue John fluorspar from Castleton. It was made and presented to the museum in the 1990's by a former curator, and is the largest known Blue John window. There is an exhibition of hats made in Stockport.

The museum's location means you can walk through two adjoining parks (Vernon and Woodbank) along the bank of the River Goyt, as far as Marple if you feel energetic.

Museum open April to September, Tuesdays to Sundays, 1 pm–5 pm. Tel: 474 4460.

Stockport War Memorial and Art Gallery

Changing exhibitions are put on at the small art gallery opposite the Town Hall in Wellington Road South. The building is partly occupied by the names of local soldiers killed in two world wars. The land was given for erection of a war memorial on condition it was used for educational purposes. Hence the art gallery.

Art Gallery open: Mon.–Fri., 11 am–5 pm. Saturday 10 m–5 pm. Tel: 474 4453.

Marple Canal Locks

The Peak Forest Canal runs through hilly Marple via a remarkable series of 16 locks. These are in good order and the walk along this stretch of canal is therefore very interesting.

The locks are on either side of the A626 from Stockport as the road plunges down to Marple Bridge. South of the A626 the canal runs through the town to its junction with the Macclesfield Canal, where there is always a colourful display of boats. North of the A626 the waterway crosses the River Goyt on a viaduct, under the higher railway viaduct, giving a spectacular viewpoint. The beautiful Marple area is an excellent centre for walking.

Etherow Country Park, Compstall

This is one of the most beautiful of the North-west's country parks. Lodge, river, feeder canal, woodlands and a hidden, tree-surrounded lake nestle in a deep valley below rugged moors. No wonder people return here again and again.

The village of Compstall lies on the B6104 between Romiley and Marple Bridge. The village was built by local industrialist George Andrew, who constructed the beautiful lodge and a feeder canal which receives water through sluice gates from the fast flowing River Etherow.

The old mill building near the lodge was built by Andrew in 1825 and at first the dyeing of yarn was carried out here. It became a cotton spinning and printing works about 1830. The textile mill closed in 1966 and three years later 165 acres of the Etherow valley became one of Britain's first country parks.

In 1986 a further 81 acres of land at Ernocroft Wood, on the east bank of the river, were acquired.

The park starts at the large lodge, where visitors can feed many types of geese and ducks. You may see Chinese, Canada, greylag, bar-headed and Egyptian geese. At times 300 geese and ducks populate this part of the park.

A path follows the feeder canal to the spectacular river weir half a mile up the valley. Then there is a lovely walk through The Keg woodlands, affording fine views of the valley below. Near the Keg Cottage, a former shooting lodge, more birds are on display in pens. The woodland walk includes the 'secret' Keg Pool, a peaceful paradise hidden from long distance view.

Park facilities: Cafeteria open daily. Angling. Braille Trail for the blind, featuring guide rails and tape recorders. Wardens: Tel: 427 6937.

Below and left: Marple

Bruntwood Park, Cheadle

This park is included because its gardens are adjacent to a vast area of grassland. The walk beside the brook that flows through the lovely gardens and across the fields is three-quarters of a mile long.

The park is heavily wooded with both evergreen and deciduous trees, inhabited

Bruntwood Park, Cheadle (continued)

by squirrels. There's an 18-hole pitch and putt course, big children's adventure playground, pets' corner, and championship BMX track. Bruntwood Hall, now a private firm's headquarters, was built in 1861 as a cotton magnate's residence.

The park's visitors enjoy a grand air show, for planes fly low over Bruntwood before landing at nearby Manchester Airport. The park's entrances at Schools Hill and Bruntwood Lane are both off the A5149 Cheadle to Cheadle Hulme road.

Bramall Hall, Bramhall

If you like old houses, make sure you visit delectable Bramall Hall and its beautiful park. There is no more arresting sight in Greater Manchester than the hall's east front. The long façade of black and white faced Elizabethan timber stands high on a knoll, overlooking the park in the valley of Micker Brook (downstream it is called Lady Brook, and eventually Norbury Brook!).

The south wing of the hall is 15th century, but most of the rest of the place was rebuilt or refashioned in late Elizabethan times. There are 10 interesting rooms open to the public, and the availability

of guided tours makes the moderate admission fee good value.

This was always the home of a branch of the Davenport family until they sold it in 1877 (they now live in the south of England). The hall was eventually sold and opened to the public in 1936. Now Stockport Council look after it.

An outstanding feature of the building are the restored wall paintings on wood and plaster which cover two walls of the ballroom or upper banqueting room. The paintings, which could date back to 1500, were done in vegetable dyes and are said

Bramall Hall, Bramhall (continued)

to be the best of their type in the North-west. They depict birds, animals, flowers and demons. This was once a form of imitation tapestry.

Charming oil paintings of some of the Davenport children, dated 1680, hang in the withdrawing room, which has a lovely plaster ceiling.

There is an imposing chapel in which services are still held. It was closed and dismantled some time between 1869 and 1890, but in 1938 was restored with money donated by a local man.

I was intrigued by a 17 ft long, 7 ft high apparent tapestry which is actually embroidery, bearing coats-of-arms. Once used to cover the long table in the Great Hall, this amazing piece of work was restored in 1979—it took 1,500 hours of work to accomplish!

▪ LADY BROOK WALK

Most visitors to Bramall Hall don't realise there is an excellent walk along the pretty valley to the east of the hall. Leave the park entrance and cross the A5102 Stockport to Bramhall road. Walk a few hundred yards up Bridge Lane from the roundabout and you will see a footpath sign on the right side of the road. From here you can follow Lady Brook as far as Poynton Pool on the Macclesfield road. At some points the brook is ideal for children to paddle.

A longer walk of nearly five miles beside the stream starts at Cheadle, passes Bramall Hall, and finishes at Poynton. I finished this walk by getting a bus from Poynton to Stockport and a second bus to Cheadle and my car.

Hall opening times: Open all year round. Tuesday to Sunday, noon to 4 pm (closed Mondays). Admission Charge. Small cafe open April to October. Tel: 485 3708.

Woodbank Park, Stockport

This big park is worth visiting because it leads down to the delights of the River Goyt. From here the walker can follow a spectacular woodland path high above the river's precipitous bank towards Marple.

Through the trees one gets lovely views of the river and the hillsides on the other side. It is an easy but beautiful walk. After a mile or so you reach a bridge which spans the wide river. One can either cross the bridge and continue towards Marple on the other side, or turn right up the glen of Poise Brook, leading up to the main Marple to Stockport road (A626). Or you can take the path at the top of the bank and return to Woodbank Park direct. Woodbank Park is at Turncroft Lane.

Roman Lakes

Bruntwood Park, Cheadle

Roman Lakes, Marple

A picturesque boating and angling lake lies in a peaceful part of the Goyt valley, and near the river. There is a shop selling drinks and food. To reach this secluded spot you drive down the rough surfaced Lakes Road from Marple (start from junction of B6102 Arkwright Road with Oldknow Road). If you prefer a pleasant walk to the lake along a lane down the valley, park your car at Marple Bridge (nearly a mile away). The walk starts at the south end of Town Street, the small shopping centre of Marple Bridge.

Chadkirk Farm Trail, Romiley

This is a signposted walk with information boards around a small dairy farm on land off the A627 road between Bredbury and Marple. The lane giving access to the car park is about 200 yards north of the River Etherow as it crosses the A627.

The well preserved 14th century Chadkirk Chapel contains an interesting picture exhibition about the old days in farming, when horses helped with ploughing, plus old farm machinery. Chadkirk was originally a monastic cell and monks tended the land. Near the chapel there is access to a charming stretch of canal to Marple aqueduct, plus woodland walks.

Werneth Low Country Park

The crest of Werneth Low, a ridge between Romiley and Broadbottom, is 800–900 feet above sea level. From the moorland walks in the country park one can enjoy fine views over Hyde and Hattersley and across to Mottram-in-Longdendale. You can drive up to Werneth Low either from Romiley or from Gee Cross, Hyde. There is a cafe and a pub on top of the hill.

Visitor Centre tel: 368 6667.

Werneth Low

Lyme Park and Hall, Disley

Lyme Park is a little on the wild side. The moors at the back rise to 1,200 ft and the area attracts a lot of ramblers. Lyme is a place to which families return again and again.

The park's attractions include the hall, gardens, and a marvellous children's playground which is hidden away in a dell near the hall. The Lyme Park Festival, lasting more than a week in early August, provides a wide variety of entertainment. Lyme Park was owned by the Legh family for 600 years, but is now run by the National Trust and Stockport Council.

■ THE HALL

This magnificent three-storey mansion is faced with buff-coloured stone from a quarry at Lyme. Parts of the building date back to the 16th century. The south front, topped with a lead statue of Neptune, overlooks a beautiful reed-fringed lake. The hall's outstanding features include three 17th century Mortlake tapestries and fine woodcarvings by Grinling Gibbons.

In 1986 one of the most important collections of English clocks went on show here. In his will Sir Francis Legh left his clocks, dating back to 1658, to the National Trust to be displayed at Lyme. Among the state apartments on show is the Mary Queen

Lyme Park and Hall, Disley (continued)

of Scots Room. Here Mary is thought to have stayed while a prisoner of Queen Elizabeth. In this room a skeleton was found in a priest's hole.

The Stag Parlour has medallions round the walls, describing the life of a typical hunk of venison. The Cheshire Gentlemen, a Jacobite society supporting the exiled Pretender, met here. The upholstery on the chair seats was made from the cloak of Charles I, and was presented to the Legh family after his execution.

Lyme has an impressive Long Gallery which was used in Elizabethan times for the taking of exercise in bad weather. There are other interesting rooms on show, and in a corridor are plaster casts of Greek friezes, depicting battle scenes. Thomas Legh of Lyme (1793–1857) helped at excavations at the Temple of Appollo at Bassae which produced a frieze dated 420 BC, which was brought to England.

Lyme Hall is open from early April to the end of October. Closed Mondays, open six days a week, afternoons only. Opening times vary according to season. Admission charge. Tel: 0663 62023.

There is a free admission visitor centre with an "Upstairs, Downstairs" theme, depicting the country house scene through servants' eyes. Visitors can "meet Lyme servants". A stepson of Piers Leigh, who lived at Lyme, wrote scripts for the famous TV series.

■ GARDENS

The gardens have a grand setting but the range of plants is restricted due to the altitude and exposed position. There is an Orangery, lake, and sunken Dutch garden.

The gardens are open throughout the year from 11 am. Small admission charge.
Location: Lyme Park's main entrance is on the A6 Stockport to Buxton road, just before you get to Disley village.

The Red Deer of Lyme

The herd of red deer at Lyme Park are rather special because they have not been 'imported'. The deer, descendants of those that once roamed Macclesfield Forest, have been at Lyme since the reign of Elizabeth the first, when the park was enclosed.

The deer, which can roam most of the park's 1,300 acres, vary in number from 230 to 300, depending on whether there has been a recent cull.

In 1969 there were 500 deer but it was decided to reduce the number because the park was not big enough to support so many.

There are in effect two herds—about 140 deer inhabit the moors at the back of Lyme Hall, while the others stick to lower ground nearer the hall. The two herds never seem to mix.

The animals are not tame and will not allow visitors to get too close. But if you walk the park in September and October you may see the bellowing stags fighting over the hinds as the mating season arrives. The hinds produce two to three calves over a period of five years, but rarely produce more than seven calves during their lives. Their average life span is 15 years, but some deer are put down earlier if their physical condition is poor.

The stags, which can weight up to 28 stones, cast their antlers in March and re-grow them by mid August. In 1980 a small number of fallow deer were reintroduced at Lyme in an enclosure at the back of the hall.

Bowdon Church

TRAFFORD

Trafford, which consists of Altrincham, Sale, Stretford, and Urmston, is mainly suburbia. But it has two very popular tourist attractions in Dunham Massey Hall and Park, and Sale Water Park and surrounding walks in the Mersey valley. Dunham Park, with its deer, was always well visited, and tourism there has positively boomed since the National Trust opened the hall to the public.

Trafford is most famous, however, for Manchester United Football Club and Lancashire County Cricket Club, and both grounds possess interesting sports museums (the museum at the cricket ground is open only to those attending matches).

A charming spot in the borough worth visiting is the village of Bowdon, a leafy-laned part of

Manchester United Museum

Altrincham. The village's parish church, St. Mary's, is a delightful building dating from the 14th century, but reconstructed in 1860. Inside there is a 17th century iron bound chest with four locks, one for each churchwarden. St. Margaret's Church, on the Dunham road, is another outstanding church, consecrated in 1855, with a 100 ft high tower. The Vicarage here is built over the Altrincham and Dunham Massey parish boundaries. Officials who used to 'beat the bounds' once walked across the vicar's study and drawing-room, with the vicar providing morning coffee.

Sadly both churches are locked most of the time, so Sundays give visitors the best chance of seeing the interiors.

Altrincham's popular main market opens on Tuesdays and Saturdays.

Urmston Meadows

I have included this spot because it is an excellent circular (or rather rectangular) walk of just over two miles through a totally unspoiled area at the end of suburbia.

Drive down Church Road from Urmston town centre to the Roebuck Hotel on the right. Turn left here down Southgate and drive to the field at the bottom. Start the walk by turning right to the River Mersey.

From the river bank there is a long walk on top of a low, winding ridge, giving good views of the fields, used for keeping horses. Eventually the path veers to the left through young trees and returns you to Southgate. You can also get to the Mersey from Queens Road, in Urmston town centre. From here one can walk all the way to Stretford along the river.

Altrincham Ice Rink

This big rink at Devonshire Road, Broadheath, is open every day of the week, with morning, afternoon and evening sessions each day. Heineken League professional ice hockey matches take place most Sunday nights between September and May (general skating after games).

For session details ring 928 1360 and 926 8316.

Dunham Massey Hall, near Altrincham

Generations of visitors to the 250 acres of Dunham Park wondered what lay behind the massive frontage of Dunham Massey Hall. Now they can find out. For the 10th and last Earl of Stamford left the hall, the park with its herd of fallow deer, and his big estates to the National Trust when he died in 1976.

The hall was opened to the public in 1980. The furnishings have, where possible, been left as they were when Roger Grey, the 10th Earl, was alive. He remained a bachelor to the end of his days.

There is some fine furniture in the imposing rooms but I was most impressed by the enormous collection of fine oil paintings of various Earls and their families. In Roger Grey's study there is a good oil painting of his father William Grey, a revered champion of noble causes.

An outstanding feature of the hall is the family's

collection of Huguenot silver. The Great Hall, part of the original Tudor house, is impressive and the Saloon and Great Gallery are long rooms of palacial proportions. There is a wonderful view of the lake-sized moat from the Great Gallery. On a window ledge a wooden plaque tells us that the north avenue of trees opposite was replanted by tenants and parishioners in memory of the last Earl.

The vast kitchen at Dunham Massey looks as if it could have been a set for the TV series, "Upstairs Downstairs". There

are pleasant ornamental gardens to complete your tour.

Dunham Massey was originally the home of the Booth family, who were created Earls of Warrington. On the death of the second Earl of Warrington in 1758, Dunham Massey passed to his only child, Mary, who had married the fourth Earl of Stamford, Lincolnshire.

Dunham Massey Hall (continued)

Dunham thus became one of the Grey family's three seats. The house was built by George Booth, second Earl of Warrington, who also planted thousands of trees in the park. A man who was very money conscious, he arranged for himself a marriage with a London heiress whom he had never seen.

The core of the house is of the late sixteenth and early 17th centuries. But the oldest complete building here is the quaint Elizabethan water mill at the end of the moat—it was built in 1616. The mill machinery, brilliantly restored, is operated occasionally, usually on Wednesdays.

scorn its shelter, even in severe winter weather. In 1987 there were about 180 deer. About 20 fawns are born each year in the bracken, away from the gaze of visitors.

■ THE STABLES

The top floor of a stable block has been turned into one of the most charming self service restaurants I have eaten in. There is also a small art gallery for visiting exhibitions.

■ THE FALLOW DEER

The park, mediaeval in origin, was already enclosed for the hunting of deer by the reign of Elizabeth I. There is a brick deer barn, dated 1740, but the deer usually

■ BOLLINGTON MILL

A short walk from the hall brings you to the River Bollin at Bollington Mill apartments. Here, in a quiet hamlet, is a beer garden at the Swan With Two Nicks.

Hall opening times: Open from April 1 to end of October. Every day except Friday, 1 pm–5 pm. Garden open 12–5.30 pm. Admission charge to house and garden. Tel: 941 1025.
Dunham Massey Hall is 2½ miles south-west of Altrincham. Drive along the A56 Chester road and turn right at Charcoal Road.

Sale Water Park

On a hot summer Sunday this place looks like the nearest thing to a seaside resort that Greater Manchester possesses. Hundreds of trippers sit on the sloping grass bank on the quayside of the lake and watch the surfers, canoeists, yachtsmen and water ski participants.

People bathe in the shallow end and anglers ply the quiet spots away from the madding crowd. This lake was created after contractors dug a half mile long hole to extract gravel for the embankment of the M63. They went down to 120 ft and today the lake has a maximum depth of 90 feet—swimming is not encouraged in these cold waters.

The water park was officially opened in 1980, and now includes a waterside leisure centre with restaurant, licensed bar and changing rooms. At the south end of the lake there is a warden-run information centre.

In 1987 jet skiing started here. The one-man craft, resembling a scooter on skis, can reach 50 mph. The 12 miles long walk round the lake can be finished off with a walk along the River Mersey to the Jackson's Boat pub, a favourite outdoor drinking spot in summer on a former bowling green surrounded by trees. The footbridge over the Mersey here was once a privately-owned toll bridge. One landlord of the pub knocked the price of the toll off a pint for visitors from the Chorlton side. The pub's name is believed to refer to a man named Jackson who operated a ferry boat on the river prior to the erection of the bridge.

To get to Sale Water Park drive along the M63 to junction 8, and drive up the lane on the north side of the M63 roundabout. From Sale approach junction 8 down Old Hall Road (A6144).
Water Park visitor centre: Tel. 905 1100. Water sports gear can be hired at the park and instruction is available.

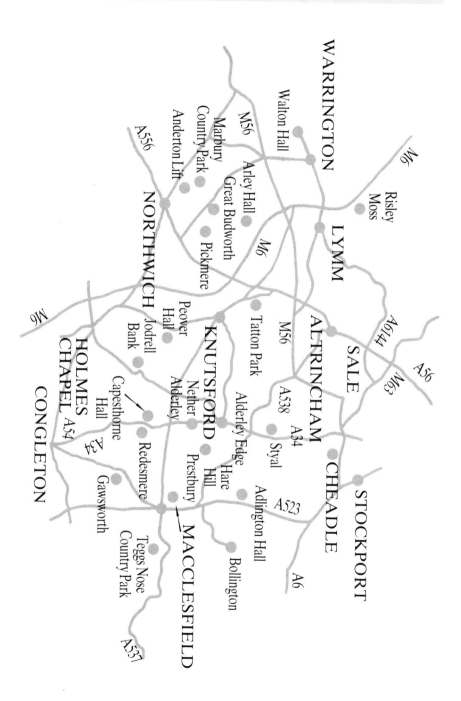

Risley Moss Nature Park

Children will enjoy this 200 acres of woodland, pools, ponds, and mossland at Birchwood, on the Manchester side of Warrington.

The site is the last preserved part of the peat bogs that once existed between Manchester and Warrington. There are woodland trails, bird hides, and an observation tower to view the surrounding landscape. At the visitor centre you can see a slide show and exhibition.

There are guided walks at 2 pm each Sunday. The free admission park is open six days a week, 9 am–4.30 pm, throughout the year (closed Fridays). Tel: 0925 824339. The best way to get there from Manchester is along M62. Leave M62 at junction 11 (signposted Warrington–Birchwood) and follow signs to park at Ordnance Avenue.

Walton Hall Gardens, near Warrington

Walton Hall, just south of Warrington and two miles north of the village of Daresbury, is a Victorian building housing some fine paintings and period furniture, formerly the home of the Greenall brewing family. The gardens are open throughout the year and feature a small children's zoo.

It is a good idea to follow a visit to Walton Hall by calling to see the parish church at Daresbury, where author Lewis Carroll (Charles Lutwidge Dodgson) was born in the vicarage. There is an Alice in Wonderland stained glass window depicting the characters from the famous book.

The Hall is open on Sunday afternoons throughout the year and on Thursdays, Fridays and Saturdays from Easter to September. Location: Off A51 at Higher Walton. Tel: 0925 601617.

Warrington Museum

This is a large museum with galleries which reflect 2,000 years of history. Opened halfway through the last century, this museum was the first to receive aid through the rates. The collection includes a shrunken head from Equador and an Egyptian mummy.

It is situated at Bold Street, off Sankey Street, open Monday to Friday and Saturday morning. Tel: 0925 444400/30550.

The Salt Museum, Northwich

The first salt museum at Northwich was opened in 1899. The present museum at Weaver Hall, London Road, was opened by the Duke of Westminster in 1981. Weaver Hall was built as a workhouse in 1837.

The story of salt extraction at Northwich from Roman times is explained, with sections on rock salt mining, wild brine pumping and solution mining. An audio visual show deals with the salt beds, the subsidence which has affected so many buildings in the area, and fights for compensation. Subsidence troubles began in 1870, and by 1880 about 900 buildings in the town had been affected, some sinking a full storey.

Visitors can get information packs for a self-guided tour of the interesting town with its jacked-up buildings.

The museum is open all year, Tuesdays to Saturdays, 2 pm to 5 pm (plus mornings as well, July and August). Open Sundays from Easter to September (2 pm–5 pm). Admission charge. Tel: 0606 41331.

Lion Salt Works, Northwich

The worlds last surviving block salt works. Founded in 1842, it used the open-pan evaporation process to make salt from natural brine. See the restoration of the Smithy, Pan Houses and steam engine on the site alongside the Trent and Mersey Canal.

B5075 one mile from junction with A 559. Over Shaw Lane, Marston new at Northwich. Open afternoons March – October . Tel: 0606 40555.

The Anderton Lift

Weaver Navigation

The little known Weaver Valley, from Winsford to the river's outflow into the Mersey estuary near Runcorn, is a fascinating mixture of the rural and the industrial. Cruises on the Weaver Navigation in a waterbus, lasting up to $2\frac{1}{2}$ hours, start from Northwich town centre. Downstream, towards Runcorn, the boat takes you to the famous Anderton Boat Lift and beyond. Upstream the trip is up the Vale Royal Cut to Newbridge, within site of Britain's only rock salt mine and brine evaporators.

The 20 miles of river from Winsford to the Mersey estuary will eventually be entirely open to the walker, as a long distance footpath is being developed. At the moment there are two stretches of path open. These are from Hunts Lock, Northwich, to Winsford Marina ($5\frac{1}{2}$ miles) and from Saltersford Locks, Barnton, to Sutton Weaver Bridge south of Frodsham (8 miles).

The Weaver and Vale Royal Water Transport Co. runs morning, afternoon, and evening trips on Tuesdays, Thursdays, Saturdays and Sundays from Easter to October. Ring 0606 76204 for times and prices.

Tatton Hall, near Knutsford

Each year about 500,000 people flock to Tatton Park—it is the most visited of the National Trust's properties. There is so much to see that if you were to view it all properly on one day your feet would be aching!

Sensibly there are moderate separate admission charges to the hall, the superb gardens, and the old mediaeval hall across the park, and to the Home Farm.

In addition to all this there is a vast deer park containing about 500 fallow deer (plus 200 red deer in a special enclosure) and lots of sheep. The park is $2\frac{1}{2}$ miles long from north to south and nearly two miles across, at its widest point. The famous Tatton Mere is almost a mile long and is used for boating and sailboarding, plus bathing from a sandy beach on the east bank. Because of the park's size, bicycles are provided for hire at the hall.

Tatton was bequeathed to the NT by Maurice Egerton, the bachelor baron, who died in 1958. He said he wanted the place preserved for the benefit of the nation.

Maurice was fond of children—he held big parties at Tatton for local boys and girls and built a boys' club in Knutsford.

■ THE HALL

William Egerton started building the mansion in 1790 to replace an earlier red brick house. Tatton Hall is only two storeys high, so despite its imposing four Corinthian columns which overlook the terrace and Italian garden, it looks slightly more like a family home than some of the stately homes I have seen.

Some of the rooms inside are magnificent, well worth the modest admission charge. The music room and adjacent drawing-rooms are chandeliered state apartments in red and gold, on the grand scale. Maurice Egerton never used these rooms, preferring more modest surroundings!

Tatton Hall, near Knutsford (continued)

The splendid library is so long as to make it larger than many public libraries. Between the 16th and 20th centuries the Egerton family collected 12,000 volumes. From the library windows the Egertons could gaze across their park and see Bosley Cloud 13 miles away, to where their vast estates once extended before they were gradually sold.

The other living-rooms, and the bedrooms and ancillary rooms complete a tour which can take an hour. I did not, however, see one painting of Maurice Egerton, although his ancestors can be seen on most of the walls. Maurice was a shy person who hated publicity!

I inspected the wine cellars and other rooms below stairs, newly opened to the public. This vast underground complex, with its tram line for trucks, is popular with children. Maurice Egerton shot game throughout the world and the heads of his victims gaze across the Tenants' Hall in an impressive display of still life.

The house is open from April 1 to October 31 (afternoons only). Admission charge. Tel: 0565 54822/3.

■ TATTON HALL GARDENS

Visit the 50 acres of gardens in late May and early June and you will see a breathtaking display of rhododendrons and azaleas, planted mainly by Maurice Egerton. Some of the bushes surround the Golden Brook pool and are reflected in the water to provide an unforgettable sight. On an island in the pool stands a Shintu temple brought from Japan and erected by Japanese workmen, who also laid out an intriguing Japanese water garden nearby, complete with tea-house.

These gardens, among the 10 best in England, provide an attractive mixture of hidden glades and paths among dense bushes and trees, plus more formal garden with immaculate lawns and lovely trees.

The gardens are open all year round. Admission charge.

■ THE OLD HALL

Experience a taste of life in the Middle Ages with a guided tour of the Old Hall, situated a mile by car from the Main Hall. The Old Hall was the mediaeval house of the Massey family, once owners of Tatton. The original 1475 wood structure gave way to red brick in 1600 but the wattle and daub walls inside remain.

The Great Hall has been restored to re-live its mediaeval atmosphere and here visitors sit in semi darkness round a log fire in the centre of the hall. When the smoke curls up some of it escapes through small holes in the roof while the rest swirls around above the Lord's balcony. Candles help to lighten the gloom, as they did in mediaeval times. Rushes cover the floor, on which people once slept on a stinking pile which was never cleared.

Old Hall opens daily (afternoons) from April 1 to October 31. Admission charge.

Nether Alderley Mill

This National Trust property on the Congleton Road is one of the oldest water-powered corn mills in Britain. It was referred to as "newly-built" when Thomas Stanley, a local landowner, died in 1591, so he probably had it built. The walls of local sandstone are topped with a sloping roof of Cheshire stone flags.

Inside you can see the original mediaeval timbers, but the working machinery on view dates from 1850 and 1870. There are two overshot wood and iron water wheels, and the rest of the machinery is constructed in the traditional manner with much timber and hundreds of wooden cogs in the gear wheels. A steam engine standing outside the mill once helped production in modern times.

The machinery is an interesting sight, and on Sundays grain is often ground to make flour for souvenirs. Behind the mill, hidden from the main road, you can see the man-made moat or reservoir, covered with lilies and surrounded by trees. The reservoir gathers water from many rivulets to feed the water-wheels. The mill was in production until 1939, although modern methods had rendered it obsolete.

A visit to this small mill will not occupy you for long, so to add interest, a visit to nearby Alderley Parish Church is suggested.

Mill opening times: April, May, June, October—Wednesdays and Sundays 2 am–5.30 pm. July, August, September—Tuesday to Sunday 2 am–5.30 pm (closed Mondays). Admission charge. Tel: 0625 523012.

Alderley Edge

One of the most famous day-trip places in the North-west, the Edge rears abruptly from the Cheshire plain, sporting outcrops of crumbling sandstone to walk over. The Edge, approached by road from the south end of the village, is covered with huge trees, mainly beech and pine, and you feel as if

you are walking in a cathedral. The trees protect you in the winter from the icy wind, and in the summer from the heat!

This National Trust property was once noted for its copper mines. Now the mansions of the rich show how Alderley Edge sprang up as a commuter town for the wealthy with the arrival of the railway. There is a wonderful panoramic view towards Manchester for residents and visitors alike. Fast and frequent trains run from Manchester.

Alderley Parish Church

St. Mary's Church, usually open, is hidden from the world up a cul-de-sac from the Congleton Road, almost opposite Nether Alderley Mill. It is a lovely building in local sandstone, the nave and porch late 14th century, the tower 16th century. In the churchyard stands a 17th century schoolhouse, now used for meetings.

There is an imposing mausoleum built for the Stanleys of Alderley, the former local landowners and lords of the manor. This powerful family used a private pew in the church, set high above the peasants, on one side of the nave, like a box at the opera. The Stanleys entered from a flight of steps outside the church, leading to the private door. Thus they did not have to mix with their tenants. They were not always popular—one Lord Stanley closed the three local pubs for good after he caught some of his workmen drinking during working hours. The "Eagle and Child", near the church, thus became a house.

A legend says that another Lord Stanley sired a child by a mistress and left the infant at the base of a tree. He went home, then took his wife for a walk. Finding the child, they then adopted the abandoned baby as their own. It was only on his deathbed that this Lord Stanley confessed to the trick he had played on his wife, the story claims. There is also a legend about an eagle picking up the abandoned child and dropping it in a field. An eagle and child have always been in the Stanley coat-of-arms.

Lymm

This attractive little town, with its famous pyramid of sandstone steps in the main street, possesses a lake of rare beauty in Lymm Dam.

A wooded path, at one point 40 feet above the water, takes you round the half-mile long lake. At one end is the A56 road, and if you cross this you can pick up another path which takes you into the centre of the village. From here a lane leads under the canal to a spectacular gorge with walls of rock plunging down to a stream. There is a short walk here along a path. Lymm is midway between Altrincham and Warrington and I recommend it for an afternoon out if you feel energetic.

Jodrell Bank Radio Telescope

About 100,000 people flock each year to see the monster Mark 1A telescope—when its bowl is vertical it is 305 feet high. The largest radio telescope in Britain has a receiving dish measuring 250 feet in diameter. The whole structure weighs 3,200 tons.

Visitors also see smaller telescopes—you can steer a 25 ft telescope yourself to pick up radio waves. The visitor centre features an exhibition of modern astronomy, including working models and space videos. I saw colour film of the Voyager–1 and Voyager–2 missions to Jupiter. There were amazing pictures of Jupiter, Saturn, and Uranus. I also watched Moscow TV live, thanks to a receiving dish in the grounds.

Jodrell Bank is a place of wonder for children—some weeks 20 to 30 coachloads from schools come here.

There is an arboretum with 20,000 shrubs and trees on the site, through which visitors can walk. The Manchester University Department of Botany was already here when the celebrated Bernard Lovell carried out his first experiments on the site in 1945. His discovery of meteor showers led to the beginnings of radio astronomy and the building of Sir Bernard's first telescope at Jodrell Bank in 1947.

Jodrell Bank is situated just off the A535 midway between Alderley Edge and Holmes Chapel. You can't miss the giant telescope—it towers over the flat Cheshire landscape, but without spoiling the view.

Latest attractions include a massive video wall with nine TV monitors, linked by computer, and a "hands on" gallery of science in which you can touch and explore.

Jodrell Bank is open seven days a week from Easter to October (10.30 am to 5.30 pm). Winter, November to March, weekends only, 2 pm–5 pm. Admission charge. Cafe. Tel: 0477 71339.

Adlington Hall

This privately owned manor house stands a few hundred yards from the Stockport to Macclesfield road (A523), four miles south of Hazel Grove. The Hall possesses a striking east wing in Elizabethan black and white. The south part of the Hall, in red brick Georgian-style, was added in 1757 and the owner, Charles Legh, lives in this part of the house.

Of the three major rooms on view the most interesting is the Great Hall, which was finished in 1505. High up on a gallery here is the largest 17th century organ in Britain. In 1805 this splendid organ was damaged and incredibly it remained silent until 1959, when it was at last restored. It is played frequently at musical evenings.

Two oak trees, standing on either side of the organ, support the east end of the Great Hall—they are all that remains of a hunting lodge that was here before Adlington Hall was built. The Great Hall has a fine hammer-beam roof, and huge murals which are undated and unsigned cover the north and west walls. These were once covered with lath and plaster, probably to protect them from destruction during the Civil War, when Adlington Hall, a Royalist garrison, was twice besieged and captured by the Parliamentarians.

In 1859 a member of the Legh family (which has owned the Hall since the 14th century) played a shuttlecock against a wall and damaged the plaster, seeing colours underneath. Then the murals were uncovered to an astonished household.

Charles Legh became the owner of Adlington in 1964 when his mother, who lived until 1983, made over the Hall and much of the estate to him to avoid death duties. Mr. Legh has further ensured that the Leghs can afford to live here by turning the huge stables block into 10 rented mews cottages, and converting an adjoining outbuilding into a banqueting site.

The Hall is open every Sunday from Good Friday to the end of September. Sundays 2 pm–5.30 pm. (August only—Wed., Sat. and Sunday, 2 pm–5.30 pm.) Admission charge. There is a tea-room in the hall. Tel: (0625) 829206.

Styal Country Park & Quarry Bank Mill

There's something for everyone at Styal Country Park, near Wilmslow. You can pay to see the textile displays in the cotton mill that Samuel Greg founded in 1784 in this beautiful part of the Bollin valley. Or you can walk round the model village that the entrepreneur built for the workers he 'imported' to his rural paradise. Or you can go for a longer walk along the river to Wilmslow, combining choice scenery with immunity from cold winter winds in the narrow defile between the trees.

The place has been a tourist mecca since the mill owners gave the mill, village, farms and woodlands to the National Trust in 1939. Production continued at the mill until 1959, but it was not until 1979 that the building was opened to the public as a museum. By 1984 the charitable trust that leased the mill from the National Trust had built up the museum so well that it received a Museum of the Year award.

■ MILL DISPLAY

Textile machinery has been brought from various mills to Styal and all of it is in working order. Former cotton mill staff demonstrate all the stages of turning raw cotton into the calico that Styal produces for sale in its shop and at other NT properties. The cloth is sent to other places to be bleached and colour printed to make tea towels, aprons, dress materials and so on. (Spinning and weaving went on here under the Gregs—finished cloth was never produced at Styal.)

The most popular machinery on show are the power looms that weave the cloth and the 90 ft long spinning Mules from a mill at Rawtenstall. There are also demonstrations of spinning by hand and weaving on a hand loom.

What the museum lacked at first was a working water-wheel. The old workhorse, a huge Fairbairn iron wheel with a diameter of 32 feet and 21 feet wide, fell into decay and was useless. But a similar wheel, rescued from a mill at Pateley Bridge in Yorkshire, was brought to Styal and restored ready for use in 1986. It is the most powerful water-wheel in use in Britain, and in 1987 the Queen Mother visited Styal to unveil a plaque in its honour!

The museum's displays of photographs and artefacts about Styal and the cotton

industry, including the former mill office and a room about the Greg family, complete a tour that takes well over an hour if you look at it properly. There is a large tea-room at the mill.

Admission charge. Open from 11 am every day, June to September. Open six days a week (closed Mondays), October to May. Tel: (0625) 527468.

Styal Country Park & Quarry Bank Mill (continued)

■ APPRENTICE HOUSE

The large detached brick cottage, five minute's walk from the mill, usually accommodated 60 boys and girls who worked 12 hours a day at the mill in its early years.

The children came from local workhouses or from parents who could not afford to maintain them. The Apprentice House has been renovated as a museum

to show exactly how the children lived here. Articles that would have been used there prior to 1847 (when child labour at Styal was phased out) are on display.

The Apprentice House is open to everyone on Saturdays and Sundays, but is mainly reserved for schools parties during the week.

■ STYAL VILLAGE

Wander round the village and see the workers' cottages that Samuel Greg built. There is also a workers' shop and a chapel. From here you can walk down to the Bollin through Styal Woods. A new bridge has been built across the river, enabling walkers to continue from what was previously a dead end by following the river downstream on the other side to the Valley Lodge Hotel a mile away on the Altrincham road. The well-known walk upstream from the mill, and its weir and pool, leads to parkland at Wilmslow called The Carrs. Styal Cricket Club boasts a ground with a tree on the field of play. If the ball strikes the tree the batsman is awarded four runs.

Paradise Silk Mill & Macclesfield Silk Museum

These museums, are a few minutes walk apart in the centre of Macclesfield. They complement each other, Paradise Mill being a working museum and Macclesfield Silk Museum being a static display.

■ PARADISE SILK MILL, PARK LANE

Paradise Mill housed Macclesfield's last handloom silk weaving business prior to its closure in 1981. The museum is on an upper floor and features 26 Jacquard handlooms in their original setting.

The museum employs a weaver in residence who shows visitors the silken arts. There is also a guide who takes you round and explains how the looms work and how other machines prepare the silk thread for weaving. The wood-framed Jacquard looms are well over 100 years old and have been restored—this type of loom was used in the garrets of houses before silk became the first textile trade to progress to the factory system.

Paradise Mill opened in 1862 and at one time both handlooms and power looms were used on different floors. In 1912 a firm called Cartwright and Sheldon took over the premises and concentrated on handloom weaving, despite being surrounded by firms using power looms.

The Jacquard loom, invented by a Frenchman in 1804, is worked by both hands and feet, with the operator standing all the time. The intricate patterns are worked by means of a punch card accounting system—it was in a sense the world's first computer. Setting up a new design on the loom occupied several days and silk produced in this way was expensive and worn generally by the rich.

■ MACCLESFIELD SILK MUSEUM, ROE STREET

This is the first museum in Britain to be devoted entirely to the study of silk. It is housed in the basement of the four-storey Macclesfield Sunday School (built 1813). There is a small theatre which screens a brilliant audio-visual display about the history of silk manufacture in Macclesfield. The screen is so wide that it fills the entire width of the theatre. In the show the points of view of both employer and worker are forcibly expressed!

The museum also features a gallery of luxury silk costumes worn by people in the 17th and 18th centuries. Silk weaving began in the homes of Macclesfield in the 1750's but did not become established on a big factory scale until the early 19th century.

In 1743 Charles Roe built the first water-powered throwing mill in Macclesfield, turning raw silk sent from London into thread ready for weaving in the capital. By the 1790's Macclesfield was an industrial town specialising in silk throwing. It was not until the 1870's that power looms

Paradise Silk Mill & Macclesfield Silk Museum (continued)

were introduced to weave plain silks. The town became Britain's foremost silk manufacturing centre, but today only a handful of firms are still turning out silk ties and ribbon, and doing silk-screen printing. The cheap silk sold in High Street shops is imported from China.

Admission charge. Roe Street museum has a cafe.
Paradise Mill Tel: 0625 618228
Open Tuesday–Sunday 1—5 pm.
Silk Museum Tel 0625 613210
Open Tuesday – Saturday 11 am–5 pm Sunday 1–5 pm.

Bollington Cycle Hire

Hire a bike and enjoy a traffic-free ride along the Middlewood Way, a former railway line. The ride starts from the Adelphi Mill, in the centre of Bollington, near Macclesfield, and takes you five miles to Middlewood, near Hazel Grove. Of course, you may cycle on the roads as well if you wish.

The hire cycles have small wheels and are suitable for inexperienced riders (children's machines available). The cycle hire set-up is run by Macclesfield Groundwork Trust, a local charity. The former gate lodge of the Adelphi Mill has been turned into a Cheshire Discovery Centre, with permanent and temporary exhibitions.

Cycles can be hired every Saturday and Sunday from April to the beginning of October. For possible midweek hire ring 0625 72681.

Gawsworth and Gawsworth Hall

There is no lovelier place than Gawsworth. Away from the modern houses up the road, the Tudor masterpiece that is Gawsworth Hall stands like a jewel on its emerald lawns. There is a fascinating old church and a former rectory, dating back to 1740, that is a sensation in black and white timbering. In the middle of all this lie three pools, one in which the church tower is reflected.

The place was largely built around 1480 and some rooms remain virtually unchanged since the days of Elizabeth I. The rooms have low ceilings, making the place cosier than palatial mansions of later ages. Old roof beams jut out everywhere. In the upstairs Gallery there is an amazing network of timbers above your head, showing how complicated the structure is. An enormous timbered truss fills the end of one bedroom.

A window of the main bedroom juts out from the wall of the hall like the stern

Open air drama at Gawsworth

superstructure of an old galleon. The bedroom's oak framing, flooring, plaster work and window glass are unchanged from Tudor days. The dining-room, which looked much the same for Elizabethan feasts, has a fine 16th century refectory table.

The chapel is the tiniest I have ever seen—it leads to a baptistry which is lit brilliantly because the walls are mostly occupied by stained glass windows depicting some of the saints. Here an old board carries sensible warnings about life. Examples are *"Avoid loud or aggressive persons, they are vexatious to the spirit"*

Gawsworth and Gawsworth Hall (continued)

and *"Exercise caution in your business affairs, the world is full of trickery"*.

Beside the hall is an area which is assumed to have been one of England's best tilting grounds. The Fitton family of Gawsworth are believed to have held jousts until the end of the 16th century.

Here lived beautiful Mary Fitton, the supposed 'Dark Lady' of Shakespeare's sonnets. She was a maid-of-honour to Queen Elizabeth, only to be sent to the Tower on becoming pregnant.

In a wood near Gawsworth Church is the grave of Samuel Johnson, actor and playwright and one of the last jesters in England. The flat stone says:

"Here, undisturbed and hid from vulgar eyes,
A wit, musician, poet, player lies."

Gawsworth also has its big "new" hall, built in the 18th century by Lord Mohun, who later fought a famous duel with the Duke of Hamilton over the Gawsworth estates. Both were killed.

Look for the gargoyles and carvings if you visit Gawsworth Church. Inside the church are statues of Sir Francis Fitton, an Elizabethan knight, his wife, and their 10 children.

Visitors can park cars in a field in the village centre. There is a cafe in a pavilion.
Gawsworth Hall: Admission charge. Tel: 0260 22345 . Open each afternoon from April to mid October.

Redesmere

This 1½-miles-long lake is near Siddington, midway between Alderley Edge and Congleton. It is a popular spot for afternoon trippers, who watch the yachting and feed the water fowl in beautiful tree-fringed surroundings. There is a footpath through the trees and along the side of the lake if you fancy a picnic.

Redesmere is just off the A34, south of its junction with the Macclesfield–Knutsford road (A537).

Capesthorne Hall

Capesthorne Hall is a stately home still lived in by the Bromley–Davenport family. The huge building an impressive and familiar sight to drivers who regularly use the nearby main road to Congleton, is not a particularly old house (the centre portion was rebuilt after a disastrous fire in 1861). The hall dates from 1719 but was altered in 1837.

Capesthorne contains a great variety of paintings, sculpture and furniture. One of its charms is that it stands in parkland crossed by a chain of man-made lakes. A beautiful Georgian chapel stands near the house, and in the stables there is a delightful 150-seat theatre which was originally used for family theatricals and which is now used regularly to present plays.

Flower gardens and a circular walk through woodland and meadow complete a pleasant day out here. There is a children's adventure playground, a site for touring caravans, a local crafts workroom and a restaurant.

Park, gardens and chapel open 12–6 pm. Hall 2 pm–5 pm. Open June to August, Tues., Wed., Thurs., Sat., Sun. May and September, Wed., Sat., Sun. April, Sundays only. Admission charge. Tel: 0625 861221.

Knutsford

Knutsford's heritage can be seen in its streets, particularly the quaint King Street with its old inns and shops, some of them Georgian but others much older.

Here Elizabeth Cleghorn Stevenson grew up to marry the Rev. William Gaskell, a Unitarian Minister, in 1832. Mrs. Gaskell made the town famous with her novel "Cranford", which first appeared in serial form in Charles Dickens' magazine "Household Words" between 1851 and 1853.

A walk round the streets that Mrs. Gaskell immortalised can be made more interesting if you obtain guide leaflets from the information centre at the Sessions House in Toft Road at the top of the town.

The "Cranford Walk" starts at the house in Gaskell Avenue at which the London born author was brought up by an aunt after her mother died when she was one year old. The walk ends at the lovely Brook Street Chapel (1689) where Mrs. Gaskell is buried. There is also a guide to a general interest walk round Knutsford's streets.

The town's tribute to the author is the Gaskell Memorial Tower and restaurant (formerly King's Coffee House). On the tower is a bust of Mrs. Gaskell, and the walls are inscribed with the titles of her

books, sayings of the famous, and the names of our kings and queens throughout the ages.

On the first Saturday in May Knutsford stages the quaintest carnival procession in the North-west. Horse-drawn carriages predominate in the May Queen parade, which, with a funfair of prodigious size draws a big influx of trippers. There is a unique custom in which pictures are drawn in sand, dyed in many colours, on the pavement outside the May Queen's house, and on other pavements in town. Knutsford has an official sandman who carries out the important sanding jobs.

Knutsford Heritage Centre, 90a King Street, Tel: 0565 50506.

Just west of Knutsford between the M6 and A 556 is the eighteenth century Tabley House with a fine collection of paintings including a Turner.

Open: April – October, Thurs – Sun. and Bank Hols. 2–5 pm. Tel: 0565 3021.

Arley Hall and Gardens

Arley Hall is tucked away off the beaten track, down little-used lanes, midway between Altrincham and Northwich.

There are separate admission charges to house and garden. The 12 acres of gardens are of most interest, featuring fine yew hedges, an outstanding double herbacious border, and 14 large ilex trees clipped to the shape of giant cylinders (thought to be unique). I was impressed by the hedges, which are like castle walls!

The present house was built about 1840, whereas the tithe barn, which is the visitors' tea-room, is 14th or 15th century. Over a doorway at Arley are inscribed the lines:

"This gate is free to all good men and true;
Right welcome thou if worthy to pass
through".

Location: Drive south from Altrincham along the A556 Chester road and cross the M6. As you leave the M6 roundabout for Chester turn immediately right into the B5391 at the Windmill Hotel. From here Arley Hall is signposted. An alternative route is via A556, A56 (to Lymm), turning left into B5159 at Broomedge. Open in the afternoons from Good Friday to early October. Closed Mondays. Tel: 056 585 353.

Hare Hill Walled Garden

This National Trust property between Prestbury and Alderley Edge consists of a walled garden and a woodland walk which in May and June is ablaze with rhododendrons and azaleas. There are good views and you can walk past a lake and on to Alderley Edge woods. At one time the NT property was a private garden attached to the adjoining Hare Hill House.

The garden is open from the beginning of April to the end of October (Wed., Thurs., Sunday only). Put the admission fee in the honesty box.
Location: Off B5087 Alderley Edge to Macclesfield road. If you visit Alderley Edge first then drive on a little towards Macclesfield, past The Wizard restaurant, then fork left for Prestbury. The garden is at Greyhound Road.

Hare Hill

Peover Hall and Gardens, near Knutsford

I am sure that most people are unaware that Peover Hall, an Elizabethan mansion built in 1585, is open to the public. This is partly because the public is admitted only on one day a week (Mondays) and for three hours only, 2 pm to 5 pm.

However, pre-booked parties of 25 people or more are shown round on other days. Guided tours at this three-storey brick built house at Over Peover usually last an hour. And then there are extensive gardens to view.

This was the home of the Mainwareing family from 1066 to 1919, when the widow of Sir Harry Mainwareing sold it. Randulph Mainwareing, the first of the line, came to England with William the Conqueror. He was given Peover, and 14 other manors, for helping to subdue the English.

The first house at Peover was built inside a moat which still retains its water today. The present mansion was occupied during the World War by General Patton and his officers (the American squaddies camped out in the parkland). The officers lived in the hall's large Georgian wing, but unfortunately a fire destroyed much of their grand residence. This Georgian wing was demolished in 1964 when the Elizabethan half of the house was restored.

Visitors are shown the Great Hall, which contains among other treasures a collection of old weapons, plus Cromwell's boot! The State bedroom boasts an enormous bed, dated 1559, from Tamworth Castle. There is a Long Gallery with original roof timbers, plus opulent living-rooms.

Outside stand the famous Carolean stables, with beautiful carvings and the magnificent plaster ceiling which is featured in books on Cheshire. The gardens include an azalea dell and a rhododendron walk.

Location: From Knutsford take the A50 Holmes Chapel road and drive south for two-and-a-quarter miles to the Shipping Stocks pub. Here turn left up Stocks Lane and drive for one mile before turning right to Peover Hall's entrance. Admission charge. Tel: 056 581 2135.

Tegg's Nose Country Park, near Macclesfield

This country park in the Cheshire highlands lies just south of the Macclesfield–Buxton road, two miles from the centre of Macclesfield.

It occupies the high ridge called Tegg's Nose, once the location of several quarries and therefore littered with rocks and rock faces. Below the south end of the hill lie the reservoirs at Langley village. From the high walks in the park there are wonderful moorland views across to Macclesfield Forest and beyond, and of the Cheshire plain to the south-west.

A display of tools, machinery and quarry products are on view here. The best quality millstone grit quarried at this spectacular place was used for building and monumental work, while the poorer gritstone and shale bands were crushed into small pieces for road construction. Legend says that this hill was once owned by an early Norse settler named Tegge. Hence Tegge's Naze on early maps, and now Tegg's Nose.

There is a refreshment kiosk and information centre here.

Prestbury

This village near Macclesfield has old coaching inns, shops and restaurants. The Priest's House, a striking black and white timbered building of 1448, has a platform over the doorway which an ejected rector used as a pulpit during the Commonwealth. The wonderful parish church is mainly 13th century and well worth a visit. There is a 1,200 years-old Saxon cross in the churchyard. The church has a striking carved doorway arch.

Pick Mere, near Northwich

If you like rowing boats, or motor boats, this is the place to be! The pear-shaped lake, $2\frac{1}{2}$ miles north of Northwich, is half a mile long and in a beautiful setting below the surrounding land. In addition to boating there are permanent fairground rides for children and a restaurant.

Location: Drive down the A5565 Chester road until you cross the M6. Immediately after the M6 roundabout turn right into the B5391 at the Windmill Hotel. Pick Mere is three miles from here.

Pick Mere

Prestbury

Rostherne Mere

Marbury Country Park, near Northwich

A walk along the bank of Budworth Mere, one of Cheshire's loveliest stretches of water, is the feature of Marbury Country Park. It is an idyllic scene when dozens of yachts are being sailed.

The lakeside path is bordered by rhododendrons and trees, a reminder that Marbury Hall, a 19th century mansion, once stood here. The country park's entrance is on the Comberbach to Barnton road, two miles north of the centre of Northwich.

Two other tourist attractions are not far away. Down the road at Anderton is the famous Anderton Lift, a metal device that hoists boats from the River Weaver Navigation to the Trent and Mersey Canal.

Near Budworth Mere stands the Tudor village of Great Budsworth, one of the most beautiful villages in the North-west. The gem of a parish church here has a wonderful interior full of quaint carvings and much more. The imposing exterior is a mass of battlements. The village's brick and timber cottages and thatched roofs complete a perfect setting.

Knutsford Villages Tour

The villages of Mobberley, Rostherne and Lower Peover are all a short drive from Knutsford, making an ideal trio for an afternoon tour. The village churches are all of great interest, so go on a Sunday afternoon when they are all likely to be open to the public.

Mobberley was the birthplace of the famous climber, George Mallory, who vanished on Mount Everest in 1924 and was never seen again. He and Scot Andrew Irvine left Camp Six at 27,000 feet for a final attempt to reach the unconquered summit. They were last spotted very near the top, and then cloud blotted out the view from below.

Rostherne

A stained glass window of great beauty in Mobberley Parish Church recalls the local hero. It depicts Mallory as a knight, with figures looking up at the Himalayas. Mobberley Church has a Jacobean gallery, a wonderful chancel screen, and much more.

Rostherne lies three miles north of Knutsford; it is a tiny but lovely place. From the churchyard you can look down on Rostherne Mere, a large lake that is an important bird sanctuary. Charlotte Egerton, a member of the family that lived at nearby Tatton Hall, was drowned in the deep lake on the eve of her wedding. There is a white marble memorial to her in Rostherne Parish Church, a striking stone building that stands next to the village cricket ground. Notice the churchyard gate of 1640, probably the oldest gate in Cheshire and a forerunner of revolving doors in hotels.

Lower Peover is three miles south of Knutsford. The superb parish church here is approached up a cobbled lane, and it is set among the fields. The stone tower is early 16th century, but much of the timber in the rest of the church could be older. There are box pews with odd doors, a lovely Jacobean pulpit and a 600 years-old font. Nearby is the famous Bells of Peover restaurant, the name of which apparently came from a man named George Bell, who was innkeeper for so long—50 years—that the place became known as Bell's.

Index of Places featured in this book

Adlington Hall	113
Alderley Edge	111
Alderley Parish Church	111
Alexandra Craft Centre	74
Altrincham Ice Rink	100
Aquatic Superstore	55
Arley Hall	122
Ashworth Valley	68
Astley Cheetham Gallery	80
Astley Green Colliery	43
Barrow Bridge	50
Boggart Hole Clough	28
Bollington Cycle Hire	117
Bolton Local History Museum	47
Bolton Museum & Gallery	47
Bolton Steam Museum	48
Bolton Town Hall	44
Bowdon Church	98
Bramhall Hall	92
Bruntwood Park	91
Bury Museum & Gallery	61
Butterfly House, Queens Park	48
Capesthorne Hall	120
Castlefield	9–11
Central Library, Manchester	15
Chadkirk Farm Trail	95
Cheesden Brook	68
Chethams School of Music	21
Chinese Arch, Manchester	6
Coach House Heritage Centre	67
Corner House, Manchester	6
Daisy Nook	73
Dinting Railway Centre	83
Dovestones Reservoir	75
Dunham Hall & Park	100
East Lancashire Railway	60
Edgeworth	50
Etherow Country Park	91
Fairfield Settlement	78
Firwood Fold	53
Fletcher Moss Botanical Gardens	25
Fletcher Moss Museum & Gallery	24
Fusiliers Museum	59
G-Mex Exhibition Centre	6
Gawsworth	118
Glossop	86
Goyt Valley	85
Granada Studios Tour	12
Haigh Country Park	42
Hall I' Th' Wood Museum	52
Hare Hill Garden	122
Hartshead Pike	76
Healey Dell Nature Trail	66
Heaton Park & Hall	27

Helmshore Textile Museums	58
Hollingworth Lake	69
Jodrell Bank	112
John Rylands Library	16
Jumbles Country Park	49
Knutsford	121
Lark Hill Place	35
Last Drop Village	55
Liverpool Road Station	14
Lower Peover	127
L S Lowry Gallery	37
Lyme Park & Hall	96
Lymm	112

Lymm

Macclesfield Silk Museum	116
Manchester Art Gallery	8
Manchester Cathedral	20
Manchester Craft Centre	18
Manchester Evening News & Guardian	18
Manchester Airport	29
Manchester Jewish Museum	25
Manchester Museum	22
Manchester Museum of Transport	26
Manchester Regimental Museum (Ashton)	80
Manchester Town Hall	15
Marbury Country Park	127
Marple	90
Melandra Castle	84
Mobberley	127
Monks Hall Museum	32
Moses Gate Country Park	55
Mottram-in-Longdendale	76
Nether Alderley Mill	110
Newton Hall	76
Oldham Art Gallery & Museum	73
Oldham Ski Centre	72
Old Man & Scythe, Bolton	44
Ordsall Hall	34
Paradise Silk Mill	116

Peel Tower	61
Pennington Flash	41
Peover Hall	123
Pick Mere	124
Piethorne Valley	68
Platt Hall	23
Portland Basin	78
Prestbury	124
Redesmere	119
Risley Moss	105
Rivington & Lever Park	54
Rochdale Art Gallery	66
Rochdale Canal	16
Rochdale Museum	66
Rochdale Town Hall	64
Roman Lakes	95
Rostherne	127
Rowarth	86
Royal Exchange	6
Saddleworth Museum	72
Sale Water Park	103
Salford Mining Museum	37
Salford Quays	32
Salt Museum	106
Sett Valley Trail	84
Shambles, Manchester	6
Ski Rossendale	59
Smithills Hall	51
Soccer Ground Tours	29
Stamford Park	76
Stockport Museum	90
Stockport Museum & Gallery	90
Stockport Town Hall	88
Styal Country Park	114
Tandle Hill	74
Tatton Hall	108
Tegg's Nose	124
Three Sisters Country Park	43
Toad Lane Museum	65
Tommyfield Market	70
Turnpike Gallery	41
Turton Tower	48
Urmston Meadows	100
Walton Hall Gardens	105
Wardle Village	67
Warrington Museum	106
Weaver Navigation	107
Werneth Low	95
Whitworth Art Gallery	22
Wigan Pier	40
Woodbank Park	93
Worsley and Worsley Woods	33
Wythenshawe Hall	23
Wythenshawe Park Horticultural Centre	24